The Art of Scandal

Modernist Literature & Culture

Kevin J. H. Dettmar & Mark Wollaeger, Series Editors

Consuming Traditions
Elizabeth Outka

Machine-Age Comedy
Michael North

The Art of Scandal
Sean Latham

The Hypothetical Mandarin
Eric Hayot

Nations of Nothing But Poetry
Matthew Hart

Modernism & Copyright
Paul K. Saint-Amour

Accented America
Joshua L. Miller

Criminal Ingenuity
Ellen Levy

Modernism's Mythic Pose
Carrie J. Preston

Pragmatic Modernism
Lisi Schoenbach

Unseasonable Youth
Jed Esty

World Views
Jon Hegglund

Americanizing Britain
Genevieve Abravanel

The Art of Scandal

Modernism, Libel Law, and the Roman à Clef

Sean Latham

Oxford University Press, Inc., publishes works that further
Oxford University's objective of excellence
in research, scholarship, and education.

Oxford New York
Auckland Cape Town Dar es Salaam Hong Kong Karachi
Kuala Lumpur Madrid Melbourne Mexico City Nairobi
New Delhi Shanghai Taipei Toronto

With offices in
Argentina Austria Brazil Chile Czech Republic France Greece
Guatemala Hungary Italy Japan Poland Portugal Singapore
South Korea Switzerland Thailand Turkey Ukraine Vietnam

Copyright © 2009 by Oxford University Press, Inc.

Published by Oxford University Press, Inc.
198 Madison Avenue, New York, New York 10016
www.oup.com

First issued as an Oxford University Press paperback, 2012.

Oxford is a registered trademark of Oxford University Press

All rights reserved. No part of this publication may be reproduced,
stored in a retrieval system, or transmitted, in any form or by any means,
electronic, mechanical, photocopying, recording, or otherwise,
without the prior permission of Oxford University Press.

Library of Congress Cataloging-in-Publication Data
Latham, Sean, 1971–
The art of scandal : modernism, libel law, and the roman à clef / Sean Latham.
p. cm. — (Modernist literature & culture ; 4)
Includes bibliographical references and index.
ISBN 978-0-19-537999-0 (hardcover); 978-0-19-992293-2 (paperback)
1. Romans à clef—Great Britain—History and criticism. 2. English fiction—20th century—
History and criticism. 3. Modernism (Literature)—Great Britain. 4. Scandals in literature.
5. Truthfulness and falsehood in literature. 6. Libel and slander in literature. 7. Law and
literature—Great Britain—History—20th century. I. Title.
PR888.M63L37 2009
820.9'112—dc22   2008033717

Printed in the United States of America
on acid-free paper

For Zoë and Sophie

Foreword

In *The Art of Scandal,* Sean Latham investigates the obscured history of the roman à clef in the last years of the nineteenth and early decades of the twentieth centuries, and identifies an important counter-discourse running underneath our traditional narratives of modernist institutions and aesthetics. The book promises to redress an imbalance in current scholarship: a symptomatic blindness created by the ideology of aesthetic autonomy that underpins so many stories about modernism. Indeed, Latham's attention to the forgotten role of the roman à clef isn't finally the most important contribution made here; rather, it's the way that restoring the roman à clef to our histories of modernism makes us reconsider the hegemony of the separation of fact and fiction, life and representation, that is foundational in so much of our thinking. *The Art of Scandal* is an intelligently argued, brilliantly researched, in some ways quiet book that has the potential to send important ripples throughout the modernist studies community. Among many other admirable qualities, it makes outstanding use of archival materials, especially those at the Harry Ransom Humanities Research Center at the University of Texas, Austin, and the special collections at the University of Tulsa. This book, then, which asks us to reconsider our facile segregation of fact from fiction, is itself built on a solid bedrock of literary fact.

Latham argues that "the scandalous boundary between fact and fiction" troubles the entire history of the novel. One can witness a kind of oscillation: early novels legitimate themselves based on a fidelity to "fact" (*Gullliver's Travels,* famously, purporting to be a true firsthand account happily discovered by its editor), whereas the modernist novel, in spite of its heavy indebtedness to realism (think of the encyclopedic realism of *Ulysses,* about which Joyce boasted at every opportunity, or the persistence of naturalism in Conrad and Hemingway), was proud of its autonomy from the "real" world, its creation, in Richard Poirier's phrase, of "a world elsewhere." Increasingly redressed in recent years, too much modernist scholarship bought the "autonomy" argument hook, line, and sinker: but our readings were thereby impoverished. Indeed, though often not thematized in quite this way, much of the best "new modernist" scholarship of the past twenty years has been characterized precisely by a refusal to take modernists at their own word, to read them according to their own mythology: the work on modernism's fraught relationship with the market and commodity culture, for instance. What's more, Latham seeks to unsettle the authority of modernism's self-descriptions through detailed attention to earlier British texts that it served the interest of modernists to ignore. A great deal of new work in modernism is dedicated to reconstructing what Michael North has called the "the scene of the modern," but little of this work performs the equally necessary task of reconstructing obscured prehistories of the modern that still await excavation.

The Art of Scandal opens with an entirely convincing argument about the way that twentieth-century readers have been trained to "believe it weirdly 'unnatural' to treat fictional characters and events as if they were real." It's one of those humble insights upon which really great critical writing is so often founded: what if we, for argument's sake, refused to take for granted that which "goes without saying"? Latham is clear about what's at stake in this nearly unanimous, and nearly unconscious, decision to sever representation from that represented: "Our good literary manners . . . have led us to obscure, abandon, or simply mischaracterize a wide array of innovative writing from the early twentieth century which openly conceals fact within fiction in order mischievously to muddle the distinction between them."

The Art of Scandal also makes an important contribution to ongoing explorations of relations between law and literature in Latham's careful articulation of the nervous dance between the novel, the roman à clef, and the changing law of libel. The law courts, we have come recently to recognize, are among those institutions of modernism that were too long effaced from our official histories, and need to be restored (just as Paul Saint-Amour, in *The Copywrights,* seeks to reinsert the law of copyright into the story of modernism). This material will be utterly new to most scholars of modernism and has, we suspect, the power to revise the received modernist narrative in ways that will go beyond what Latham has done with it here: it will almost certainly prove to be foundational in new lines of research.

Working through readings of Wilde and Freud, Joyce and Lewis, Huxley, Lawrence, and Rhys, Latham builds a convincing case for the importance of recognizing the critical, dialectical role played by the roman à clef in the construction of a modernist aesthetics. The readings of individual writers and novels here are always fresh, often revelatory. The material on Joyce alone will certainly get the attention of modernist (and of course Joyce) scholars; and the readings of, at either end of the study, Freud and Rhys, are wonderfully suggestive.

The Art of Scandal is a truly important book for the field of modernist studies; and its argument will, we believe, quickly enter our discussions of modernism. We're pleased to bring it to you in the Modernist Literature & Culture series.

KEVIN J. H. DETTMAR AND MARK WOLLAEGER

Acknowledgments

In *Ravelstein,* his artfully tender roman à clef about Allan Bloom, Saul Bellow writes that "love of scandal makes people ingenious." Just where this genius resides, of course, remains delightfully ambiguous, shared as it is between writers who might encode their secrets in novels and readers seeking to recover—indeed, even invent—fact from fiction. *The Art of Scandal* uses that strangest of genres, the roman à clef, to trace this errant creativity in so unlikely a collection of places as Joyce's *Ulysses,* Freud's examining room, Ottoline Morrell's sumptuous estate at Garsington, and even British courtrooms. In ranging so widely, of course, I accrued many debts to those who listened patiently, argued sharply, and so often gave unselfishly of their time, talents, and ideas. In a scholarly study about skillfully hidden identities, I do want to name those often unintentional collaborators as openly as I can. So scattered a list of thanks cannot discharge my debts to them, but it can suggest just how much of this book belongs to them.

Unfortunately, the two most important debts I owe must remain anonymous. The first is to some intrepid bibliographer who over a decade ago posted a query to the first modernism listserv. It asked the list's readers to post the titles of any romans à clef published in the first half of the twentieth century. The subsequent replies surprised me with the sheer number of books that fit this description, and my own love of scandal set me reading my way through them. Unfortunately, I cannot locate that original posting, though remain grateful for this relatively simple question that kept me thinking about these books for so long. The second anonymous debt I owe is to the many students, non-majors all of them, whom I first taught in graduate school. I remember talking with my fellow section leaders, lamenting the fact that we had to drum so ceaselessly into the heads of our students the fact that characters in fiction were not real people and needed therefore to be treated as textual effects rather than historical subjects. The problem, I only gradually found, is that the harder I tried to convince my wisely skeptical students of this critical truism, the less certain I became of it myself. These students unknowingly taught me to be a better reader, and this book about that troubled line between fact and fiction is my own belated attempt to answer the questions they so shrewdly put to me.

In following the strangely intermittent life of the roman à clef, I found myself venturing into often alien intellectual terrain, places I might not have dared without the close contact between faculty a smallish place like the University of Tulsa allows. Chuck Adams patiently led me on an extremely useful journey through the law library and, thanks to his own work on civil procedure, helped reveal the artful complexities of defamation law. Bob Spoo also provided crucial help on libel law while providing an ideal model for how to work between law and literature. When my interests turned from case law to case studies, Elana Newman too provided invaluable help, sounding out her own colleagues to help me trace that still fuzzy moment when medical writers began concealing the names of their patients behind pseudonyms like "Dora." Laura Stevens and Kate Adams also provided invaluable ideas and bibliographies. Such casual kindnesses as these made this book far stronger and more ambitious than it otherwise would have been.

I owe debts not only to these people, but to larger institutions and the often thankless work of administrators who make sure they function. My colleagues in English at the University of Tulsa all helped in ways large and small, as did my patient chair, Lars Engle, and my supportive dean, Tom Bendediktson. I'm also extremely grateful for the grants that made my research possible. The National Endowment for the Humanities, the South Central Modern Language Association, the Mellon Foundation, the Harry Ransom Humanities Research Center, and the Oklahoma Humanities Council all provided significant awards funding my travel to distant archives where I could dig up dirt on any number of literary scandals. A series of faculty development grants from the University of Tulsa also proved invaluable, as did the feedback from the referees and colleagues who read these various grant proposals. Marc Carlson and Lori Curtis never ceased to amaze me with their command of McFarlin Library's Special Collections, making it a joy to riffle through the papers of Rhys and Ellmann. Sandy Vice, our departmental secretary, helped me master the jujitsu of paperwork and administration and it's only thanks to her that I could finish *The Art of Scandal* while serving as director of graduate studies. Similarly, Carol Kealiher tirelessly devoted herself to keeping good care of the *James Joyce Quarterly,* patiently fending for it during those times when I needed to focus solely on writing. Similarly, Richard Black did an exemplary job managing the Modernist Journals Project as it continued to expand. To all of these people and institutions, I am deeply grateful for their humbling faith and unflagging generosity.

Over the last five years I have been extremely fortunate that so many people were willing to listen to the conference papers, lectures, and talks in which *The Art of Scandal* slowly took shape. Hard questions from these varied audiences led to hard thinking, whether about the precise kind of constraints libel law places upon writers or about the subtle differences between a salon and a coterie. The ideas here have been usefully tempered in crucibles ranging from undergraduate survey courses to lecture halls in Dublin, Cambridge, Santa Barbara, and Seattle. I've been fortunate as well in the readers who devoted their time to this manuscript at its varied stages of completion. As has always been the case, Bob Scholes helped me at every stage along the way, from a hastily compiled bibliography we built over lunch to his final reading that made me see some deep flaws I wanted so badly to ignore. The anonymous reader for this manuscript returned an astonishing report: nine single-spaced pages in length, it guided me through revisions large and small that made this thing clearer, more concise, and certainly better than it would have been. Similarly, Kevin Dettmar and Mark Wollaeger urged me to bring this book to completion while proving to be tough readers and thoughtful editors. I'm honored that they selected it to help launch the Modernist Literature and Culture series.

My deepest thanks, finally, are to those whose acts of generosity, inspiration, and support seemed the most casual—even though this book would have been impossible without them. Jen has always and again been the calm center of my life, from whom springs love and grace. She's taught me to find a peaceful strength amidst the seeming chaos of our lives. And then there's Zoë and Sophie. They've grown up with me always scribbling away on this thing in the background, patiently accepting my hours at the computer, a brief move to Austin, and my too frequent travels. Though never really certain about this book, so devoid of illustrations, adventure, and magic, they made sure I got it done. It's for them.

Contents

Foreword vii

1. Introduction: Fact, Fiction, and Pleasure 3
2. True Fictions and False Histories: The Secret Rise of the Roman à Clef 21
3. Open Secrets and Hidden Truths: Wilde and Freud 43
4. Libel: Policing the Laws of Fiction 69
5. The Novel at the Bar: Joyce, Lewis, and Libel 89
6. The Coterie as Commodity: Huxley, Lawrence, Rhys, and the Business of Revenge 124

Notes 167
Select Bibliography of Modernist Romans à Clef 193
Index 197

The Art of Scandal

1. Introduction
Fact, Fiction, and Pleasure

Be warned: this book commits one of literary criticism's deadliest sins by treating seemingly fictional works from the early twentieth century as if they contained real facts about real people and events. Those professional readers who write and teach literature within the university strenuously insist that their students first learn to separate fiction from biography and thus treat the text as an enclosed and self-authorizing aesthetic object. Even the most innovative reading strategies, whether rooted in post-structuralism, neo-pragmatism, the new aestheticism, or cultural studies, all tend to share this fundamental assumption about the autonomy of fiction. The modernist text, in particular, enshrines what Richard Poirier calls "a world elsewhere," freed by language and style from the dreary "environment already accredited by history and society."[1] As Brett Bourbon elegantly puts it in *Finding a Replacement for the Soul,* "We accept that we cannot infer from a fiction the beliefs of the author in the way we might if he or she were speaking in his or her own voice. We naturally speak of characters and events in fiction as distinct from persons and events outside fiction. Fictions, unlike nonfictions, do not make specific claims about the world."[2] The "we" in this sentence, however, is troublingly imperial, for what if one does not read or speak about fiction in this way? Who, after all, has not paused in the midst of a novel or story to wonder if the author has experienced the events described in the text? Or if some particularly villainous character is not, in fact, based on a real person?

Surely such questions, along with the kind of readerly pleasures they generate, are not unnatural; after all, they come easily to most anyone who picks up a novel.

The "intentional fallacy," that sturdy foundation stone of the modern critical enterprise upon which the author and his or her intentions have been ritually sacrificed, has long proven a reliable bulwark against such reading strategies, insisting as it does on a firm divide between fiction and nonfiction, between the worlds inside and outside the text. Far from a natural practice, however, this mode of reading has to be regularly drummed into literature students. James Joyce is no more Stephen Dedalus, we confidently assure them, than Ernest Hemingway is Jake Barnes or Virginia Woolf is Clarissa Dalloway. That this principle is taught rather than simply intuited, however, suggests that it is *not* a natural way to read, that it is a disciplined intellectual skill rather than some natural aesthetic instinct.

In a 1976 interview with *Playboy*, Truman Capote pithily makes this same point, taking a jab at professors and critics by cattily assuring the magazine's readers that "*all* literature is gossip."[3] Rather than an autonomous object of critical contemplation, Capote suggests that even the most difficult novels can be all too easily read as titillating memoirs or even private diaries in which authors make private scandals into public commodities. In a roughly contemporary piece, "Novelists as Inspired Gossips," Margaret Drabble similarly insists that fiction cannot be so easily quarantined behind the intentional fallacy since it so often "speculates on little evidence, inventing elaborate and artistic explanations of little incidents and overheard remarks that often leave the evidence far behind."[4] Readers commonly proceed in this forensic sort of way, working backward from such "explanations" in hope of finding the singular detail that might reveal some rousing fact about the author and those who have passed through his or her life. This is certainly true of such openly scandalous (and wildly popular) books as *The Nanny Diaries* or *The Devil Wears Prada*, both of which generate a voyeuristic frisson by allowing us a covert yet very public glimpse into their exclusive social circles. In 2004, the *New York Times* Sunday Styles section noted with some chagrin the developing vogue for this kind of writing (one that has only been further spurred by the release of major studio films based on both these works): "In the last two years, the publishing industry has embraced a genre that might be described as 'gossip lit,' turning out a flotilla of best-selling novels that rely less on the craft of literature than on the recycling of rumor and on their author's well-positioned perches."[5] In the eyes of this reviewer, herself so clearly steeped in a modernist aesthetic of imaginative supremacy, merely "recycling" one's experience is degrading; and because the author hides her malice behind the flimsiest veil of fiction, such works lack even the presumably more honest authority of a journal or memoir. Such complaints about the allegedly thinning boundary between fact and fiction are hardly new. Following the publication of books like *The Company* and *The Washington Fringe*

Benefit in 1976, *Time Magazine* loudly lamented its own "Age of Psst!" in which the private scandals of the Nixon era were artlessly hidden in public works.[6]

Far from the distinctive product of the late 1970s or the opening years of the twenty-first century, this mode of reading and writing contains its own distinctive array of creative energies that spark productively across the gaps between fact and fiction, between "a world elsewhere" and our own. This book seeks to energize these networks by tracing the strange career of the roman à clef, a counter-form to the novel that emerged in the 1890s and helped constitute the legal, aesthetic, and ethical challenges we associate with some of the early twentieth century's most monumental literary productions. After all, Joyce scholars have been involved in a now decades-long debate about the precise relationship between Stephen Dedalus and his author, arguing often fiercely over where precisely to draw the boundary between fiction and autobiography. In Oscar Wilde's first criminal trial for gross indecency in 1895, his novel *The Picture of Dorian Gray* was introduced as a piece of evidence against him, the jurors invited to see in its pages a lurid autobiographical description of the author's own homosexual affairs. The judge ordered that the book be disregarded since "the question of literature is . . . entirely different" than the question of guilt, but the mere fact that such a legal opinion had to be registered at all indicates that jurors might naturally conflate fiction and fact in their deliberations.[7]

The demand that fiction's autonomy be preserved from fact's crude intrusions, however, issues exclusively neither from critics nor from the bench, but from a surprising array of early-twentieth-century writers often surprised by the very energies they had released. "Cannot those who criticize books and write about books," H. G. Wells asks in the preface to *The World of William Clissold*, "cease to pander to that favorite amusement of vulgar, half-educated, curious, but ill-informed people, the hunt for the 'imaginary' originals of every fictitious character?"[8] To read novels as gossip is cast here as a dangerously vacuous pursuit, characteristic of crass and undisciplined readers who cannot even make the most basic distinctions between fact and fiction. Sewell Stokes, an infamous society columnist in the 1920s and '30s, found such claims disingenuous, waspishly insisting in the preface to his *Pilloried!* that gossip and fiction cannot be so easily disentangled: "In fiction, the more realistic an author makes his characters the more he is praised. . . . Yet when the same critic is confronted by a realistic (but not always complimentary) fact about a living personality, he does not like it. Most novelists, however, take characters for their stories from among their friends and acquaintances, 'writing them up' until the only fictitious thing left about them is their name. H. G. Wells, Arnold Bennett, Michael Arlen, Osbert Sitwell, and 'Elizabeth,' are only a few examples of authors who constantly do this."⁹ Stokes claims that he is really not much different than a novelist and that "the personality in the pillory is more naturally exposed than the one in a picture-frame."¹⁰ This abruptly reduces the generic distinction between fiction and gossip to a question of manners: Stokes boldly risks telling the truth about prominent figures from Dorothy Gish to Rebecca West, while the timorous novelist hides his or her assaults behind the thin façade of fiction in which only the names are changed to protect the guilty. Even Wells, in the midst of his screed, admits as much, decrying the attempt to decipher the origins of seemingly fictitious characters not because it is impossible or errant, but because it is simply rude.¹¹ After all, the very book in which this lament appears contains devastating and widely recognized portraits of Winston Churchill and Margot Asquith, a fact that prompted D. H. Lawrence to argue in a review that this kind of coy and gossipy writing "is simply not good enough to be called a novel."¹²

H. M. Paull, whose widely read *Literary Ethics: A Study in the Growth of Literary Conscience* ran though multiple editions in the first few decades of the twentieth century, treats such reading and writing practices not simply as a question of manners, but of morals. In a section of her work headed "Literary Misdemeanors," she devotes an entire chapter to "Actual Persons in Fiction in Drama" and warns aspiring writers to resist the allure of turning a profit on private scandals, condemning "the malicious writer" who "is often tempted to use his opportunities of gratifying his malice by a caricature which he can deny was intended for the individual generally recognized."¹³ Portraiture in general, she counsels, must be avoided by any novelist who recognizes that "his business is to create a character" and that "a copy cannot claim to be a creation."¹⁴ To confuse literature with gossip is cast as unethical and also unprofessional because it undermines the romantic ideal of the writer as a purely creative being able to draw characters and events from out of his or her imagination. The fact that Paull has to issue such advice at all again suggests that this was by no means a commonly shared view of the novelist's vocation, and, like Wells, she hastens to condemn "the readiness with which many people jump to the conclusion that they can recognize the originals of the author's characters."¹⁵ Well aware that texts can take on peculiar and sometimes anarchic social lives of their own, Paull apportions the blame for such degraded practices evenly between writers who fail their professional obligation and readers who seek to indulge their appetite for gossip and scandal. She reassures us that any attempt to cross the boundary between fiction and nonfiction is a "misdemeanor," an ethical failure to be firmly yet easily corrected. This is precisely the role literary criticism has come to play, training generations of readers to believe it weirdly "unnatural" to treat fictional characters and events as if they were real.

Our good literary manners, however, have too often led to us to obscure, abandon, or simply mischaracterize a wide array of the most innovative writing from the early twentieth century that openly conceals fact within fiction in order mischievously to muddle the distinction between them. In the process, sadly, we have dampened some of reading's very real pleasures while simultaneously suppressing the ways in which readers themselves have helped constitute the limits and usefulness of fiction as an aesthetic and pragmatic category. The novel itself, after all, emerged from a fascination with gossip, and once it attained a recognizably distinct status as a proper aesthetic object, the scandalous modes of reading and writing that helped to shape it quietly dissipated behind a haze of fussy propriety and emergent professionalism. But in the late nineteenth and early twentieth centuries, this consensus collapsed as writers and readers alike revived an earlier and much more chaotic narrative form that sought to engage a collapsing public sphere[16] by using "gossip lit" to break down the separation between fact and fiction. Paull, in fact, closes her chapter on the ethics of literary portraiture by lamenting the return to prominence of this most despised and unprofessional of genres: "The roman-a-clef is a form of art which many would like to see abandoned, and I must confess that I am one of their number."[17] Yet this mode of writing nonetheless played a generative albeit unexamined role in the twentieth-century renovation of the novel, providing passage beyond Victorian realism and into a far murkier field where fact and fiction pleasurably—and sometimes dangerously—intertwine.

From the French for "novel with a key," the roman à clef is a reviled and disruptive literary form, thriving as it does on duplicity and an appetite for scandal. Almost always published and marketed as works of pure fiction, such narratives actually encode salacious gossip about a particular clique or coterie. To unlock these delicious secrets, a key is required, one that matches the names of characters to the real-life figures upon whom they are based. These keys are complex and often obscure objects: they might be circulated privately by the author among a circle of intimates; excavated decades later by scholars studying the notes scribbled in the pages of an author's drafts (see figure 1.1); or simply invented by readers themselves. In the seventeenth century, they were regularly published as separate documents that could then be bound together with the original text. In the twentieth century, however, the mechanisms of mass culture and celebrity often helped circulate a more informal kind of key. Book reviewers, gossip columnists, journalists, and even dust jacket blurbs, for example, might unlock a roman à clef, inviting the reader to probe more deeply in searching out historical analogues for allegedly fictional characters. Uncovering the secret that Octavia Lee is really Rosalind Brooks in Compton Mackenzie's best-selling *Extraordinary Women* may require

8 THE ART OF SCANDAL

Fig. 1.1. From a custom-bound edition of Compton Mackenzie's 1928 roman à clef, *Vestal Fire*. Here and throughout the book the author's wife cropped photographs of friends and pasted them onto pages facing the initial appearance of their veiled textual doubles. The fictional names appear in heavy blank ink, the real ones in a light silver. From the Compton Mackenzie Collection, HRHRC.

an insider's knowledge, for example, while the secrets of *Ulysses* or *Vile Bodies* are more or less hidden in plain sight.[18] Even more troubling, the keys capable of unlocking a roman à clef (and thereby transmuting fiction into fact) might themselves be elaborate but erroneous inventions, the accidental products of readers seeking to turn a novel into a veiled autobiography or memoir. Indeed, such contingencies often lead directly to courtroom confrontations where an increasingly complex body of libel laws struggles to maintain a firm boundary not only between fact and fiction, but between proper and improper modes of reading and interpretation.

Dismissed by Henry James as a mere "tissue of personalities," the roman à clef profoundly troubles any easy attempt at categorization since it must be defined, in part, by its duplicity. On the one hand, it can strategically employ the conventions of the novel—including an almost obsessive focus on detailed description—to pass itself off as fiction. For those who possess (or imagine themselves to possess) a key, on the other hand, these very same textual elements are transmuted from realistic simulacra into genuine facts about real people. Furthermore, unlike the memoir or the journal, the roman à clef ultimately depends for definition on the conditions of its reception and circulation. Able to pass as a novel, it becomes a roman à clef only through the introduction of a key that lies beyond the diegesis itself. Such elusiveness, in fact, constitutes part of its appeal, for those in possession of the key (indeed, even those who only imagine themselves to posses a key) derive a snobbish pleasure from knowing a privileged secret and being part of an exclusive group able to share in the text's gossipy delights. To learn the key is to encounter a different text, one in which matters of form, character, and symbol give way to questions about motive, veracity, and revenge. Neither quite fiction nor nonfiction, it tests the self-sufficiency of these categories and thereby undermines the modernist novel's ability to construct "a world elsewhere." Able to masquerade variously as both a novel and a history, the genre deeply troubles our most basic assumptions about the aesthetics of fiction and the ethics of reading. Is it any wonder that craftsmen like Paull and James simply wished it would go away?

Far from an aberration, however, the roman à clef has shadowed the novel from the very moment of its invention and played a crucial role in the new genre's founding attempt to distinguish itself from both romance and history. Having served such a catalytic role in the rise of the novel, however, the once vibrant roman à clef was quickly transformed into the garbage bin of literary history and used to dispose of those writers and readers unable to grant fictional texts the full autonomy of proper aesthetic objects. By the end of the eighteenth century, treating the novel as a history or biography had become a crude and vulgar act, despite the fact that this very mode of interpretation contributed so crucially to its rise. The novel thus came into its own by repressing any sense of potential ambiguity about the relation between fact and fiction. Yet it remains unable to free itself entirely from the suspicion that it is nothing more than a glorified memoir, an anxiety that has been periodically heightened thanks to the scandals stirred up by books as various as Lady Caroline Lamb's *Glenarvon,* Evelyn Waugh's *Vile Bodies,* and Saul Bellow's *Ravelstein.* Regularly denounced by critics as romans à clef, these works are the novel's bad conscience, abject sites excluded from the more prestigious genre in order to cement its own claims to authority and autonomy. The wide popularity and stubborn persistence of the roman à clef, however, suggests that, far from being a sclerotic literary form, it continues to energize the imagination of readers and writers unable or unwilling to accept the novel's isolation from the world of fact. Despite its disruptive powers, the roman à clef nevertheless remains surprisingly difficult to define, since it takes shape through acts of both creation and reception. It is thus a pragmatic rather than purely analytic category, its provisional status dependent less upon clear generic criteria than upon complex networks of circulation and reception. Returning, as Michael North urges we do, to "the scene of the modern" thus enables us to begin elaborating this complex alchemy of reading and writing that has been obscured by the myth of modernist genius. Yet this historical return requires not just a greater elaboration of cultural context, but a carefully nuanced and ultimately pragmatic theory of genre.[19]

Claudio Guillén, in *Literature as System: Essays toward the Theory of Literary History,* defines a genre as "a problem-solving model on the level of form."[20] This basic theoretical concept has deeply shaped our histories and theories of the novel by providing a particularly flexible and widely adaptable way of thinking beyond the singularity of aesthetic production. It has allowed us to cast the novel as a mechanism for mediating between the public and private spheres; for creating the materials of modern subjectivity; for internalizing and disciplining emotion; and for instructing readers in codes of class, taste, and distinction.[21] The works of the great novelists, from Fielding, Austen, and Richardson to Dickens, the Brontës, and Eliot, have all been powerfully interpreted in this mode, revealing the social, political, and psychic work they have performed. What, however, of the roman à clef? What kind of work does it do? What problems does its form attempt to solve? And why has it proven so stubbornly persistent, despite a centuries-long attempt to remove it from the bounds of propriety? Such questions are more than the mere arcana of literary history, for the roman à clef reemerges in the late-nineteenth century with resounding success, its tentacles entwining the bestseller markets, while also reaching into even the most highbrow texts.

As I argue at greater length in chapter 2, Oscar Wilde's *The Picture of Dorian Gray* illustrates both the difficulty of defining this genre and the importance of reviving it as a crucial stimulus of modernist innovation. No single key directly unlocks its secrets, but the intertwining of Wilde's pubic persona with his fictional characters transformed the book retroactively into a roman à clef as readers and critics sought clues that might expose the secrets of London's gay subculture and its social elites. Its author certainly disavowed such readings, but he was nevertheless eventually called to the stand and asked to confess Dorian's crimes as his own. Understanding how this could happen means thinking about genre as an essentially pragmatic rather than positivistic category, as a particular relationship of both production *and* consumption fully delimited by neither authorial intention nor ideological function. Wilde may not have intended to write a roman à clef and the book itself can be read more easily and comfortably as a novel. Nevertheless, its initial reception and retroactive transformation into a record of its author's life helped unleash a flood of derivative works, including E. F. Benson's *Dodo*, Robert Hichens's *The Green Carnation*, Elizabeth von Arnim's *Elizabeth and Her German Garden*, and later Michael Arlen's wildly popular work, *The Green Hat*. Now largely forgotten or dismissed as frivolously indulgent, these were all international best-sellers that transformed their authors into celebrities who were themselves often then parodied or ridiculed in an ever-expanding web of romans à clef.

The public's apparent appetite for scandal and its fascination with the lives of the wealthy in Mayfair and Manhattan bred, in turn, an interest in the equally captivating artistic coteries of Paris, London, Berlin, and Capri. One of the most vibrant literary markets of the early twentieth century, in fact, was for works that offered glimpses into such bohemian affairs. Journalists and gossip columnists regularly reported on these groups, mixing the taint of scandal with a healthy dose of moral indignation. Such a position, however, always meant that they were outsiders, cultural tourists who could never fully penetrate the group to extract its most alluring secrets. Instead, it was the members of the coteries themselves who offered up this gossip through the genre of the roman à clef. Aldous Huxley notoriously made a career for himself in precisely this fashion, penning caustic accounts of Ottoline Morrell's coterie in not one but three separate books. D. H. Lawrence too seized upon this opportunity, creating such a callous portrait of Morrell in *Women in Love* that the book was nearly suppressed. Just as Oscar Wilde offered a glimpse into the homoeroticism of London's West End, so too Radclyff Hall and Compton MacKenzie used the roman à clef to expose—in one case tragically and in the other comically—the still furtive lesbian communities of the 1920s. Somerset Maugham, Jean Rhys, Ford Madox Ford, Osbert Sitwell, Evelyn Waugh, and Wyndham Lewis, along with scores of other writers both within and beyond the canonical bounds of literary modernism, also experimented with this genre, publishing books they consistently claimed were entirely imaginative but that aggressively exploited the roman à clef's illicit pleasures.

Despite the variety and popularity of such works, however, critics and historians alike have largely ignored them, erasing the scandalous appeal of a few in order to recuperate them for the canon while dismissing the rest as mere ephemera. Even genre criticism has largely ignored the modernist obsession with the roman à clef, inventing often torturous or bizarre terms to distance various experiments in the novel from its disreputable yet persistent double. Thus, Joyce's *A Portrait of the Artist as a Young Man* and *Ulysses,* for example, as well as similarly monumental works like Proust's *À la recherche du temps perdu,* Butler's *The Way of All Flesh,* and Woolf's *Orlando,* are typically sorted into less frivolous-sounding generic categories such as the Bildungsroman or the entirely oxymoronic "autobiographical fiction." This latter term, in fact, is an official subject heading used to catalog works in the Library of Congress, but "roman à clef" is not. Nevertheless, the latter most accurately describes a significant array of early-twentieth-century prose writing.

The reasons for this suppression are complex and will be explored at greater length in subsequent chapters, but it is not difficult to make some initial suppositions about the neglect of this vital genre. Surely part of the problem is that even so methodical a critic as Northrop Frye could not find a way to fit the roman à clef's structural ambiguity into his typologies. In *The Anatomy of Criticism* he constructs what remains one of the best taxonomic systems for sorting various kinds of prose writing and the relationships between them. Acknowledging the often unstable boundary between fact and fiction, he contends that "autobiography . . . merges with the novel by a series of insensible gradations" and that their point of intersection is the "fictional autobiography," which he deems "introverted" and "intellectual."[22] By this, he means that such writing is interested in ideas rather than relationships and in the ways in which a singular consciousness processes them. Though an apt description of the journal and the memoir, this simply does not fit the roman à clef—a genre that here is largely ignored. Using the example of Aldous Huxley's *Point Counter Point* (a widely recognized roman à clef), Frye instead associates it with the "extroverted" category of "Menippean satire," which "resembles the confession in its ability to handle abstract ideas and theories, and differs from the novel in its characterization, which is stylized rather than naturalistic, and presents people as mouthpieces of the ideas they represent."[23] This is somewhat more useful; as we will see, authors accused of writing romans à clef inevitably fall back on the defense that they have merely satirized a general type rather than a genuine person. The fact is, however, that even if these characters may appear as types, they are nevertheless derived in the roman à clef from very real people and are thus far less "intellectual" and abstract than Frye's analysis allows. Indeed, for those authors seeking to trade on their relationship to these often well-known figures as well as for audiences seeking access to their private scandals, it is the actual person rather than the satirical type that is the compelling, albeit concealed, center of the book.

Neither memoir nor autobiography, the roman à clef also remains distinct from the two other fictional forms Frye identifies: the satire and novel. It typically lacks the often highly stylized characterization of the former, yet resists, through its sly pursuit of extradiegetic aims, the latter's tendency "to dissolve all theory into personal relationships."[24] Instead, it occupies an ambiguous critical space by seeming to insist on itself as fiction while encoding scandalous and often disturbing facts about real people and events. The problem, of course, is that even those in possession of a key have no idea where precisely to redraw the line between fact and fiction, discovering in such texts not what Frye calls the "integrated pattern" of autobiography, but a chaotic array of claims that cannot be easily sorted. Consider again the case of *Ulysses*. We may know, for example, that Buck Mulligan is really Oliver St. John Gogarty, who did indeed briefly share a Martello Tower with James Joyce on Dublin's Sandymount Strand. But we also know that this actually occurred some months before the events described on June 16, leaving us uncertain about whether or not the two friends discussed the death of Stephen's mother or shared a conspiratorial desire to exploit the imperial romanticism of the Englishman who lived with them. This curious and often frustrating doubleness has delighted generations of Joyce scholars who never tire of drawing ever-shifting lines in the sand between the facts and the fictions of the text, but it is by no means unique to *Ulysses*. Such ambiguity is instead the very essence of the roman à clef and is therefore the quality of a widely recognized genre rather than the unique aesthetic experiment of a singular author. The often probing theoretical questions we pose about the relationship between fiction and fact in *Ulysses,* in other words, are the same ones any reader poses to books with similarly open secrets.

In "Language, Narrative, and Anti-Narrative," Robert Scholes, himself an astute critic of genre, maintains that narratology must recognize a basic generic distinction between history and fiction. The former, he contends, "is a narrative discourse with different rules than those that govern fiction. The producer of a historical text affirms that the events entextualized did indeed occur prior to entextualization. Thus it is quite proper to bring extratextual information to bear on those events when interpreting and evaluating a historical narrative."[25] We thus recognize historical narrative primarily by a shared assumption that it is always a secondary description of events that preceded its narration. Even the historical novel shares this sense of temporal priority, insisting that certain events—say the fall of Rome or the French Revolution—exist outside the text, even if the characters experiencing them do not. Fiction, however, is "certainly otherwise, for in fiction the events may be said to be created by and with the text. They have no prior temporal existence, even though they are presented as if they did."[26] The roman à clef's tantalizing ambiguity, however, prevents us from making even this most basic distinction, particularly since—unlike the historical novel—it tends to focus less on epic events than on intimate relationships. It is not that those who possess a key gain access to a publicly authenticated history preceding entextualization. Instead, they paradoxically find themselves locked inside a labyrinthine text, finding that though in possession of a key, they cannot be certain which doors open onto fact and which onto fancy.

The roman à clef thus straddles a critical gap in our narratological taxonomies, one that yawns even wider when we realize the ambiguous relationship between fact and fiction it generates is not alone sufficient to define the genre. After all, for some readers such works are simply fictions: not a mystery to be unlocked with a closely guarded key, but novels in the most traditional vein. It is, in fact, tempting to cast the roman à clef as a deconstructive principle of contamination and reversal rather than a distinct genre. Its unstable oscillations between fact and fiction reveal the interdependence of these two categories, allowing it to collapse Frye's analytic categories. Through its distinctively doubled operation as a mode of writing about the world, it renders novels into facts, histories into fictions. As Derrida argues in "The Law of Genre," "as soon as genre announces itself, one must respect a norm, one must not cross a line of demarcation, one must not risk impurity, anomaly, or monstrosity."[27] The roman à clef thus reveals the artificial, indeed monstrous quality of all genres. Yet reducing it to this sort of abstract post-structural principle obscures the social functions of the genre—the pressing and quite particular historical conditions of its rise and fall as well as its eventual resurgence at the heart of modernism. The attempt to define the roman à clef, in other words, requires us to ask about the ways it was self-consciously used not only by writers but, even more importantly, by readers as well. As Wai Chee Dimock argues in her reassessment of genre theory more generally, such a pragmatic approach can move us productively away from modernism's fetish for originality by "giving pride of place instead to the art of receiving, and affirm it as an art: crafty, experimental, and even risk-taking."[28] Although not explicitly a book about genre theory, *The Art of Scandal* nevertheless contributes to this resurgent field by pursuing what John Frow calls the "social life of forms" in their densely articulated historical context. It thus integrates close readings of individual texts—some familiar and others much less so—with biography, legal history, and the sociology of reading in order to articulate the various uses to which the roman à clef was put in the twentieth century's opening decades. Simply stated, I am more interested in the often improvisational ways a variety of producers and consumers deployed the genre than in its deep ideological structures or its epistemological status.

This pragmatic approach to genre nevertheless requires its own admittedly provisional taxonomy: an initial attempt to define those elements producers and consumers might bring to bear in creating a roman à clef. First, the genre is distinguished by what Gérard Genette calls "conditional fictionality," meaning that the narrative that for some readers is true for others is pure fiction.[29] Spanning the gap between history and the novel, it can theoretically be reduced to neither fact nor fiction yet can be mistaken for both. Second, in its pages plot matters less than the most subtly nuanced details. For the astute reader, after all, it is often the telling description of an individual's idiosyncrasies—a characteristic laugh, for example, or a unique turn of phrase—that reveals the real person concealed in the text. Such details may appear to be novelistic in helping to build up a richly described world within the book, but they actually point beyond fiction to the density of reality itself. As we will see, libel suits often focus on exactly such details and are regularly avoided by making almost imperceptible changes to textual descriptions. Finally, unlike other genres, the roman à clef is infectious and threatens unremittingly to transform any fictional text into a narrative of fact. Its claims to historical accuracy and thus an uncanny social agency can remain latent until energized by its passage through networks of reading and reception. Attending to the "social life" of this form thus means seeking out the particular communal structures that activate this latent content and thus (sometimes even retroactively) constitute the genre itself. The addition of a brief preface, for example, the release of private letters, and even a wily public denial that a particular character is based on a real person can be enough to unleash this viral quality. And once exposed, the genre can mutate in unexpected ways, undermining even the most vehement assertions of authorial intention or critical rectitude. This is precisely why writers like James and Wells so despised the genre: once released, it has the ability to the taint all their work, potentially transforming powerful aesthetic objects into what they consider mere glib entertainments. The proliferation of mass media at the end of the nineteenth century, and the congruent development of widely distributed celebrity cultures, further multiplied the channels through which this kind of infection might spread to a reading public eager to revel in the public exposure of private scandal. Some of the most innovative writers of the modernist period, I contend, helped released this infection—and later found themselves often overwhelmed by its toxic effects.

Literary professionalism and the accompanying ideal of aesthetic autonomy have nevertheless proven effective prophylactics against the roman à clef, even for those writers who experimented with the form. Gustave Flaubert, whose own uncompromising professionalism has helped to single him out as one of the modern novel's most compelling godfathers, famously wrote to Louise Colet of his desire to write "a book about nothing, a book dependent on nothing external, which would be held together by the strength of its style."[30] This dream of transforming the novel into a fully autonomous aesthetic object is still deeply resonant and continues to shape our understanding of modernism as that "world elsewhere." "I refuse," Flaubert would later write, "to consider Art a drain-pipe for passion, a kind of chamber pot, a slightly more elegant substitute for gossip and confidences."[31] *The Art of Scandal* seeks to wake us from Flaubert's beautiful dream by recovering the ways in which modernist writers and readers used the roman à clef to sift the contents of such literary chamber pots. Deliberately duplicitous in its masquerade, this genre both offers and disavows the promise of a social utility for art that law courts and literary critics have often sought to keep in check. Taking the roman à clef seriously therefore means challenging some of our most basic assumptions about both the sanctioned and illicit pleasures of reading modernist texts, and about the authority and autonomy of the fictional world itself.

This is not a matter of just recovering a few neglected texts, though the argument I make tacks between highly canonical works such as Joyce's *Ulysses* and others, like Aldous Huxley's *Those Barren Leaves,* which require us to draw what Ann Ardis calls "a much more detailed and nuanced topographical mapping of the period than modernism's classic narratives of rupture have ever provided."[32] This imaginative cartography allows us to survey more accurately the ways early-twentieth-century writers sought to test the boundaries of the literary field by examining the constitutive exclusions shaping their aesthetic enterprise. "To utter in public the true nature of the field and its mechanisms," Pierre Bourdieu argues in *The Field of Cultural Production,* "is sacrilege par excellence, the unforgivable sin which all the censorships constituting the field seek to repress. These are things that can only be said in such a way that they are not said."[33] This description of the constitutive secret at the heart of the literary field aptly defines as well the roman à clef's own "conditional fictionality," its riddling strategy for saying things in such a way that they are not really said. To ask about the secrets behind the roman à clef, I shall argue, is to ask questions about the contingent practices, pleasures, and aesthetics it at once exploits and disavows. In rereading modern literature through the prism of the roman à clef, therefore, this book simultaneously reveals the open secrets and illicit pleasures of modern critical practice as well. From television programs "ripped from the headlines" to best-selling novels, the roman à clef remains stubbornly with us, still shadowing our fictions with the suspicion that they have concealed within their pages a scandalous kernel of history or biography to be either pleasurably extracted or haughtily dismissed.

The Art of Scandal is not a bibliography of the roman à clef in the early twentieth century, nor does it even pretend to touch on every major work in the period that might fall under this category. Indeed, the genre becomes so pervasive—and so infectious—that any such survey becomes essentially encyclopedic.[34] This book instead offers a theory of the roman à clef that functions simultaneously as a counter-theory of the novel. It weaves together the threads of literary criticism, sociology, legal theory, and intellectual history. Chapter 2 picks up the first of these strands, following it through the genre's original seventeenth- and eighteenth-century contexts where it at once contested and facilitated the emergent novel's claim to moral authority and aesthetic autonomy. Both the roman à clef and the novel developed unique yet interrelated strategies for negotiating the expanding divide between history and fiction. The latter's eventual rise, in fact, came to depend precisely on its ability to suppress and eventually supplant the far more disruptive—and even innovative—energies of the roman à clef. Throughout the eighteenth century, the two genres remained deeply intertwined with one another as even seminal texts like *Moll Flanders* and *Clarissa* continued to shade productively, if often dangerously, into the skillfully concealed facts of the roman à clef. The novel eventually succeeded as brilliantly as it did in the early nineteenth century only by covertly incorporating its shadowy double, which was, in turn, roundly denigrated and repressed as inartistic and insipid. The earlier genre did not disappear entirely, however, but continued to stalk the novel in works like Dickens's *Bleak House* and Disraeli's *Coningsby*. Such books stand out precisely because they seem so exceptional, the troubling remnants of an earlier organization of the literary field that did not pit fact so starkly against fiction.

By the end of the nineteenth century, however, the novel's mode of organizing social, historical, and aesthetic knowledge came under increasing pressure as the roman à clef abruptly emerged from the historical margins, amidst a rapidly expanding, mass-mediated celebrity culture. Chapter 3 examines two key figures—Sigmund Freud and Oscar Wilde—who mark the onset of modernism, in part, by turning toward this long neglected genre, only to find that it possessed social and narrative powers well beyond their control. Unlike most of his predecessors, Freud regularly adopted the conventions of the roman à clef for his case studies, using this device as a way to mask (and sometimes multilate) the identities of his patients while nevertheless revealing the most intimate details of their private sexual and psychic lives. In his 1901 study, *Dora: An Analysis of a Case of Hysteria,* this generic experimentation becomes essential, helping to organize one of the founding texts of psychoanalysis around the ambiguous, indeed neurotic, tension between history and fiction. Wilde too exploits these same ambiguities throughout his work. Like Freud, he attempts to cultivate and to exploit a central, organizing secret in his work that articulates the provisional identities and social practices hovering imprecisely between history and the novel.

Wilde's disastrous libel trial eventually revealed the limits of such ambiguity, as well the unpredictable agency of genre itself. Just as Freud did in his analysis of Dora, the courts firmly decided that the roman à clef's constitutive secret could all too easily be transformed into the open secret of homosexual desire. As disruptive and even deconstructive as the genre might be, in other words, it could abruptly congeal in sometimes comic, sometimes tragic, and sometimes dangerous ways as historical fact. The debates over the meaning of Dorian Gray's sin in the first libel trial opened the door to what would become an increasingly disruptive battle over the legal definition of fiction in the twentieth century and the curious agency of readers in creating and sustaining the roman à clef. Indeed, despite the often heroic narratives of modernism's campaign against antiobscenity laws, writers in the period were much more likely to run afoul of libel suits sometimes brought successfully by plaintiffs entirely unknown to them. Chapter 4 thus surveys the surprisingly rich yet almost entirely unexplored intersection between literature and libel in the period. As writers increasingly experimented with the roman à clef's "conditional fictionality," judges, juries, and eventually legislators in Great Britain struggled to maintain a clear legal conception of fiction—and the consequences were broad and far-reaching. Publishers sometimes demanded vast changes to manuscripts, and the inherent conservatism of libel law became, in the words of one commentator, a "terror to authorship." Following the particularly far-reaching case of *E. Hulton and Co. v. Jones* in 1909, the novel itself seemed to teeter on the edge of illegality as the courts proved almost incapable of meeting both the legal and aesthetic challenges posed by the roman à clef's ability to broach the public sphere.

For writers of the period, this legal crisis was serious. Chapter 5 explores how James Joyce and Wyndham Lewis negotiated the consequences of their own deliberately provocative narrative experiments with so infectious a genre. Both drew heavily on their own lives—as well as those of nearly everyone they knew—to launch a deliberate critique of the fact–fiction divide, transforming it into a fundamental aspect of their high modernist aesthetics. The interpenetration of world and text in books like *The Apes of God* and *Ulysses*, however, also led both men into often grave legal trouble, putting their books in limbo and, in Lewis's case, leading to a seemingly endless string of crippling libel suits. Far from purely extraliterary events, these legal entanglements are instead an organizing component of the works themselves: the core element of a largely forgotten modernism structured around social, aesthetic, and legal contests between fiction and reality. Forged and circulated in this complex field of force, these experimental texts not only exploit the ambiguities of libel law but are themselves inevitably constrained by its potent ability to adjudicate fact and thereby define the limits of fiction.

The history of critical and legal attempts to fix the unsettling ambiguities of the roman à clef provide the necessary background for the final chapter's study of the genre's reemergence within a highly segmented marketplace where elite culture became a site of both production and mass consumption. Many modernist romans à clef were often dismissed merely as the products of literary coteries, written for the pleasure of a few insiders and sometimes privately printed for their own consumption.[35] The continuing expansion of the mass media in the twentieth century, however, and particularly the emergence of modern celebrity culture, meant that an ever-growing audience imagined they had access to even the most exclusive literary and cultural circles. Gossip columns—like those penned by Sewell Stokes—catered extensively to this fascination, making the private friendships of such figures as Lady Ottoline Morrell and Oscar Wilde into very public news. Uniquely positioned to exploit this fraught tension between the public and the private thanks to its own structural ambiguities, the roman à clef became an increasingly popular genre, catering to a market hungry for scandal and snobbery. Chapter 6 focuses narrowly on two such coteries, one in England and the other in Paris. The first organized itself around the imposing figure of Ottoline Morrell, a woman who shaped the lives and careers of many of Britain's most important modern writers and artists. Despite her generosity, however, she was the subject of brutal satires in at least nine romans à clef penned by, among others, D. H. Lawrence, Aldous Huxley, and W. J. Turner. Far from being simpleminded acts of brutality or revenge, these works instead deliberately exploit the genre's aesthetics of detail in order to cross the boundary between the hermetic aestheticism of highbrow modernism and the considerable rewards—both social and financial—of the wider literary marketplace. In the deep reaches of expatriate Paris, Jean Rhys deployed the roman à clef in similarly strategic ways, using the masochistic protagonist in a book like *Quartet* to attack Ford Madox Ford and the misogynistic culture of his bohemianism. Poised at the boundary between public and private, the roman à clef thus becomes a potent site of intersection and contradiction where gender, genre, modernism, and celebrity become densely entangled.

At its core, *The Art of Scandal* makes a simple claim with far-reaching consequences: writers throughout the early twentieth century revived the roman à clef as part of a larger movement to renovate fiction by loosing it from the strictures of a conservative realism. In the process, the genre took on an uncanny agency of its own with far-reaching consequences for the legal, social, financial, and aesthetic structures of the novel. Within the crucible of modernism, as well as the celebrity cultures of modernity in which it was embedded, this genre's volatile energies were rekindled. Yet the often chaotic and still resonant results of such experimentation have largely been ignored, repressed, or condemned as inartistic and inauthentic. By developing a distinctive art of scandal, however, writers and readers found a way to resist aesthetic autonomization by working at the complicated nexus of coterie culture, the mass market, cultural analysis, and the courts of law. To treat the roman à clef seriously, therefore, requires us to press at the very boundaries of intellectual propriety, to reveal in the ambiguities of its open secrets those things that we ourselves do not wish to confess about the structures and canons of the literary field. "The novelist," H. M. Paull regretfully informs her readers, "must reckon with the readiness with which many people jump to the conclusion that they can recognize the originals of the author's characters."[36] Rather than frowning upon such impropriety, this book instead indulges in it precisely because so many people do indeed read this way. In doing so, they activate the latent critical energies of the novel that were there at its very invention and that still command the power to alter fundamentally our bedrock assumptions—as readers, writers, and critics—about the aesthetics and the ethics of fiction.

2. True Fictions and False Histories
The Secret Rise of the Roman à Clef

Can a novel be true? Answering this simple question is anything but easy since it is structured around an obvious paradox. On the one hand, it is in the very nature of a novel to be fundamentally untrue, to be, in other words, a work of fiction. Thus are reader and author alike freed from a crude forensic adherence to the truth as the text unfolds in the parallel yet autonomous realm of the imagination. This is not to say novels cannot contain facts about the world, only that these facts are themselves always secondary to a special kind of truth—about the nature of love, for example, or the complexity of personal relationships. Even in a historical novel like Scott's *Waverly,* which places particular emphasis on its fidelity to the Jacobite Rebellion, this alternative kind of truth emerges outside of a verifiable past in the eponymous hero's relationship with Flora Mac-Ivor. Similarly, the worlds constructed in the social-problem novels of the nineteenth century, like Gaskell's *Mary Barton,* may have been drawn extensively from Parliamentary blue books, but nevertheless are populated with invented characters. We have no doubt learned to love this nebulous relationship between the novel and the truth, but it also continues to bedevil us. Where, after all, does fiction stop and fact begin when reading any work of fiction? Modernist texts tackle this question aggressively in their experiments with the roman à clef's "conditional fictionality," but its roots run deep into the novel's eighteenth-century origins.

Daniel Defoe in his 1719 "Preface" to *Robinson Crusoe,* arguably the first English novel, claims he is not an author but an editor, and that he has collected "a just history of facts; neither is there any appearance of fiction in it."[1] Everything in the book—from that eerie footprint in the sand to the mariner's incredible luck in securing the cargo of a wrecked ship—is plainly designated as historical truth. His "Preface" to *The Further Adventures of Robinson Crusoe,* published only four months after the success of the first volume, mounts an even stronger claim for the text's absolute veracity: "All the endeavours of envious people to reproach it with being a romance, to search it for errors in geography, inconsistency in the relation, and contradictions in the fact, have proved abortive, and as impotent as malicious."[2] Lightly dismissing the critics, Defoe reassures his readers that the text is indeed a history rooted in strict adherence to facts he has diligently gathered rather than simply invented. Surprisingly, this same concern with preserving the proper distinction between fact and fiction is apparent two centuries later in Virginia Woolf's *The Voyage Out,* although the valence of these two terms has shifted radically. Terence Hewett, one of the book's central figures, describes his desire to write something fundamentally new, "a novel about Silence." He attributes the difficulty and even the impossibility of such a project precisely to the uncertain boundary between fiction and history exploited equally by novelists and their audiences: "Nobody cares. All you read a novel for is to see what sort of person the writer is, and, if you know him, which of his friends he has put in."[3] Like Defoe, Woolf's Hewett insists on drawing a sharp distinction between fiction and history and implicitly excoriates the maliciousness of any reader brash enough to confuse the two.

In the two hundred years that separate Defoe's and Woolf's first forays into the novel, the moral weight of fiction clearly changed, though the novel's epistemological instability persisted. Struggling unconsciously to create a fundamentally new genre of writing, Defoe felt compelled to stake his work on a claim to truth so absolute that even his own role as author was minimized, reducing him to an editor of testamentary documents. He would, in fact, keep up this practice throughout his career, lamenting in the 1722 "Preface" to *Moll Flanders* that "the World is so taken up of late with Novels and Romances, that it will be hard for a private History to be taken for Genuine, where the Names and other Circumstances of the Person are concealed; and on this Account we must be content to leave the Reader to pass his own Opinion upon the ensuing Sheets, and take it just as he pleases."[4] Poor Daniel Defoe: no one will believe that he is merely a journalist or an editor, trying to protect his confidential sources through the simple expediency of changing a few key names. Woolf's Terence Hewett has an identical yet isomorphic problem: everyone reading his imagined novel about "Silence" will nevertheless believe that he is little more than a journalist or an editor who is protecting his sources by changing a few key names. Indeed, the very fact that readers so often treat Hewett and Rachel Vinrace as ciphers for Woolf herself only makes this confusion that much more pressing. On the one hand, therefore, it is obvious that the networks of reception through which imaginative texts move underwent a radical change soon after the novel's invention, so that Hewett (and through him, perhaps Woolf) seeks to claim the freedom of his work from the very world of factual events to which Defoe tied his narrative star. On the other hand, both Hewett and Defoe remain embedded in the same fundamental struggle to prevent the infection of fact with fiction. Defoe assures his readers that his works are essentially romans à clef and that he holds the interpretive key, while Hewett laments the fact that his novel will always be mistaken for a roman à clef to which his own private relationships provide a hidden key.

Both writers are enmeshed in a troubling bind that, over the course of its long history, the novel has been able to suppress but never quite resolve. "One question that novels repeatedly ask," J. Paul Hunter argues, is "How do you know? Most novels seem to begin in epistemology; certainly most address issues in ways that suggest urgent involvement."[5] But is it not simply novels that engage this question—so too do the legal and aesthetic institutions that both shape and are themselves shaped by their production and reception. The Scots-Frenchman John Barclay deliberately exploited the ambiguous relationship between truth and fiction in his 1621 work *Argenis*.[6] Published in France and written in Latin, this book is arguably the first roman à clef, and though written in a language guaranteed to secure only an elite and educated audience, it enjoyed enormous popularity when first published.[7] In his "Preface," Barclay does not attempt to draw any clear distinction between fact and fiction, but instead assures his readers that the two have been delightfully mingled so that moral virtue and decorum can take precedence over a purely factual adherence to the truth. This mannered approach nevertheless has a sting:

> [N]o man's character shall be simply set down: I shall find many things to conceal them which would not well agree with them if they were made known. For I, that bind not myself religiously to the writing of a true history, may take this liberty. So shall the vices, not the men, be struck; neither can any man take exception, but such as shall with a most shameful confession discover his own naughtiness. Besides, I will have here and there imaginary names, to signify several vices and virtues, so that he may be as much deceived, that would draw all in my writing, as he that would nothing, to the truth of any late or present passage of state.[8]

Barclay here acknowledges all the central elements of a roman à clef: its "conditional fictionality," its devious manipulation of seemingly insignificant details, and even its infectiousness. After all, he brazenly concludes by daring his readers to (mis)recognize themselves and thereby admit their own scandalous behavior. Similarly, Osbert Sitwell in his "Author's Preface" to a 1914 collection of stories entitled *Triple Fugue* exploits these very same conventions. "In humbly presenting the following tales of the Old and New worlds," he coyly writes, "I would at the same time wish to warn my readers that any character failing to recognize himself will immediately be prosecuted for libel."[9] Sitwell is confident that his readers *will* mistake his fictions for facts, and like Barclay he dares them to recognize themselves, knowing that to do so is to admit the essential veracity of his caustic portraits. If the novel, as Hunter contends, begins in epistemology, then we can likewise say that it remains haunted by a productive and entertaining doubt about the kind of knowledge it produces and the uses to which it might be put by both authors and readers.

Such ambiguity is not merely the stuff of literary theory or delicious gossip since, as Sitwell implies, there is always the possibility that these uncertainties will be resolved by juries called to courts of law. Here, where the novel enters into the realm of ethical and legal debate, the coy games of the roman à clef become potentially criminal and civil offenses. While this issue will be considered in greater detail in chapters 2 and 3, one more parallel between the fictions of the eighteenth and early twentieth centuries proves revealing. John Richetti notes that "in terms of numbers, at least, the market for fiction in the first forty years or so of the eighteenth century was clearly dominated by amatory fiction, narratives (mostly short, novella length) often subtitled histories or secret histories of memoirs."[10] Among the most famous of these was Mary Delarivier Manley's 1709 roman à clef, *The New Atalantis*, a scandalous account of the Whig government and its insidious influence on Queen Anne.[11] For her troubles, the Earl of Sutherland ordered Manley's arrest and trial for seditious libel. On the stand, at least according to her autobiography (itself published as a roman à clef), she claimed to have defeated the charge by invoking both her gender and her ability to preserve some vital sense of doubt about the veracity of her work. Thus, she is uncertain "Whether the Persons in Power were ashamed to bring a Woman to her Trial for writing a few amorous Trifles purely for her own Amusement, or that our Laws are defective, as most Persons conceiv'd, because she had serv'd her self with Romantick Names, and a feign'd Scene of Action."[12] The text's delicate ambiguity and "conditional fictionality" effectively stymied the legal system itself, exposing "defective" laws that would continue to founder in their often tortured attempts definitively to separate fact from fiction. In 1895, in an event that marks at least one point of origin for literary modernism, Oscar Wilde also found himself in a courtroom struggling to manipulate these same juridical defects for rather different ends. His libel trial eventually led to his prosecution for indecency, and *The Picture of Dorian Gray* was introduced as evidence of his crimes by prosecutors who claimed that characters in the text were thinly disguised stand-ins for Wilde and his lovers. He would, of course, famously be condemned to hard labor on the basis of soiled sheets, but as was the case in the Manley trial, the book entered into evidence remained an obdurate object, its status as either a novel or a roman à clef never fully resolved.

The parallels I have drawn here—between Defoe and Hewett, between Barclay and Sitwell, and between Manley and Wilde—all reveal a surprising affinity between the fictional practices that contributed to the rise of the novel in the early eighteenth century and the series of often radical innovations that transformed the genre in the aesthetic crucible of twentieth-century modernism. This chapter unravels from the history of the novel one surprisingly resilient thread linking these otherwise disparate cultural moments: the strange and persistent social life of the roman à clef as the novel's troubling and disruptive double. The more totalizing any history of the novel claims to be, as William Warner argues, the more gaps and fissure inevitably open in an edifice unable to account fully for "what is contingent and arbitrary in the ideological confrontation of early modern culture."[13] One such contingent artifact is the roman à clef, a genre that has received only intermittent attention from critics and historians who typically collapse it into a hodgepodge that expands or contracts to include such archaic forms as the *chronique scandaleuse*, the true history, and the *histoire amoureuse*. The roman à clef, however, is not just an ancestor to the novel that long ago withered on the genealogical tree; it is instead a creative and stubbornly persistent counter-form to the novel. As we will see, its resurgence in the last decade of the nineteenth century disrupts the novel's narrow claims to authority by reviving the set of legal, ethical, and aesthetic contradictions that the realist novel managed only temporarily to suspend rather than resolve. Rather than attempting to provide an alternative or corrective history of the novel, therefore, this chapter will instead outline briefly the roman à clef's shadowy and discontinuous history as it too emerged in the eighteenth century and interwove itself through the novel's rise and consolidation in Victorian realism.

The Rise of the Novel and the Fall of the Roman à Clef

Unlike the roman à clef, the novel's historical rise depended on its apparent ability to resolve the sort of opposition between fact and fiction that so troubled Defoe; its great genius, theorists generally agree, resides in its singular ability to generate an aesthetic solution to an interdependent set of legal, ethical, and epistemological problems. Yet as it first took shape in the eighteenth century, this distinctive compromise remained vague and inchoate. Such instability is readily evident, for example, in Charles Gildon's 1719 "Epistle to Daniel Defoe" published just after *Robinson Crusoe* appeared. Declaring himself no "Enemy to the Writers of Fables," Gildon disputes the book's claim to be merely an edited factual history and takes its author to task for "throwing in needless Absurdities to make the Truth of your Story still more doubted."[14] The urge to preserve the moral priority of fact is evident here, and he concedes that there is nothing wrong with composing an entirely fanciful story. Indeed, in a postscript to the letter added after *The Further Adventures of Robinson Crusoe* appeared, Gildon claims suddenly to understand that the "Book is nothing but a Romance." In shifting the debate over genre away from both fable and history, he resolves his uneasiness by realizing that Defoe has been writing fiction all along while dishonestly trying to pass it off as something morally serious and ethically legitimate. The befuddled Gildon, however, continues to be worried by a paradox that also troubled a wide array of seventeenth and eighteenth-century writers and critics: the ability of such fanciful narratives nevertheless to tell a distinctive kind of truth. Defoe himself confesses that he has altered parts of the story, but only with the intention of providing such sound moral instruction that "all the Part that may be call'd Invention, or Parable in the Story" can be legitimated.[15] Gildon seizes on this apparent confusion about genre, contending that "the Publication of this Book was not sufficient to justify and make Truth of what you allow to be Fiction and Fable . . . unless you would have us think, that the Manner of your telling a Lie will make it a Truth."[16] For modern readers, of course, Gildon seems delightfully naïve since we now so readily accept the irony that fiction's lies can indeed be made to tell certain kinds of truths.

J. Paul Hunter argues in *Before Novels: The Cultural Contexts of Eighteenth-Century Fiction* that, like Gildon, "readers, writers, and arbiters of taste remained nervous about fictitiousness for more than a century and into the nineteenth century novelists remained defensive about their invented worlds, even while always insisting that mimetic accuracy was less important than the uses a story was put to."[17] Hunter implies that by the twentieth century the problem of fictitiousness had somehow abated, facilitated perhaps by a combination of habituation, an Eliotic insistence on impersonality, and the sometimes subtle and sometimes overt operations of the intentional fallacy. The abrupt return of the roman à clef in the 1890s, however, deeply troubles this narrative about the novel's success, reminding us that the ability to sort fact from fiction in imaginative texts is no more stable now than it ever has been. "Fictionality," Brett Bourbon argues, is ultimately a "metaconceptual judgment or stance that is specifically descriptive not of some special relation between the world and the fiction, but of how we understand ourselves relative to these words."[18] Readers, in other words, may find themselves constrained at any given historical moment by particular legal and critical institutions seeking to police proper modes of reading, but these forces ultimately command a very weak power at best. Thus does the roman à clef continue to stalk the novel, providing an alternative yet still largely invisible way of negotiating the boundary between history and fiction. Indeed, its infectiousness suggests just how tenuous the novel remains, subject as it is to changing habits of reading and reception.

The roman à clef, unlike the novel, does not insist on the full autonomy of its characters from the world of historical fact. This not only produces a series of ethical and interpretive quandaries, but also disrupts the mystifying pleasures of identification. Many such works, in fact, are often narrated by a magical voyeur able to move invisibly in and out of private settings while commenting (often, though not always, satirically) on the events recorded. The reader is thus consistently made aware of him or herself as a self-conscious yet "secret observer of a hidden scene"[19] rather than undergoing what Marie-Laure Ryan calls the process of "recentering" the consciousness in "non-actual possible worlds."[20] The novel rises so quickly to prominence, Deirdre Lynch argues, because it dwells "on the notion that it is (as Sterne puts it) 'nonsensical minutiae' and 'the small sweet courtesies of life' that exhibit the truth of character most tellingly."[21] When confronting the roman à clef, readers certainly attend to the same "nonsensical minutiae" associated with characterization and individuality in novels, but they do so in a sleuthlike effort to decode the identity of the historical antecedents for the constructs on the page. This idiosyncratic mode of reading is thus based on spectacle and speculation rather than identification and interpellation. What I call throughout this book the "aesthetics of detail" is essential to both the novel and the roman à clef—indeed, that's why one can so easily pass for the other. This mechanism, however is deployed for starkly different ends in the two genres, one leading inward toward an autonomous fictional space and the other beyond the diegesis to the historical world. Tracing the roman à clef's often obscure social life as well as the unique kind of reading practices it generates reveals the strange persistence of a form that competes with the novel by challenging its legal and aesthetic stability.

Ian Watt's influential 1957 *The Rise of the Novel* established a remarkably durable set of terms for explaining the abrupt emergence and consolidation of this genre, linking it to a series of sweeping technological and sociological changes intertwined with the rise of the middle-class in eighteenth-century England. As the title suggests, it tells a heroic story and contains within its scintillating title a sense of inevitability, what Lennard Davis calls "a signification of destiny and power."[22] At the center of this story is the bourgeois individual, a historically contingent figure that requires a new set of narrative forms to legitimate its expansive economic and political power. In its simplest form, what Hunter calls the "triple-rise thesis," Watt's narrative explains that the expansion of an affluent English middle-class produced rising literacy rates and a concomitant demand for new kinds of reading material.[23] In this model, the roman à clef fades from existence both because it is associated with aristocratic coteries and because its claims to truth remain too explicit. By turning to the historical archive, Hunter's *Before Novels* challenges key elements of Watt's theory, effectively mining the foundations upon which the novel's rise had been based. "There is serious difficulty," he writes, "for the triple-rise thesis in the matter of timing: the quantitative information we now have suggests that the steepest acceleration in literacy occurred early on in the seventeenth century, at least three generations before the novel began in any meaningful sense to emerge."[24] This unexpectedly wide gap clearly disallows any easy correlation of the rise of middle-class literacy with the creation of the novel. The challenge for the literary historian thus resides in the need to explain why this particular genre among the many other kinds of writing being avidly produced and widely disseminated achieved cultural dominance by the end of the eighteenth century. Hunter surveys a welter of published and private work in order to contend that the novel did not arise heroically with the rapid ascent of the English middle classes, but was instead generated from a relatively slow accretion of various reading and writing practices. Moving deftly between primary documents, cultural history, and literary sociology, this analysis demonstrates the ways in which biographies, diaries, sermons, travel narratives, journalism, and other literary modes all eventually succumbed to "the novel's imperialism."[25] Among the most potent of these narrative precursors were those works claiming to penetrate the private realms of individual lives. Emphasizing the vogue for diary writing in the late 1600s, for example, Hunter argues that a "cultural climate receptive to issues of privacy" arose and that "revelations that would have caused profound embarrassment—even shame—a generation earlier began to find their way into print."[26] This fascination with privacy clearly feeds into many of the discursive dynamics a critic like Nancy Armstrong identifies in *Desire and Domestic Fiction*, but it does not explain why such accounts must necessarily be fictional.[27] Though few private diaries were actually published, the widespread practice of "lifewriting" itself generated a kind of curiosity about what others might be recording. Hunter notes that although the novel sought to provide such a peep into another's life, it nevertheless "seemed to preserve a cloak of decency by keeping human secrets in private places and times."²⁸ This protective cloak, of course, was generated by the curious power of fiction itself to tell truths about subjective experience that nevertheless did not impinge upon the historical world of real people. Even when more deeply imbricated in the textual productions of the late seventeenth century, therefore, the novel's distinctive power continues to reside in its ability to police a firm boundary between fictional and historical worlds, between Robinson Crusoe, for example, and Daniel Defoe.

As Hunter reveals in his account of this complex historical moment, however, the public trade in private life was thriving well beyond the writing of Richardson, Smollett, and Fielding. In fact, the rise of the novel was both accompanied and contested by the roman à clef and other similar kinds of texts that Lennard Davis calls "factual fictions." Such works deliberately erect a "covert frame," creating for the reader an "ambivalent reaction—an uncertainty as to the factual or fictional reality of the work."²⁹ Defoe provides only the most famous example of this when he insists that nearly all his long works are based in fact; and in doing so he was merely following what had become a relatively familiar convention. Barclay's *Satyricon* also explicitly deployed this kind of frame and by the late seventeenth century the scandalous and infectious appeal of such ambiguous readings prompted a surprising renovation of the original classical satire by Petronius. As David Fleming argues, few commentators sought to link specific characters in the original *Satyricon* to particular characters in Nero's Rome. Yet by 1694 numerous keys suddenly appeared in print and essentially transformed the ancient text from fiction into fact.³⁰ The very earliest romans à clef, like the *Satyricon*, first emerged in France, and Barclay's work was later followed by the even more scandalous works of Roger de Bussy-Rabutin, whose 1660 *Histoire amoureuse des Gaules* cloaked explicit political attacks behind lightly disguised classical pseudonyms. Indeed, the key in this case proved too easy to decipher, and Bussy was first imprisoned in the Bastille then exiled from Paris. Later writers sought to navigate these risks more carefully, though Grandchamp's 1701 *Telemaque moderne* explicitly evokes a similar kind of frame. "Les Heros qui va paroistre ici masque sur la Scene," he writes in the preface, "sous le nom de Telemaque Moderne, a fait tant de bruit dans le monde par ses Intrigues, que le Public n'aura pas de peine a le recconoistre: Il ne faut pas mesme de Clef pour l'intelligence de cet Ouvrage." He goes on to note, however, that "le respect qu'on doit aux Augustes Peronnes, qui sont les principaux Acteurs de cette Scene, ne permettoit de les nominer."³¹

Perhaps the most famous of the French authors to exploit the roman à clef's "conditional fictionality" and infectious appeal was Mlle. de Scudéry, whose 1664 work, *Artamene ou Le Grand Cyrus*, became a sensation in both France and

England. In its pages the increasingly transparent insistence that an apparently fictional work is, in fact, based upon genuine historical sources is enfolded with the ambiguous frame of the work and then satirized. She writes that if her assurance of the text's historical authenticity "does not fully satisfy the scrupulous, they have only to imagine—to put their minds at rest—that my work is taken from an old Greek manuscript in the Vatican Library—but one so precious and rare that it has never been printed and never will be."[32] Such misdirection transforms the work into a maddening yet pleasurable hall of mirrors in which no clear boundary between fact and fiction can be discerned. Initially, it appears to be a kind of fiction rooted in the heroic tradition of the romance. Its preface, however, undermines this claim by asserting its historicity even while ironically invoking that fanciful Vatican document. This is similar to Defoe's prefaces, which also claim (albeit with a good deal less obvious irony) that his works are historical accounts of real events. The popularity of de Scudéry's book, however, lay precisely in the fact that it was a roman à clef in which the "lineaments of her most renowned contemporaries and the salient lines of their careers may be traced, and were easily traced by her readers, in the figures of ancient conquerors, princes, and incomparable queens."[33] In other words, *Artamene* does indeed describe real people and real events, drawn not from secret Vatican documents, but from the lives of de Scudéry's famous contemporaries. Yet the preface wittily critiques those texts claiming to provide an historical ground for otherwise obvious fictions, again frustrating any attempt decisively to separate fact from fiction.

In his history of the novel, Davis emphasizes de Scudéry's mockery, attributing to it what would become one of the dominant novelistic practices of the early eighteenth century. Her joke about secret Vatican papers, he argues, "becomes over the next hundred years the insistent convention of the novel."[34] Indeed, English and French writers alike increasingly claimed their works were essentially true, their stories generated from found documents, first-person accounts, or private diaries. Seen from this vantage, the roman à clef again becomes less a form in its own right than a mere precursor to the novel, functioning in this model to resolve what Davis describes as a Puritan bias against fiction. This moralistic anxiety, in fact, generates a temporary paradox in which a literary work (such as a roman à clef) that wanted to comment on the public sphere "had to adjure that it was fiction, while for a pure fiction to appear in print it had to claim to be true."[35] Thus, Defoe's prefaces claiming their historicity are balanced against an alternative narrative mode exemplified in the period by the work of Mary Delarivier Manley, whose wildly popular *Secret History of Queen Zarah* (1705) seemed deliberately to invoke the same ironies evident in de Scudéry's work by claiming in its subtitle to be "*Faithfully*

Transcribed From the Italian Copy Now Lodged in the Vatican at Rome, and Never Before Printed in Any Language." A precursor to the later *New Atalantis* narratives that would land her in jail, this too is a roman à clef whose key was later printed and often bound with the original book. Davis claims that this text and others like it were essentially pieces of political journalism, part of what he calls a "news/novels discourse," that made some slight claim to fictionality only to protect its author from imprisonment for sedition. Over the next hundred years or so, he concludes, this discourse would eventually resolve itself into two distinct forms: factual political narratives on the one hand and fictional works on the other.

This otherwise neat history, however, neglects Mrs. Manley's troublesome subtitle, which does not stake any claim to fictional autonomy. Instead, just as de Scudéry did, she generates another interpretive hall of mirrors in which no firm boundary between fact and fiction can be established. The very fact that Manley would later be found innocent of libel by a court only reinforces the difficulties facing both her contemporary readers and later critics. Ros Ballaster contends that such writing is far more troublesome to the history of the novel than even Davis allows: "Manley's fiction stands perpetually on the borders of what are perceived as discrete discursive territories. The political and the personal, the erotic and the pathetic, the real and the fictive, scandal and satire, all undergo a series of inversions and re-articulations until their supposed exclusivity is undermined."[36] It is not simply a matter, as Davis would have it, of two emergent discourses becoming only temporarily entangled before emerging in orderly opposition as "news" and novels." This assumes, like most histories of the novel, that the roman à clef simply disappears into the widening gap between fact and fiction after catalyzing their differentiation. Like Hunter and Watt then, Davis too constructs a history of the novel that treats the roman à clef as historically and generically retrograde. Its "conditional fictionality" and its thinly veiled revelation of private scandals are thus resolved when "by virtue of abandoning such devices as authorial disavowal and the 'found' document, Fielding can shift his median past tense closer to contemporary reality."[37] The novel, in such a model, essentially suppresses the readerly and writerly anxieties generated by the roman à clef, allowing it to claim a now familiar autonomy from the world of politics and history. By cutting itself free from any direct association with real historical people and events, the novel thus insists on the resolution of that key ambiguity Davis identifies in the very concept of a "factual fiction."

Despite the novel's fragile claims to a new kind of truth that is neither empirical nor historical, the roman à clef does not simply disappear, nor do the kinds of reading practices upon which it depends. Most narratives of the novel's rise to prominence as an objective and autonomous aesthetic object nevertheless seek to exorcise this counter-form and thus immunize the emergent genre from the ambiguities teasingly exploited by Manley, de Scudéry, and even Defoe. As Michael McKeon argues in *The Origins of the English Novel, 1600–1740,* for such fictional realism to emerge "the quality of being history-like must become separable from the fact of being a history and acquire a validity of its own."[38] In McKeon's account, the roman à clef plays an instrumental rather than a contingent or accretive role in this process, acting as a textual catalyst that eventually helps precipitate the novel from the otherwise inert mixture of idealistic romances and classical histories. Eighteenth-century narrative texts, he claims, were caught in the moral and aesthetic discourse of the period "between the traditional, Augustinian strategy of mediating an essential truth by contingent means, and the historicist identification of truth with historical truth."[39] The romance, in particular, was strongly condemned for its failure to preserve truth of any kind, so that it was neither an allegorical expression of timeless values nor an authentic documentation of real events. Within this context, the roman à clef emerges in France as part of "the romance attempt to internalize a modestly historicizing self-critique."[40] Drawing as it does on the public secret that it is an only slightly fictionalized account of real events, it recuperates the romance through "a pronounced claim to historicity," adopting the posture of "autobiographical memoir, secret history, or authenticated document."[41] The roman à clef, McKeon claims, possesses a distinct social life of its own that nevertheless sets in motion a historical dialectic capable of sublating eighteenth-century anxieties about the ambiguous relationship between fiction and fact in the novel. This new genre is thoroughly infused with the language and structures of history and thus overcomes the idealism of romance; yet preserved as an autonomous fiction, it simultaneously insists that the people and events it describes have no existence prior to or beyond the text. A charmed object, the novel squares the circle that Defoe, Manley, and others tried to resolve by insisting that their fictional works were supported by documentary evidence or first-person confessions.

McKeon's dialectical account of the novel has provoked a good deal of often heated debate, in part because it is so totalizing that "it seems that nothing *could* get lost or lose its way, least of all the dialectic, which guides history toward one culmination in the novel."[42] The roman à clef, despite the singularly instrumental role McKeon assigns to it, is again a casualty of this irresistible drive toward the novel; and it must be sacrificed to effect the larger epistemological synthesis. As was the case in the work of Watt, Hunter, and Davis, this conditionally fictional form is first suppressed then erased—as if the roman à clef simply ceased to exist.

Were it to survive, after all, the dialectical synthesis would collapse, exposing once again the paradoxical truth-telling lies of the novel while arresting the march of literary history toward an apparently inevitable realism. McKeon himself seems to sense this problem when he positions the novel as a necessary bulwark against what he calls the "extreme skepticism" about fiction that prompted writers to authenticate their works by asserting that they were derived from genuine historical documents. Were the novel to fail in this historical role, then the roman à clef's ambiguities would again become infectious, fomenting what he can only imagine as a disastrous collapse of generic and epistemological categories: "Extreme skepticism," he writes, "can easily seem not the final, teleological triumph of the revolt against romance idealism that was crudely engendered by naïve empiricism, but the untenably negative midpoint between these two opposed positions, in constant danger of becoming each of them by turns."[43] The problem with McKeon's model is not simply that its dialectic proves so incredibly totalizing—a fault that archival critics like Hunter and Davis labor to correct—but that it depends on the eventual arrest and stabilization of the very skepticism that initially set it in motion. The roman à clef becomes, he argues, an untenable genre precisely because it swerves too wildly between idealism and empiricism, leaving the reader uncertain about where to draw the line between the text and the world. Thus, it drops out of his account altogether, so that the novel can proceed apace to its idealized (and apparently final) embodiment in the great works of nineteenth-century realism.

The parallels between the eighteenth and twentieth centuries I briefly drew at the beginning of this chapter, however, suggest that the roman à clef did not go so very gently into the good night of literary history. Indeed, that "untenably negative midpoint" McKeon dismisses as a kind of nightmarish space of cynicism, doubt, and anxiety could serve reasonably well as a compelling definition of the modernist novel. In the intervening period between, say the publication of *Tom Jones* (1749) and *The Picture of Dorian Gray* (1891), the novel alleviated only temporarily the "epistemological squeeze" experienced by early eighteenth-century readers. The line between fact and fiction was increasingly policed by legal and aesthetico-moral sets of injunctions that distanced the novel from history by confining it to a relatively autonomous aesthetic realm. In the process, the roman à clef and the ambiguities it deliberately exploits necessarily became either archival artifacts or simply bad art: a blind narrative alley in some accounts, a precursor to the novel, in others, and in some cases just a fashionable continental import whose vogue quickly passed. The fact that we still use the French term, roman à clef, for such texts further compounds this sense of obsolescence, as if the genre is entirely outside the English-speaking tradition and is, at best, an accidental import from the continent.

Despite their often striking differences, Hunter, Davis, McKeon, Lynch, and many other leading theorists of the novel all agree that this genre follows a particular historical trajectory and reaches its apotheosis in nineteenth-century realism. Here, it seems, the novel reaches its logical end. Pushing the historical horizon for analysis into the twentieth century, however, exposes the ever-present fault lines that led so abruptly to the collapse of the consensus underpinning the novel's success. The roman à clef, after all, did not wither away with the rise of the novel nor was it sublated in the dialectics of literary history. Widely reviled throughout the nineteenth century, it became a kind of monster locked in the novel's basement: an ugly, scandalous, and even illegal form consistently dismissed as amateurish and vulgar. Nevertheless, it emerges in the twentieth century to initiate a radical series of narrative innovations every bit as disruptive as those that first set the novel in motion.

The Rumbling Monster

The loudest rumbles issued by the roman à clef in the nineteenth century tended to echo around books that exploited the genre's "conditional fictionality" and its obsession with apparently insignificant detail in order to win some measure of profit from a celebrity culture still in its nascent stages. The most remarkable of these emerged as passing and historically delimited vogues in both Great Britain and the United States. The "silver-fork" novels of the 1820s and 1830s, for example, not only helped develop the figure of the English dandy, but also drew on the same voyeuristic qualities of the seventeenth-century roman à clef to provide readers a glimpse into the lives of Regency aristocrats. In "The Dandy School," William Hazlitt rails against what he considers this deliberately archaic mode of writing that does not seek "to enlarge the bounds of knowledge and feeling." Such books, he continues, narrow human sympathy "to a single point, the admiration of the folly, caprice, insolence, and affectation of a certain class;—so that with the exception of people who ride in their carriages, you are taught to look down upon the rest of the species with indifference, abhorrence, or contempt."[44] Although these novels rarely contained recognizable portraits of real people, their often titled authors—including Benjamin Disraeli and Edward Bulwer Lytton—traded on the idea that their unique access to the most exclusive social circles might indeed mean readers could extract some delicious yet skillfully concealed facts.

In other cases, writers drew even more explicitly on the duplicity of the roman à clef. Lady Caroline Lamb's *Glenarvon,* for example, appeared anonymously in 1816 and began to sell quickly after it became clear that the eponymous hero was, in fact, a satiric portrait of Byron.[45] The poet himself tellingly dismissed the book as a poorly executed romance rather than a novel: "If the authoress had written the truth, and nothing but the truth—the whole truth—the romance would not only have been more romantic, but more entertaining. As for the likeness, the picture can't be good—I did not sit long enough."[46] With characteristic wit, Byron manages here to assert both the factual and fictional accuracy of the book, lodging it successfully in the still unstable gap between the novel and biography. Indeed, according to John Clubbe, it was regularly treated as a "fictional biography" that might itself "reveal the mysterious author of *Childe Harold I* and *II.*"[47] The instability proliferating around the dissonance between Byron's public persona and his private life, in fact, points not only to *Glenarvon*'s ambiguous truth claims, but to the roman à clef's potential infectiousness—what Barbara Judson calls the "predations" of a form "that imbricates romance and reportage."[48] Its creation and success were largely products of Byron's own fame since the key that unlocked the text's secrets was not itself published, but instead constituted as an open secret made available through an increasingly sophisticated array of both private channels and mass-mediated networks. These are the same networks, in fact, on which a writer like Thomas Love Peacock depended, so that his own satirical portraits (including the 1818 *Nightmare Abbey,* which also contained a portrait of Byron) could gain purchase as direct interventions in the public sphere rather than as autonomous works of art.[49]

An emergent celebrity culture in the United States also led to periodic eruptions of the roman à clef, its infectious threat held only partially in check by the compromises implicit in the realist novel. Two such books appeared in the 1850s, one looking back to the eighteenth century while the other anticipated the ability of celebrity culture to undermine the novel's presumed autonomy. The first of these was Nathaniel Hawthorne's 1852 *The Blithedale Romance,* which offered an often caustic description of his experiences in the Fourier community at Brook Farm. Its preface refers directly to these events and enigmatically claims the story itself is "essentially a day-dream, and yet a fact—and thus offer[s] an available foothold between fiction and reality."[50] Even while starkly confessing the text's lack of autonomy, Hawthorne nevertheless then immediately asserts that the "characters . . . are entirely fictitious" and he deems it a "grievous wrong . . . were the author to allow it to be supposed that he has been sketching any of their likenesses."[51] Such claims may be disingenuous, but in making them Hawthorne (like Byron) turns explicitly away from the "aesthetics of detail" characteristic of both the novel and the roman à clef and insists instead that his book is an eighteenth-century romance: a moral tale centered on ideal types rather than a mimetic representation of the world.

So mannered a frame may have helped lend the text a kind of dignity in the author's mind, but the fine generic distinction he sought to draw was largely lost on an audience that eagerly received the book explicitly as a roman à clef. Like Byron and his circle, the Brook Farm group had gained enough celebrity that serious profits could be won by the marketing of their private lives. Indeed, two years later, in 1854, *The Blithedale Romance* was followed by an even more wildly popular book that abandoned entirely any pretense to romance. Fanny Fern (a pseudonym for Sarah Willis Eldridge Parton) released *Ruth Hall* with the aid of what Debby Applegate calls "an entirely new marketing form (the first modern 'blockbuster' campaign), based on new principles of motivation."[52] Her innovative publishers circulated flyers at once heralding the book as a best-selling novel and posing the question "IS RUTH HALL AUTOBIOGRAPHICAL?"[53] Unlike *Glenarvon* and *The Blithedale Romance*, however, Fern's book does not actually point to any easily recognizable historical figures beyond the obscure (indeed fictional) author herself; instead it simply trades on the *potential* scandal of its "conditional fictionality." Deliberately routed through the institutions of celebrity culture, it exploited the roman à clef's infectiousness, inculcating reading habits of the sort novelists like Herman Melville struggled at the same moment to escape.[54]

Ruth Hall, Glenarvon, and *The Blithedale Romance* reveal the novel's instability amid the growing energies of celebrity culture, but they are nevertheless relatively exceptional works. The fault-lines they reveal, however, are still faintly evident even in those nineteenth-century texts that otherwise mark the realist novel's apotheosis. Mary Shelley's *Frankenstein,* for example, begins with the words, "Letter I," its gothic excesses carefully framed in an authenticating epistolary format. Like Defoe's insistence that he is only an editor rather than an author, so too Shelley here implicitly casts her narrative as an unmediated relation of true, historical events. By 1818, of course, this had become merely a convention, but its stubborn survival suggests that the consensus underpinning the novel remained fragile. Similarly, Emily Brontë's *Wuthering Heights* contains a framing narrative, this one filtering the text's events through an eyewitness account rather than through found letters. The anomalous date that begins the work's first sentence heightens this effect, making Lockwood's narrative read either as a diary entry or as a personal confession: "1801.—I have just returned from a visit to my landlord—the solitary neighbor that I shall be troubled with."[55] Even her sister's less gothic *Jane Eyre* describes itself on the title page as "an autobiography" rather than a novel, a generic marker that again seems by 1848 to be little more than an archaic remnant of the genre's origins. After mid-century, even these vestigial textual elements began to disappear so that works of long fiction could simply begin *in medias res*, without the need for epistolary frames or eyewitness narratives. What Garrett Stewart calls "conscripted reading," in which the reader is addressed directly either in a preface or by the narrative voice, instead gives way to "impressed attention."[56] Readers, that is, no longer had to be reassured about their relationship to the text, but were instead interpellated into a mimetic world possessed of an autonomy no longer rooted in found documents or personal diaries. In his 1929 history of the English novel, Ford Madox Ford reveals just how pervasive this erasure of eighteenth-century anxieties had become when he explains to his audience the quirky nature of Defoe's "Preface" to *Robinson Crusoe*: "Whether you set out to hypnotize the public into believing for the time being that they have attended at a scene or trick them into believing that they have read real memoirs when the memoirs are fictitious the artistic, if not the ethical, results are nearly equal."[57] The potential problem of the text's fidelity to historical fact is here dismissed out of hand as a niggling question that has nothing to do with the work's aesthetic integrity.

The heroic arc theorized by Watt, Davis, and McKeon thus reaches its apogee in a nineteenth-century realism finally able to divest itself of any lingering skepticism about fiction's entanglement with fact. As prefaces, letters, and framing narratives began to disappear, novels themselves became closed off into their own complex mimetic world and could not be mistaken for "a straightforward assertion by the author."[58] The roman à clef stubbornly persisted, however, as a mode of reception capable of sometimes surprising writers who found their works accruing an unpredictable and sometimes even libelous factitiousness. Even Charles Dickens, whose canon of work helps establish the high-water mark of the novel in English, found himself accused of Paull's "literary misdemeanor" when numerous critics claimed that the character of Skimpole in *Bleak House* was a portrait of Leigh Hunt. In letters both public and private Dickens ardently decried this charge, defending the integrity of his art and dismissing any suggestion that he was engaged in mere literary portraiture. Writing in *All the Year Round,* Dickens (referring to himself in the third person) says that

> he yielded to the temptation of too often making the character SPEAK like his old friend. He no more thought, God forgive him! that the admired original would ever be charged with the imaginary vices of the fictitious creature, than he has himself ever thought of charging the blood of Desdemona

and Othello, on the innocent Academy model who sat for Iago's leg in the picture. Even as to the mere occasional manner, he meant to be so cautious and conscientious, that he privately referred the proof sheets of the first number of that book to two intimate literary friends of Leigh Hunt (both still living), and altered the whole of that part of the text on their discovering too strong a resemblance to his "way."[59]

He draws a telling distinction here, in fact, between an "aesthetics of detail" pointing beyond the text and what one critic calls instead a novelistic "type of writing that tendered the deepest, truest knowledge of character."[60] Taking great pains to distance himself from the suggestion that one of his greatest works may, in fact, be a roman à clef, Dickens goes so far as to fault his own artistry rather than admit that one of his characters has a historical correlate.

Jane Austen's works also neatly embody the novel's cathartic release from discourses of history, news, and autobiography. Originally, both *Sense and Sensibility* and *Pride and Prejudice* had been drafted as epistolary texts, their vibrant prose still deeply embedded in an increasingly outmoded form bearing all the anxieties of the novel's origins. Austen, however, abandoned these early drafts and instead produced two magnificent works that continue to exemplify the novel's aesthetic potential. As Deirdre Lynch argues, it is writers like Austen and her near contemporaries who "first succeed in prompting their readers to conceive of them as beings who take on lives of their own and who thereby escape their social as well as their textual contexts."[61] In striking out the epistolary content of her work Austen simultaneously claimed a complete autonomy for her invented world and shut it off from the authority of historical or autobiographical witness. Her books thereby generated an image of the real world, but they did so only by suppressing the generic and narrative markers that might literally ground them in the existence of real individuals.

This transformation of the novel from an epistolary form to a realist one both within and beyond the works of Austen constitutes part of the genre's distinct power of incorporation, its ability—as Terry Eagleton colorfully puts it—to "cannibalize other literary modes."[62] Rather than the carefully tailored structure of older narrative forms such as epic and tragedy, the novel is youthful, vigorous, and "anarchic," engaged in a struggle to convert "its literary ancestors into mere components of itself in a kind of Oedipal vengeance on them."[63] This essentially Bakhtinian model transforms the novel from simply one narrative form among many into the form to end all forms, the "sole genre that continues to develop, that is as yet uncompleted."[64] Breathlessly modern, it appears to defy definition since it can always become something more. It is, Bakhtin argues, "plasticity itself. It is a genre that is ever questing, ever examining itself and subjecting its established forms to review. Such, indeed, is the only possibility open to a genre that structures itself in a zone of direct contact with developing reality."[65] This proximity to reality may grant the novel its distinct incorporative power, but it is a curiously circumscribed one, premised on its isolation from other narrative modes such as journalism, history, and autobiography. The novel can and does continue to develop, but it does so within the closed circuit of a purified fiction that can generate an almost perfect reproduction of historical reality that is not to be mistaken for a factual account of the world. Writers like Austen, Dickens, and the Brontës deliberately attempt to cut their texts off from the historical world, confining their characters to a simulacrum that everywhere resembles but nowhere impinges on the reality beyond the text. Even historical novels, like *Waverly* and *A Tale of Two Cities,* may describe actual places and events, but the line between fact and fiction remains clearly marked. Dickens, for example, may give us a powerful image of London that accords with our perception of the city, but by no means do we expect to meet Oliver Twist or Paul Dombey on its streets. These novels do, however, work diligently to make us see those avenues, to absorb us in the text so completely that we are transported through the medium of language from our armchairs to the city itself. In attempting to produce an image of the world, in other words, the nineteenth-century novel does indeed become anarchic and vigorous, absorbing not only particular descriptive details about the geography of London, for example, but fragments of plays, poems, tragedies, and other traditional genres.[66]

In appropriating these other types of writing, the novel appears gradually to slough off eighteenth-century anxieties about its unstable relationship to fact and history, developing instead along its own increasingly autonomous and institutionalized trajectory. The "extreme skepticism" McKeon argues was so essential to its creation gives way to the confidence of the Victorian realists who became increasingly absorbed not with the generic identity of the novel but with its ability to produce intricately detailed and powerfully immersive reading experiences. The epistemological unease so potently encoded in the roman à clef was thereby temporarily displaced onto a much narrower concern with the relationship between word and world. Novelists unquestionably remained anxious about their craft, but these worries were essentially linguistic and increasingly abstract as they struggled to forge a realism that George Levine defines as "a self-conscious effort, usually in the name of some moral enterprise of truth telling and extending the limits of human sympathy, to make literature appear to be describing directly not some other language but reality itself."[67] This is a subtle yet profound shift in emphasis, as Defoe's factual fictions give way to the immersive worlds of Dickens. The old anxieties surrounding the novel's ability to produce genuine knowledge about the world remained firmly in place, as is evident in Levine's description of the genre's continuing commitment to "some moral enterprise of truth telling." The realist novel, however, does not attempt to tell historical truths about the world; at best, as Bourbon puts its, "a sentence about some posited possible world could only mean about that fictional world."[68]

The realist aesthetic of the nineteenth-century novel requires the preservation of an essential critical distance between the simulacrum on the page and the historical world that the reader and writer share. Marie-Laure Ryan in her study of immersion describes the gap this way: "The difference between fiction and nonfiction is not a matter of displaying the image of a world versus displaying the world itself, since both project a world image, but a matter of the function ascribed to the image: in one case, contemplating the textual world is an end in itself, while in the other, the textual world must be evaluated in terms of its accuracy with respect to an external reference world known to the reader through other channels of information."[69] This distance, in fact, generates the uniquely anarchic and appropriative powers Bakhtin describes while simultaneously generating a relatively constrained space in which McKeon's "extreme skepticism" becomes narrowly focused on the limitations of language. As Caroline Levine argues in *The Serious Pleasures of Suspense,* realism was far from a confident aesthetic, but its anxieties remained confined essentially to the space of the page: "The realists worked, first, to gesture to the radical otherness of the world, and they did so by pointing to the failures of representation. But this effort to acknowledge alterity slowly yielded to a sense of the impossibility of getting at an otherness outside the languages of representation—and the realist experiment turned inward, to investigate its own rhetorical practices."[70] This agonistic encounter between language and world has become part of a familiar story about the development of modernism, which seized on these ambiguities and transformed them into a radical series of textual experiments. Levine compellingly argues that the Victorian novelists themselves realized the troubling failure of signification, tracing the aesthetic crisis of the twentieth century back into these earlier works. The disruptive potential of this linguistic turn, however, is essentially delimited by the autonomous nature of the novel as an institution, for while such skepticism may be evident in the works of, say, George Eliot, it does not appear to extend to a larger culture in which knowledge was being increasingly aggregated in distinct intellectual disciplines.[71] Thus, even the severely limited skepticism that helped drive the creation of the novel was, by the nineteenth century, not only narrowed to a problem of language and representation, but simultaneously confined to an isolated aesthetic space largely cut off from the discourses of science, history, and law.

The consolidation of the realist novel's power as, in Bakhtin's words, the "sole genre that continues to develop," requires that the roman à clef be suppressed. This would appear to be an odd, even paradoxical outcome, if only because the roman à clef offers even more direct contact with a developing reality of the kind Eagleton encourages and admires. Precisely because of its ability to link explicitly its narrative to the historical world beyond the text, the roman à clef is uniquely able to provide some needed relief from the developing *agon* between word and world. Defoe's insistence, after all, that there is a real figure behind Robinson Crusoe or Moll Flanders means that the signifier does indeed have a referent, that it can come to rest in the very historical reality shared by the reader and author rather than floating in the uncertain void Caroline Levine describes. The problem, however, emerges from the roman à clef's conditionality, its teasing ability to conceal as fiction its scandalous and sometimes even illegal historical claims. Eagleton implicitly rules the genre out of bounds as he attempts to stake his own charged history of the novel on a crude distinction between fiction and history. "It is not fiction which leads to madness," he writes, "but forgetting the fictionality of fiction . . . A fiction which knows itself to be a fiction is perfectly sane."[72] By this standard, of course, the roman à clef is an insane genre, and it was precisely this sort of logic that essentially led to its long confinement throughout the nineteenth century. It trades, after all, on the inability to distinguish fact from fiction and thereby disrupts the aesthetic autonomy through which the realist novel develops. Lodged at the intersection between history and fiction, the roman à clef opens the otherwise closed circuit of realism, unleashing the "extreme skepticism" the novel had tenuously constrained by the end of the eighteenth century.

As we will see, the roman à clef so effectively challenges the novel's epistemological and aesthetic autonomy because its aesthetic of detail produces its own distinctive realist mode. The novel, which traces its developmental arc from the epistolary works of Richardson to its Victorian apex in Dickens, Gaskell, and Eliot, lays claim to an authority that, as Lynch contends, rests on the creation of intricately described characters with whom we can identify, but who do not lead lives beyond the page. Profoundly shaped by critical accounts refracted through the work of Michel Foucault, this image of the novel as a laboratory for the creation and disciplining of modern subjects has placed particular emphasis on modes of realism that shape discourses of privacy, identification, and immersion. An alternative and competing realism, however, more typically characteristic of the roman à clef, finds its telos not in the emotionally wrought realism of the nineteenth-century novel, but in the conditionally fictional works of James Joyce, Marcel Proust, Jean Rhys, Wyndham Lewis, and many of their contemporaries. Such texts offer an alternative concept of realism derived less from the special truths of an invented character than from publicly authenticated historical and biographical fact. They emphasize spectacle rather than immersion, voyeurism rather than identification, and celebrity rather than privacy. The full blossoming of celebrity culture—first facilitated by the expansion of print culture in the eighteenth century and later expanded through the multiplying media of the nineteenth century—helps sustain this counter-form to the traditional novel. As texts increasingly circulated through an intricately networked marketplace, the roman à clef's infectious powers gained new vectors of dissemination in the early decades of the twentieth century. Reviewers, gossip columnists, and enterprising cultural producers of all types used these mechanisms to reap considerable profits by rendering all kinds of fiction intensely realistic, yet suddenly conditional. Like the enterprising advertisers who asked "IS RUTH HALL AUTOBIOGRAPHICAL?" they developed new and often legally fraught strategies for marketing private lives to a public audience no longer dependent upon the fragile ethical compromises that underwrote the novel's invention. These experiments, furthermore, often unexpectedly exceeded the control of their creators, as the roman à clef pursued its own strange social life amidst complex new networks of circulation and reception.

3. Open Secrets and Hidden Truths
Wilde and Freud

For the roman à clef, celebrity culture acts as a catalytic medium, activating the form's distinctive energies by transferring interpretive power to ever more widely dispersed audiences. Private lives quickly become public properties so that, as Sewell Stokes argued, the boundary between gossip and the novel begins to dissolve. This accounts, in large part, for the roman à clef's reputation as a degraded form since, rather than relating the special truths of the realist novel, it comes perilously close to something like reportage or even social stenography. Even when treating it seriously, critics still lament the fact that it draws from the stagnant shallows of actual events rather than from the deep wells of the creative imagination. Reviewing Evelyn Toynton's 2000 roman à clef, *Modern Art,* the novelist Francine Prose laments in the *New York Times Book Review* "how frequently we will be disturbed and jarred awake from the dream of art by the nagging, inescapable question of reality: How much of this story is true?"[1] She then goes on to praise the book as a success, but only because the author writes "intelligently" enough to "transcend the limitations of the *roman à clef.*" That is, we eventually become absorbed enough in the veiled portraits Toynton draws of Lee Krasner and Jackson Pollock to quit worrying about anything so déclassé as reality and become fully immersed in a world rich and intelligent enough to approach the status of realist fiction. The paradox here is obvious and reveals just how badly dulled the once "anarchic" force of the novel has become. Despite its immense incorporative powers, a novel can be judged a critical success only when it stops just short of actually creating portraits of real people, when it manages fully to suppress the very question that underwrote its very rise three centuries earlier: "How much of this story is true?"

Such a question inevitably introduces the "extreme skepticism" McKeon claims the novel barely repressed and which assumed a new sense of urgency as the nineteenth century drew to a close. Writers, readers, critics, publishers, even medical scientists and ultimately jurists all found themselves increasingly caught up in a renewed debate about the limits of fiction, as the roman à clef once again emerged from the shadows to unsettle the aesthetic, ethical, and legal consensus underwriting the novel. Initially, writers were drawn to certain elements of the form because they offered a way to reconfigure history and fiction and thereby challenge the realist novel's claims to a self-sufficient autonomy. This generated a new and heady kind of social agency: a means of engaging the public sphere not though political discourse, but rather through emergent networks of celebrity culture and mass mediation. After all, a book trading on an author's fame and social connections could spark political scandals, foment lawsuits, and sometimes make or shatter individual reputations. The roman à clef's unique ability to rework the opposition between fact and fiction, furthermore, extended its influence well beyond questions of aesthetics. As we will see, early sexologists deliberately employed its structures in order to publish their revolutionary studies, making the genre itself an integral part of what Judith Ryan calls "the simultaneous emergence of modern psychology and modernist literature."[2] The anonymous case history, in fact, emerges in psychiatric discourse at almost the same moment that Oscar Wilde and others begin to experiment with the roman à clef. Science and art alike cast about for a set of narrative tools capable of generating new modes of knowledge by productively renegotiating the boundary between fact and fiction.

But these early innovators also failed to grasp the infectious nature of the roman à clef as a social form: its uniquely disruptive ability to transfer interpretive authority from writers to readers. In borrowing particular narrative elements—like openly encoded names and "conditional fictionality"—these texts energized the genre as a whole. Early cases studies, which first concealed the names of patients behind pseudonyms, became not just scientific documents, but gossip sheets that the scandalized public sought to decipher. Far from protecting an individual's identity, in other words, the changed names in such works aroused a forensic curiosity that echoed through diverse networks of reading and reception. Thus Havelock Ellis found himself redacting one of his most important works to calm the fears of an anxious family, while Freud himself grew so frustrated that he eventually abandoned the form altogether. The habits of reading reactivated by the roman à clef's resurgence further enabled the transformation of a novel like Wilde's *The Picture of Dorian Gray* into a secretly encoded account of its author's life. Although it actually contains very little real biographical detail, the book nevertheless acquired a troubling agency of its own that emanated precisely from its retroactive reception as a roman à clef encoding the author's own misdeeds. Wilde himself may have initially invited such a misreading, but he too failed to understand just how powerfully the form's "conditional fictionality" could rewrite the facts of his own life. Like other writers at the end of the nineteenth century, he painfully learned that within an emergent mass culture, the roman à clef was less a rigidly defined genre than a pragmatic social form that could be called suddenly into existence with sometimes dangerous results.

Deeply immersed in a burgeoning celebrity culture increasingly invested in the public trade on private scandal, the roman à clef proliferated wildly in the 1890s and played an essential role in modernism's deliberately self-historicizing rupture with the past. Robert Hichens, Marie Corelli, and George du Maurier all exploited the form in books that sold millions of copies to readers eager to savor its genuine comic appeal while also seeking out its latent, gossipy secrets.[3] This initial round of experimentation began with Oscar Wilde's *The Picture of Dorian Gray* in 1891 and quickly reached full flower in E. F. Benson's *Dodo, a Detail of the Day*. Published in 1893, *Dodo* offers a portrait of the wealthy socialite Margot Tennant, an attractive and well-connected woman who eventually married English Prime Minister H. H. Asquith. The book ran promptly to twelve editions and made Benson—himself the son of the Archbishop of Canterbury—an instant celebrity. The Prince of Wales addressed Margot as "Miss Dodo" at a royal ball and, according to Benson's biographer, Lord Rosebery advised Asquith when his engagement was announced "to read *Dodo* if you have not already done so—there's a great deal of truth in it."[4] Typically treated (if treated at all) as nothing more than a faddish society entertainment, *Dodo* initiated what would become a decades-long experiment with the roman à clef and inspired a raft of imitators suddenly eager to transform their social knowledge into financial success. Not only did Benson's book attempt to rework the boundary between fact and fiction, it also helped legitimate the sorts of reading practices the realist novel sought to suppress. As a consequence of the roman à clef's infectiousness, the public increasingly began to treat a wide variety of other books as potentially covert ciphers concealing scandal and intrigue that— with the proper gossipy knowledge—could be expertly decoded.

Such innovative modes of both reading and writing, however, were by no means confined solely to the novel or even to the aesthetic sphere. At just the moment

Benson, Hichens, and Wilde began their experiments, so too did an entirely different set of writers, themselves seeking to renegotiate the fact–fiction binary—albeit from the other side of this divide. In the emerging fields of psychology and sexology, Havelock Ellis, Richard von Krafft-Ebing, Josef Breuer, and Sigmund Freud all exploited elements of the roman à clef to develop a new and deeply influential genre of scientific writing: the anonymous case study. Its "conditional fictionality" and aesthetics of detail permitted them to describe authoritatively the most intimate details of their patients' lives while nevertheless seeming to protect them from public scrutiny. Eschewing statistics and aggregated data, these researchers instead published dazzlingly scandalous stories about the sexual practices, intimate secrets, and private dreams of their patients. Paradoxically, to lend their accounts the authority of fact, they cast them as romans à clef: accounts of real events in which only the names had been changed. Indeed, unlike *Dodo* or *Trilby,* these studies begin by explicitly articulating the need to develop a new narrative technology capable of expressing a still emergent knowledge about the mind. Here, for example, is the second paragraph of Breuer and Freud's foundational work, *Studies on Hysteria:*

> We have appended . . . a series of case histories, the selection of which could not unfortunately be determined on purely scientific grounds. Our experience is derived from private practice in an educated and literate social class, and the subject matter with which we deal often touches upon our patients' most intimate lives and histories. It would be a grave breach of confidence to publish material of this kind, with the risk of the patients being recognized and their acquaintances becoming informed of facts which were confided only to a physician. It has therefore been impossible for us to make use of some of the most instructive and convincing of our observations.[5]

As tantalizing as any roman à clef, this passage insists on the ambiguity of what follows, promising simultaneously to reveal and withhold illuminating secrets. The case history itself thus seeks to reconfigure the news/novel divide, deploying narrative techniques typically reserved for the novel in order to develop both a new kind of knowledge and the forms necessary to communicate its hermetic contents to a wider public. Yet these innovative experiments also proved unexpectedly disruptive, quickly escaping the control of their authors to assume an unruly social life of their own.

Linking Freud to Wilde through the circuit of genre, this chapter argues that the roman à clef reemerges in the waning years of the nineteenth century not as a self-consciously deployed form, but as an initially disordered array of narrative technologies for creating new configurations of fiction and fact. For Oscar Wilde, these new tools offered a way to challenge the limits of an ossified Victorian realism by integrating art and politics as well as public and private life, and he uses the roman à clef's "conditional fictionality" to articulate emergent sexual identities. Freud sought to use these same narrative techniques to tap the secrets of the unconscious. Concealing names and revealing details behind a fictional screen permitted him to publicize and even to invent new kinds of knowledge about the most intimate private behavior. Neither Wilde nor Freud set out explicitly to write romans à clef, but both found that the narrative form they had each adapted possessed a disquieting agency of its own. Indeed, their infamous popularity helped usher in the regimes of reading and interpretation that quickly facilitated the rise of the roman à clef as a distinctive modernist form. Freud indignantly abandoned the anonymous case study—the very form he helped pioneer—when he found that readers pursued the secret identities of his patients as ardently as they did the hidden meaning of dreams. Wilde at first believed himself more fully in command of his materials and openly invited readers to see *The Picture of Dorian Gray* as a moralistic tale about the dangers of confusing art and life. As was the case with Freud, however, he failed to grasp the potential hazards emanating from the genre's inherent infectiousness—its powerful ability to transfer interpretive authority from writers to mass-mediated networks of reception. As a result, Wilde found himself in the dock, tragically defending himself from a genre he could not fully control.

Case Histories

In *Axel's Castle*, that early study of a still emergent high modernism, Edmund Wilson draws a clear line through Marcel Proust's *À la recherché du temps perdu* linking the roman à clef to the psychoanalytic case study: "Superb as are the qualities of objective dramatic imagination which have gone into" the book, he writes, "it was never quite disengaged from his sick-room."[6] After lavishing further praise on the text, he can't help but pause and ask, is Proust "telling us his own case history with symbols?" The answer of course is both yes and no, but the question captures an underlying suspicion of what Martin Jay calls "the specter of psychologism" in modernism.[7] For Wilson and other theorists seeking to articulate a new aesthetics, this ghostly presence carries with it "connotations of reductionism, contamination, and relativism" since it threatens to entwine author and character too closely, reviving the eighteenth-century skepticism about the novel's autonomy.[8] It drove critics like Wilson and T. S. Eliot to embrace instead an impersonal formalism capable of preserving aesthetics from the taint of historical and individual contingency. The roman à clef, however, is an intensely personal genre, its pleasures and powers dependent, to some degree, both upon celebrity authors and what Arthur Bauman called in *The Fortnightly Review* "a taste for indecent curiosity in the private lives of unimportant neighbors."[9] Indeed, this helps explains why it dropped so precipitously out of New Critical accounts of the period. But the genre's insistent exploration of private life entangles it with those strands of modernist cultural production that sought to make an aesthetic of personality itself. Proust, Joyce, and even Freud wove their own lives insistently through their own texts, blurring the boundary between fact and fiction. More even than the novel, the roman à clef offered them the narrative tools to develop this new mode of writing, providing ways of reconfiguring fact and fiction as well as public and private life. For Freud and other early innovators in the field of psychology, the genre's ambiguity promised to extend the reach of a scientific discourse that could not otherwise breach the secrets of sexual life and the unconscious. Faced with the paradoxical need to preserve the confidentiality of their patients while nevertheless relating the most intimate of private details, they fell back on the roman à clef as a regrettably crude but seemingly necessary aid.

Surprisingly, Freud, in some of his earliest work in psychoanalysis, sounds a lot like Eliot and other modernist writers who at once lamented and embraced the end of the realist novel. Just as Eliot announces that the "narrative method" (and with it the realist novel) "ended with Flaubert and James,"[10] so too Freud acknowledges that current psychiatric rhetoric had reached a crucial limit. The rudiments of the "talking cure" he initially developed with Breuer led to remarkable results in the case of "Anna O.," but he immediately ran into difficulties in trying to implement them. Thus, in the opening preface to *Dora: An Analysis of a Case Study of Hysteria,* Freud begins casting about for a new way to synthesize the otherwise bewildering collection of symptoms, instances of repression, and other psychological phenomena he finds in his patient. This slim text initially casts psychoanalysis as a narrative tool necessary for restoring the psychic unity destroyed both by the case's famous incompleteness and by the bewildering nature of the unconscious itself. "I have restored what is missing," Freud writes, following "the example of those discoverers whose good fortune it is to bring to the light of day after their long burial the priceless though mutilated relics of antiquity."[11] This restorative process, however, is inevitably artificial since it requires the analyst to invent material to fill in the gaps that plague the afflicted patient. As literary critics have long recognized, this renders "Freud . . . as much a novelist as an analyst"[12] who weaves together his own fictions to fill out the facts of an individual neurosis. But *Dora*, of course, is not really a novel; it purports to be the accurate record of Freud's sessions with a young woman named Ida Bauer conducted in the closing months of 1900, just after the publication of *The Interpretation of Dreams*.[13] And while Freud may be trying to use psychoanalysis to "restore what is missing" in his ill patient, he is simultaneously trying to develop a narrative form capable of filling out the very same lacunae in his still evolving theories of hysteria and the unconscious. To do so, he resorts not to the novel, but to the roman à clef, a genre that much more effectively permits the self-conscious suturing of fiction onto fact.

As the 1905 preface to *Dora* makes clear, reading Freud's text as a roman à clef is all too easy an exercise: "I am aware," he laments, "that—in this town, at least—there are many physicians who (revolting though it may seem) choose to read a case history of this kind not as a contribution to the psychopathology of neuroses, but as a roman à clef designed for their private delectation" (3). Replacing Ida with "Dora," of course, is essential to the publication of this case since it is the only way he can safely yet accurately relay the sexual secrets and traumas of a bourgeois family. But as the text enters circulation, this substitution itself undermines the very objectivity it is meant to guarantee, threatening not only his patient's trust but his own dispassionate authority. Without publishing accurate notes or transcriptions, after all, readers can't help but wonder what else might have been changed—wonder, that is, just where the act of fictional substitution comes to an end. Indeed, on the very first page Freud rushes to address this concern, one which had troubled a good deal of his earlier work, including *Studies in Hysteria*. He writes that "whereas before I was accused of giving no information about my patients, now I shall be accused of giving information about my patients which ought not be given" (1). This excess of intimate detail is meant here to act as a guarantor of Freud's own objectivity and thereby delimit the study's reception by authorizing it as genuinely scientific discourse. The more spectacular the secrets he discloses, however, the more dogged his readers become in their attempts to ferret out the real identity of the Viennese family wracked by such scandal.

As we will see in a moment, Freud helped pioneer the use of the anonymous case study, and his writings were among the very first psychological texts that substituted fictional names to convey real facts. Yet he remained deeply suspicious of this form and was prescient about its potential instability once passed along to a reading public fascinated with sexual scandal. Indeed, it is somewhat surprising to realize he wrote only a few such studies himself, turning instead to increasingly more abstract works rooted primarily in theory rather than practice.[14] Part of the problem, of course, was his own growing celebrity, which brought with it what he called "the irksome attentions of a city that focuses quite particularly on my work as a physician."[15] As was the case with Dora, the patients he includes in his case studies themselves become objects of intense public scrutiny, feeding that same curiosity about "the private lives of unimportant neighbors" Baumann critiques in the *Fortnightly Review*. Fed into the mass-mediated networks generating his own fame, they too find themselves potentially transformed from psychiatric patients into international celebrities.[16] But Freud is also concerned that the narrative elements of the roman à clef he employs ultimately threaten to distort his findings by making clinical facts and narrative fictions dangerously interdependent. One of his final case studies, "Some Remarks on a Case of Obsessive-Compulsive Neurosis," makes this point explicitly: "I find the kind of distortions . . . to which one normally has recourse [in writing a case study] increasingly inappropriate and reprehensible. If they are only minor ones they do not fulfill their intended purpose of protecting the patient from indiscreet curiosity, and if they are more substantial then the sacrifice is too great, for they ruin our understanding of the overall logic of the case, which derives precisely from the petty realities of everyday life."[17] Freud finds himself stymied here by the resurgence of the roman à clef—both as a mode of reception and as resource for his writing. To publish the most intimate secrets of his patients' lives, he must resort to a narrative technique that allows for an artful blending of fact into fiction. Though openly acknowledging this act of concealment, however, he simultaneously finds that the very secrets he wishes to tell threaten to reveal the identity of his patients. The quotidian nature of psychopathology—the way in which the seemingly most mundane details of an individual's life inadvertently reveal sexual trauma—threatens to turn every anonymous case history into a roman à clef.

Freud had good reason to be concerned about the unexpected social life of his work and the ability of the case study to acquire an agency of its own. The Hippocratic Oath, after all, unambiguously commands the physician to silence: "All that may come to my knowledge in the exercise of my profession or in daily commerce with men, which ought not to be spread abroad, I will keep secret and will never reveal."[18] Yet the history of medicine in general—and more particularly of psychiatry—turns precisely on the need to divulge the most intimate details of a patient's life and history. Throughout the nineteenth and even early twentieth centuries, case studies generally made no attempt to preserve the anonymity of the patients, many of whom were women and often institutionalized members of the working class. James Braid, the Scottish physician and inventor of hypnotism, for example, made regular use of real names in his 1843 study, *Neurypnology; or, the Rationale of Nervous Sleep*. He records the case of "Mrs. Slater," a thirty-three year-old woman who loses the use of her legs after a traumatic pregnancy only to have their full function restored by hypnosis. "In recording cases," Braid writes, "I consider it my duty to report *facts as I have found them,* and to make no compromise for the sake of accommodating them to the preconceived notions or prejudices of anyone."[19] Though he is defending himself here against the charge that hypnotism is a fraud, his rigorous adherence to "facts" plainly extends to providing not only the name of his patient but extensive details about her personal life as well. Similarly, the renowned French physician Jean-Martin Charcot, one of Freud's own teachers, often lectured and toured with his patients, particularly "Blanche" Wittmann, who was popularly dubbed "The Queen of Hysterics."[20] These sessions are, in fact, the subject of a well-known 1887 painting entitled *Une leçon clinique à la Salpêtrière* by André Brouillet featuring Wittmann in the grips of a hysterical seizure.[21] Far from protecting his patient's privacy, he instead puts her vividly on display both for paying audiences and for the viewers of this heroic image that still hangs in the hospital.

Even as Charcot's theatrical presentations became well-known, however, the practice of so openly breaching a patient's confidentiality began to wane. In the December 1886 issue of *Le Revue Philosophique*, one of Freud's most important predecessors, Pierre Janet, published an article about a young woman plagued by hysteria and sleepwalking. "We will designate her by the letter L.," he writes, before going on to argue that his experiments on her reveal the existence of something "outside of consciousness" where "there is memory which persists, attention which is always awake."[22] This rudimentary description of the unconscious—the revelation, that is, of another kind of subjectivity operating within the patient—is itself accompanied by one of the earliest uses of a pseudonym in a case study. Just as the girl's deeper self is hidden or obscured from her, in other words, so is her identity more effectively hidden from the reader, transforming her from a historical actor into a literary construct. Janet, moreover, was not the only one to begin experimenting with this new form for the case study. Nearly simultaneously another of Freud's teachers, Richard von Krafft-Ebing, published his landmark study, *Psychopathia Sexualis*. A compendium of "the pathological manifestations of the sexual life," the book contains potentially explosive materials and the preface warns that "the author saw himself compelled to chose a title understood only by the learned, and also, where possible, to express himself in *terminis technicis*."[23] He also chose to conceal the identities of his patients, either citing their self-narrated case-studies in the anonymous first person or using single letters as in "Case 125": "On May 1, 1880, G., Ph.D., and a writer, was brought to the clinic for mental diseases at Graz, by the public authorities. While on his return from Italy, G. found a soldier in Graz who gave himself up to him for hire, but ultimately denounced G. to the police, because G. had openly announced his love for men" (300). Like Janet's "L.," this patient too finds himself suddenly entangled in a confusing configuration of secrecy and disclosure, revealing here not the operation of the unconscious mind but of what Eve Kosofsky Sedgwick calls the "epistemology of the closet."[24] He directly resists Krafft-Ebing's attempts to diagnose him as somehow ill, prompting the physician to describe the man as cynical, while using the conventions of the roman à clef to gesture toward even more scandalous secrets: "This was the extent of G.'s disclosures, whose mental condition was certainly congenitally abnormal. As proof of this may be cited his cynicism [and] his incredible frivolity in his application of his vices to religion, in which direction we cannot follow him without overstepping the bounds set by scientific inquiry" (302). The problem here is that the patient, in his frank admission and discussion of homosexual desire, discloses too much information, threatening to turn Krafft-Ebing's rhetorically disciplined scientific discourse (complete with all those Latin words), into a roman à clef that trades on the power and pleasure of secrecy.

Paradoxically, then, the introduction of pseudonymous names and initials in psychological case studies leads to an excess of knowledge, this narrative device suddenly revealing new possibilities and ontologies troubling even to those who employ it. The unconscious mind (for Janet) and homosexual desire (for Krafft-Ebing) both reveal the structuring power of a central secret at the core of human subjectivity, one suddenly exposed by the narrative conventions and reading habits of the roman à clef. As a site where desire can be both addressed and disciplined, the roman à clef plays an important role in what Foucault calls the "discursive explosion" of talk about sex in the nineteenth century.[25] Rather than leading simply to some greater revelation of truth or accuracy, however, the authors of these studies found themselves operating at an increasingly fluid boundary between fact and fiction. Seeking to reveal some deeper truth about human identity, they resorted to the conventions of narrative fiction in order to obscure their patients' identities—both from the reader looking for scandals and even from the subjects themselves. This is particularly true of Havelock Ellis, who begins his monumental *Studies in the Psychology of Sex* by gratefully acknowledging those who "have furnished me with intimate personal records" and lamenting that "I cannot make my thanks more specific."[26] This preface candidly admits that the text functions inevitably as a kind of roman à clef, its secret identities secured behind the screen of a "conditional fictionality": "I have tried hard to get at the facts, and, having got at the facts, to look them simply and squarely in the face. If I cannot perhaps turn the lock myself, I bring the key which can alone in the end rightly open the door: the key of sincerity" (xxviii).[27] Ellis, of course, does possess a particular kind of interpretive key that promises (or threatens) to reveal the real identities openly hidden behind letters like "Z" and "Q." But this same key also has the power, the preface suggests, to reveal other kinds of secrets openly hidden in the public sphere, secrets about homosexuality, sado-masochism, and auto-eroticism. Using the conventions of the roman à clef to withhold one kind of secret thus opens the possibility of exposing others as the book enters into networks of reading and reception beyond the control of both the author and the scientific discourse he seeks to control. The initial confusion of fact and fiction designed to protect a tantalizing anonymity quickly becomes both infectious and pervasive as the case study becomes entangled in emergent debates about the legal and moral status of such writing.

For Ellis, in particular, this attempt to use the roman à clef as a narrative tool capable of revealing "the psychology of sex" led precipitously from the exam room to the courtroom. These early volumes, in fact, have long been acknowledged as key texts in early-twentieth-century debates about both sexuality and obscenity since they led to the trial of English publisher and book-dealer George Bedborough in October 1898. He was charged with conspiring "to vitiate and corrupt the morals of the liege subjects of our Lady the Queen, to debauch and poison the minds of divers of the liege subjects of our said Lady the Queen, and to raise and create in them lustful desires" (xvii). Before what Ellis called this "epoch-making case" (xvi), however, the book had already encountered another kind of difficulty following its initial publication in Germany. For the section titled "Sexual Inversion," Ellis had secured a number of his case studies from the English author and poet John Addington Symonds—the man who appears in the text as "Z." He provided Ellis narratives from "many more or less distinguished inverts" as did his wife, whose own same-sex relationships were also fed into the text. In addition to these case studies, Symonds also contributed other material on the history, ethics, and culture of male–male desire. Accordingly, his name appeared alongside Ellis's own on the title page both in this initial 1886 German edition and in the first English edition printed a decade later.

Symonds, however, had been struck down by influenza in 1893, and his literary executor, Horatio Brown, withdrew permission to publish the material at the very last moment. In the immediate wake of Oscar Wilde's conviction, it became clear that this scientific study could all too easily be read as a roman à clef, and that Symonds's name—though protected by that pseudonymous initial in the case studies—was nevertheless hidden too plainly in sight on the title page. The genre's infectiousness meant that it had the potential to reveal not just "Z" but, though association, the identities of the friends, colleagues, and collaborators whose narratives he had also recorded. Brown and the Symonds family therefore purchased and destroyed the entire initial print run, leaving Ellis to revise the text heavily, removing his coauthor's name and the materials he had added—with the crucial exception of the case studies themselves.[28] These remained to constitute the core of the volume on *Sexual Inversion,* which was published later that year. The suppression of Symonds's name reveals just how pervasive the roman à clef and its habits had become, inviting readers to investigate the very boundary between fact and fiction that the altered names had initially been meant to secure. Ironically, by presumably enabling writers to probe more deeply into the secrets of sexuality and human identity, the use of pseudonyms simultaneously—and unexpectedly—exerted new pressures on the fact–fiction divide.

Like Ellis, Freud too quickly ran afoul of the roman à clef's anarchic streak, its ability to assume a life of its own as a social form that cannot be fully controlled or constrained by its creator. His decision to substitute the name "Dora" for Ida Bauer is essential to the case study and to the very invention of the psychoanalytic method since "it is certain that patients would never have spoken if it had occurred to them that their admissions might possibly be put to scientific uses; and it is equally certain that to ask them themselves for leave to publish their case would be quite unavailing" (2). To relate the truth of hysteria, in other words, he has to resort to the roman à clef, consoling himself and his readers with the assurance that fact and fiction are mingled only in the name of science. In "Some Remarks on a Case of Obsessive-Compulsive Neurosis," his anxieties about the use of this technique become even more pointed: "I cannot provide a complete treatment history because this would require too detailed an account of my patient's circumstances. The irksome attentions of a city that focuses quite particularly on my activities as a physician preclude the possibility of any entirely faithful account."[29] Indeed, Freud actually published very few case studies in the course of his career, and this preface to his account of the "Ratman" suggests some of the limits his narrative experiments with genre impressed upon him. In Dora's case, however, such concerns quickly give way to his determined efforts to root out the secrets he believes she had skillfully hidden from herself. That is, he not only employs the narrative elements of the roman à clef in writing the case history, but tries to read Dora herself as this same kind of ambiguous text—one in which the unconscious mind employs its own generic codes to tell a vital truth while nevertheless concealing its content. Just as Freud conceals the real identity of his patient, so too, he believes, does Dora conceal what he calls her "intention to be ill" (38). Getting at this suppressed intention thus requires him to develop new interpretive techniques for negotiating not only this case but the complicated form of the roman à clef itself—a form that now shadows not only the novel but the unconscious mind as well.

As Neil Herz argues, Freud's narrative falls afoul of what I have called the roman à clef's infectiousness, that "thoroughgoing epistemological promiscuity in which lines . . . blur between what Dora knew and what Freud knew."[30] This puts the case too simply, however, since the very boundaries between fact and fiction, as well as between the case study and the novel, are also at stake. In fabricating the truth of Dora's illness, Freud weaves an increasingly elaborate fiction that he attempts to impress both on us and on the girl herself as the fact of an underlying illness. There is always the danger, however, that this story will fail, that it will be exposed as an elaborate invention rather than genuine scientific knowledge. In the text, therefore, it's not just that the boundary between fact and fiction becomes blurred, but that Freud attempts constantly to switch the two—to avoid the inevitable "epistemological promiscuity" inherent in the case study by simply reversing the narrative's polarity. The facts of Herr K.'s sexual abuse thus become fictions thrown up by Dora's own unconscious as a way of concealing the deeper truth of her own sexual desires. At the end of 1900, however, Dora decided to leave treatment, thereby rejecting Freud's analytic method and its proposed solutions to her suffering. As Jen Shelton argues, as "Freud takes his revenge on Dora by narrativizing her," a new kind of modernist writing, "obsessed with authority," emerges.[31] His case study seeks to control the narrative ambiguities on which it depends by using "Dora" to fill the gap left by Ida Bauer's departure. The roman à clef thus becomes not merely an analytic tool designed to help the analyst "restore what is missing," but an interpretive technique capable of creating a new kind of knowledge about the self.

Freud soon discovers, however, that this narrative form possesses a social life of its own and that his celebrity, or what he calls, "the irksome attentions of a city that focuses quite particularly on my work as a physician," threatens to undermine the interpretive authority he seized from his patient.[32] The work of hiding identities, he worries, obscures crucial facts about his cases while inviting readers to treat serious scientific work as a kind of social gossip, a point he makes explicitly in his introduction to the "Ratman" case: "I find the kind of distortions . . . to which one normally has recourse [in writing a case study] increasingly inappropriate and reprehensible. If they are only minor ones they do not fulfill their intended purpose of protecting the patient from indiscreet curiosity, and if they are more substantial then the sacrifice is too great, for they ruin our understanding of the overall logic of the case, which derives precisely from the petty realities of everyday life" (126). The psychoanalytic case study, in effect, depends on the aesthetics of detail, on an attentiveness to what Freud calls "the most harmless and banal features." These are what give critical insight into a patient's neurosis even as they make him or her most easily "recognizable to all" (*Ratman* 126). Yet this is also an essential element of the roman à clef as a genre: an obsession with identifying those seemingly innocuous textual details that can abruptly turn fiction into gossip. Freud's innovative case studies took full advantage of the roman a clef's innovative potential, but it activated dormant modes of reading and reception that had been largely quiescent throughout the nineteenth century. Surprised by the roman à clef's anarchic social life, he sought quickly to constrain its energies, turning in his own work away from such narratives toward more abstract and anecdotal forms. This proved, however, an impossible task, since the roman à clef and the case study alike remain vitally productive genres that helped generate new kinds of reading and writing within a burgeoning modernism.

Oscar Wilde's Open Secrets

In transforming Dora—both the girl and the case study itself—into a roman à clef, Freud contaminated fact with fiction, creating an ambiguously open secret at the heart of the text. As he notes in his postscript to this fragmentary case history, "I can only repeat over and over again—for I never find it otherwise—that sexuality is the key to the problem of psychoneuroses and . . . no one who disdains the key will ever be able to unlock the door" (105). But according to Freud, the key here is not so much sexuality broadly conceived, as it is homosexuality. Dora, he insists in a famously startling footnote, is in love not the with the creepy and abusive Herr K., but with the man's wife, a secret that "was the strongest unconscious current in her mental life" (110). The analyst comes to this realization, in fact, only after the girl's treatment has ended and he has "learnt the importance of the homosexual current of feeling in psychoneurotics" (110). Freud thus seeks to reestablish his own interpretive authority in this note by fixing the boundary between fact and fiction—which heretofore had defined neurosis—on the identification of same-sex desire. Indeed, he apparently imagines a series of erotic exchanges between Dora and Frau K. that provided the girl with "her knowledge of sexual matters" (110). Earlier in the case study, Freud had already repeatedly insisted that in seeking to "guess her secret" he had not introduced any sexual knowledge the girl did not already possess (65).[33] "Her knowing all about such things," he then claims in that climatic footnote, "and, at the same time, her always pretending not to know where her knowledge came from was really too remarkable" (110). Dora's neurotic confusion of fact and fiction, in short, becomes both sign and symptom of what Colleen Lamos calls the "pathenogenic secret" of homosexuality.[34] If Freud's case study provocatively mixes fact with fiction in order to produce a new kind of knowledge, it does so here by displacing the secrets of the roman à clef (who is Dora?) onto the equally unstable secret of homosexuality (what is Dora?).

In the end, the fragmentary nature of the text and Dora's abrupt decision to terminate her treatment indicate that as a narrative technology, the roman à clef fails. This owes less to the particulars of the individual case, however, than to Freud's own inability to grasp the power of the device he had appropriated. He seeks, after all, to discard the roman à clef's "conditional fictionality" and thereby realign fact and fiction into an antagonistic binary, making Dora "whole" by revealing "her secret." Such revelations become the basis of psychoanalytic treatment in which the patients are given the necessary "key" to unlock the facts they have deliberately (albeit unconsciously) concealed behind a fictional armor of dreams, symptoms, and fantasies. In this early text, however, Freud fails to realize that the roman à clef becomes a kind of narrative prosthesis, what Tim Armstrong calls "a self-mastering mutilation in which the whole is rejected rather than recovered."[35] This resurgent genre structurally refuses resolution, resting on a duplicity that cannot be resolved without destroying its unique pleasures and powers. His final, desperate attempt to make Dora "whole" by introducing the secret of homosexuality thus not only fails to provide a cure, but simultaneously reveals the close connection between the "open secrets" of this narrative form and the equally duplicitous structures of the homosexual closet. Just as the roman à clef depends on the constitutive creation of a secret at the heart of the text, so too, as Eve Sedgwick argues, a new kind of sexuality was emerging that "was distinctly constituted *as* secrecy."[36]

If Freud sought finally to delimit and thereby control the roman à clef's powers by making both Dora and *Dora* whole again, Oscar Wilde employed the same textual and sexual devices to exploit more fully this emergent array of "self-mastering mutilations." Just as the case study deliberately manipulates the conventions of fiction in order to develop and disseminate a new set of facts about the human subject, so too Wilde deliberately blurs the boundary between fact and fiction in an effort to escape what he calls, in *The Decay of Lying*, "the prison-house of realism."[37] Appending elements of his own celebrity persona to seemingly fictional texts, he uses the roman à clef to reactivate the "extreme skepticism" the realist novel sought to control. His "entire oeuvre," Rhoda Garelick argues, "is dedicated precisely to collapsing distinctions between private and public, life and work, artist and celebrity," exploiting the roman à clef's structures to pose again that vexing question, "How much of this story is true?" Where Freud seeks unity and a "key," however, Wilde instead attempts to preserve what Michael Patrick Gillespie calls a "hypostatically suspended" truth, one that depends on the genre's "conditional fictionality" and infectiousness.[38] Such playfulness has its limits, however, and Wilde, like Dora, finds that the ambiguous secrets of his own texts can themselves be forcibly aligned around the epistemology of the closet. In the courtroom, fact and fiction would be painfully disarticulated in a way that helped define a decades-long engagement with the roman à clef.

Wilde's experiments with this anarchic narrative form both propagated and depended on his celebrity. Theatrical audiences urged him onto the stage after his premieres to take a bow—not only as the playwright but as the alter-ego of fictional dandies like Viscount Goring and Lord Darlington.[39] In his 1891 novella *The Picture of Dorian Gray*, the painter Basil Hallward at once acknowledges this public appetite for Wilde's celebrity while simultaneously disavowing it. In deciding not to exhibit the stunning portrait of his young friend, he bemoans the fact that "we live in an age when men treat art as if it were meant to be a form of autobiography."[40] He then concludes with a longer defense of aesthetic autonomy and of his own goals as an artist: "We have lost the abstract sense of beauty. Some day I will show the world what it is; and for that reason the world shall never see my portrait of Dorian Gray" (11). Hallward's reasoning here is enigmatic, acknowledging that this portrait not only can but perhaps should be read autobiographically since it lacks the alienating qualities of an "abstract" aesthetic—a point he earlier acknowledged in allowing that the picture contained "the secret of my own soul" (5). The painter's friend, Lord Henry Wotton (who serves as a textual double for Wilde's public persona), finds this lament baffling too, saying "I think you are wrong, Basil, but I won't argue with you" (11). It is not clear, however, just where the painter's error lies: in the vogue for autobiography? The essentially abstract quality of beauty? Or simply the decision not to exhibit the painting? This deliberately vague response captures effectively the roman à clef's ambiguity and the unique narrative resources it offers. After all, the text mounts a defense of aesthetic autonomy through the figure of the artist while simultaneously undermining the claim through the words of the character most closely associated with the author himself.[41] The celebrity persona is here pitted against the artist, and the encounter's "conditional fictionality" frustrates any attempt to adjudicate between them.

With increasing ingenuity, Wilde strategically deployed the roman à clef throughout his writing to mount a critique of both Victorian realism and the kind of proto-modernist abstraction Hallward praises. Both aesthetic modes, after all, depend on preserving a central, organizing autonomy that cleaves fact and fiction into two mutually opposed realms. This is the very distinction Wilde sought to challenge, however, and his critical writing during the 1890s turns on the deliberate attempt to muddle this divide, from the dizzying pursuit of Shakespeare's inspiration for the sonnets in "The Portrait of Mr W. H." to the witty dialogue in "The Decay of Lying." This latter work, in particular, contends that the realist novel has all but exhausted its energy in what Vivian (the Wilde-like figure in the piece) describes as a perilous obsession with mimeticism. In a passage that initially sounds like a critique of the roman à clef, he argues that "the modern novelist presents us with dull facts under the guise of fiction": "He insists on going directly to life for everything, and ultimately, between encyclopedias and personal experience, he comes to the ground, having drawn his types from the family circle or from the weekly washerwoman" (293). In the attempt to capture reality, in other words, art has become indistinguishable from history, the novel having collapsed entirely into a kind of crude sociology satirically linked here to Herbert Spencer and the Royal Society. The only response, Vivian asserts, is to embrace what he calls society's "lost leader, the cultured and fascinating liar" (305) who can invent new kinds of fiction without regard to dull and dreary facts.

Crucially, however, in associating the artist with the liar, Vivian avoids a simplistic defense of aesthetic autonomy in order to engage instead the ambiguities of the roman à clef. Structured as a dialogue laced with witticisms, the text counts on our ability to discern the persona of Wilde himself in the character of Vivian.[42] Thus, when he argues that "the only real people are the people who never existed," a paradox emerges as Vivian disavows the very confusion between reality and fiction animating the text itself. "If a novelist," he continues, "is base enough to go to life for his personages he should at least pretend that they are creations, and not boast of them as copies" (297). This is an apt description of "conditional fictionality" as it emerged amidst the celebrity culture of the late nineteenth century: a factual text "pretending" to be fiction, its author's own disavowal embedded—like Wilde's—within the narrative itself. Vivian, in the "Decay of Lying," thus extends the roman à clef into the public sphere so as to reactivate the "extreme skepticism" the novel struggles to contain. "Literature," Vivian claims, "always anticipates life. It does not copy it, but moulds it to its purpose" (308–9). Far from a defense of the realist novel's autonomy, this argument insists that the roman à clef permits certain kinds of narrative to reach into the world of fact, prompting his own creative rereading of the literary canon: "Schopenhauer has analysed the pessimism that characterises modern thought, but Hamlet invented it. The world has become sad because a puppet was once melancholy. The Nihilist, that strange martyr who has no faith, who goes to the stake without enthusiasm, and dies for what he does not believe in, is a purely literary product. He was invented by Tourgénieff, and completed by Dostoieffski. Robespierre came out of the pages of Rousseau as surely as the People's Palace rose out of the *debris* of a novel" (308). Vivian's hermeneutic refuses to prioritize fact or fiction since the resurgent roman à clef cuts both ways, rewiring the circuits running between readers, writers, and texts. When turning to Thackeray's *Vanity Fair,* for example, he treats it first as a traditionally conceived roman à clef in which real details can be extracted from a fictional façade: "I once asked a lady, who knew Thackeray intimately, whether he had any model for Becky Sharp. She told me that Becky was an invention, but that the idea of the character had been partly suggested by a governess who lived in the neighborhood of Kensington Square, and was the companion of a very selfish and rich old woman." Here fiction and reality are initially aligned so that the latter emerges as the text's hidden truth, its necessary but concealed origin. Vivian goes on to relate, however, that after the appearance of *Vanity Fair,* this governess morphs into her fictional counterpart, "and for a short time made a great splash in society, quite in Mrs. Rawdon Crawley's style, and entirely by Mrs. Rawdon Crawley's methods" (309). Like Dora, the governess finds herself exposed to the roman à clef's infectiousness, subject to the unexpected imbrication of fantasy and reality by a book that begins to write her own life for her.

Wilde published "The Decay of Lying" in 1891, the same year in which *The Picture of Dorian Gray* appeared in book form as an experiment in the resurgent narrative form outlined by Vivian.[43] Like earlier romans à clef framed around celebrity circles, including *Glenarvon* and *The Blithedale Romance,* the book was received as scandalous delectation, met with outrage by critics and enthusiasm by a public eager to peer into Wilde's elegant and sophisticated world. Yet it also revealed the dangers inherent in the roman à clef. Its ability to inject an "extreme skepticism" about fiction's boundaries grew so disruptive that its own author eventually found himself—like Thackeray's governess—struggling against a fiction that began to script his own life. It was in this same year, after all, that Wilde began the affair with Lord Alfred Douglas that eventually led to his trial, imprisonment, and lonely exile. At only their second meeting, Wilde presented to his new friend a signed, presentation copy of *Dorian Gray.* In what would become a powerful demonstration of the roman à clef's infectious potential, this novella would later be entered into evidence in Wilde's trials and essentially treated as if it described the affair that actually followed its publication.

The magical painting around which the book's plot rotates is itself a "self-mastering mutilation" that absorbs Dorian's increasingly terrifying sins so he can remain eternally youthful and beautiful. Pursuing a career of riot and hedonism from the town houses of Kensington to the East End docks, he seeks to become a pure fiction, locking the painting registering the horrifying reality of his actions in an attic so that he can "become the spectator of one's own life" and thereby "escape the suffering of life" (110). Because he does not bear the marks of history in his flesh, his mutilated self can experience new kinds of pleasures and knowledge. He "sought to elaborate some new scheme of life that would have its reasoned philosophy and its ordered principles, and find in the spiritualizing of the senses its highest realization" (130). Dorian's elaborate defense of what Henry Wotton calls the "new Hedonism," however, depends on separating the fact of degradation from the fiction of his beauty (130). Like Vivian's nascent theory of the roman à clef, Wilde's text subtly insists on the ambiguous reconfiguration of the news/novel divide. Thus, Dorian finds himself constantly lamenting "the tragedy of his own soul," indulging his own brand of skepticism, which prompts him to flee parties and study the painting locked securely in his attic (135). The magical canvas, in other words, does not permanently sever the connection between fact and fiction, but only further destabilizes it, creating a longing for organic unity just as alluring as the new kind of experience it offers. This renders the painting itself less a deeply suppressed truth than a dangerously open secret. Dorian is finally destroyed only at the moment he attempts to slash the painting and thereby restore the precedence of his aestheticized self over the "monstrous soul-life" emblazoned on the canvas (223). In assaulting the painting, Dorian rips away the ambiguity integral to his identity. As he dies, the "conditional fictionality" of his life suddenly collapses and the history of his crimes are inscribed upon an unrecognizable corpse watched impassively by the suddenly autonomous portrait.

Dorian's attack on the painting may mark the end of the text, but the energies released by its experiment with the roman à clef resonated widely. Just as the protagonist's friends in some fundamental way misread him, so too Wilde's public found themselves struggling to resolve the book's own tantalizingly open secrets about its author's life. Trying to link Wilde both to Dorian and to Henry Wotton, critics in the *St. James Gazette*, the *Daily Chronicle*, *Punch*, and the *Scots Observer* all decried the book as morally corrosive, shocking, and even dangerous. Wilde's now well-known responses to these allegations sharply turn this critique on the readers and reviewers themselves by arguing that "there is a terrible moral in Dorian Gray—a moral which the prurient will not be able to find in it, but which will be revealed to all whose minds are healthy."[44] The interpretive burden is rhetorically shifted here from author to reader, so that troubled reviewers found themselves accused of the very immorality they had tried to discern in Wilde himself. Such a move is predicated on the roman à clef's "conditional fictionality" and insists that the book does indeed contain some kind of destabilizing secret truth that nevertheless cannot be definitively separated from its fiction. When the story appears in book form, Wilde further extends the roman à clef's reach in his famous preface, which, in a series of epigrams, defines with surprising precision the evolving structure of the modernist roman à clef. "All art," he writes, "is at once surface and symbol," and he warns of the "peril" of trying to resolve this seemingly deconstructive tension in favor of one or the other (xxiii). Insisting that the text function either as an autonomous fiction or a morally fraught history risks revealing not the text's secrets, but the reader's own. "It is the spectator," he writes echoing his initial responses to the book's reviews, "and not life, that art really mirrors" (xxiv). Here then is both the cost and promise Wilde's experiment with the roman à clef proffers: deliberately confusing the boundary between fact and fiction makes reading itself an increasingly anarchic and infectious exercise since the secrets we unlock might be our own. What he tragically fails to grasp, however, is that this epistemological ambiguity has legal as well as aesthetic dimensions that can be dangerously resolved when it passes beyond his interpretive control.

Hidden Truths

After the publication of *The Picture of Dorian Gray,* Wilde experimented ever more creatively with this kind of open yet risky secrecy. The plots in his brilliant social comedies all depend on the preservation of scandalous secrets whose eventual revelation serves not to realign the moral and amorous worlds of the play, but to insist on the endless interpenetration of fact and fiction. In *The Importance of Being Earnest,* for example, secret identities proliferate seemingly without point or purpose since love, marriage, and identity finally come to depend less on some essential, factual self than on the fiction of individual names. Thus, both protagonists seek to be rechristened as Earnest, and one even discovers that he had quite literally been swapped with a novel at birth. And since suave and witty Wilde-like characters move effortlessly through these plays, the boundary between fact and fiction becomes even more porous. Famously, the author himself would regularly appear on stage after the performance, seeming to step out of the play's fictions to entertain the audience beyond the limits of the scripted text. Garelick argues that for Wilde "the on- and off-stage—or literary and extraliterary—narratives were identical."[45] Such a claim, however, is too simplistic, missing the most daring element of Wilde's narrative innovation. Far from making fact and fiction "identical," he sought instead to extend each into the other without resolving the structural tension between them. Rather than aligning on- and off-stage worlds, these texts instead activated the creative possibilities emerging from a resurgent skepticism about the news/novel divide.

On the page and in performance Wilde pushed the conditional limits of his fictions, testing the roman à clef's infectiousness as well as its extension into the historical world. At the London premiere of *Lady Windermere's Fan* in February 1892, for example, several men arrived wearing green carnation boutonnières, which had briefly been a symbol of homosexuality in Paris the year before; most in the audience were mystified, as Wilde had predicted they would be in a conversation with W. Graham Robertson: "A young man on the stage will wear a green carnation; people will stare at it and wonder. Then they will look round the house and see here and there more and more specks of mystic green. 'This must be some secret symbol,' they will say: 'What on earth can it mean?'" The point, Wilde tells Robertson, is that the carnation means "nothing whatever."[46] And at the end of the performance, Wilde himself appeared on stage, folding the perplexed audience into the play itself by extending his congratulations on the "great success of your performance."[47] The boundary between fact and fiction here does not collapse, but instead becomes conditional—even neurotic—as the audience finds itself linked to the fiction onstage while trying to piece together the apparently open secret of the green carnations around them. This may, of course, have been a joke largely at their expense, an instance of Sedgwick's "glass closet," which both manages to reveal and to conceal homosexuality simultaneously. Crucially, however, Wilde insists on the symbol's fundamental lack of meaning, its suspension between fact and fiction or between "surface" and "symbol." The flower, in short becomes a narrative element Wilde grafts onto his own play about secrets in high society in order to plunge the audience into the hermeneutic confusion Wilde believes essential to the roman à clef.

The brilliance of these experiments in genre and performance, however, depends on preserving the roman à clef's anarchic potential; Wilde managed skillfully throughout the 1890s to generate the kind of secrets that, like those dyed flowers, could successfully mean both everything and "nothing whatever." Indeed, in the wake of *Dorian Gray* and *Lady Windermere's Fan*, similar kinds of texts began to appear, including E. F. Benson's *Dodo* in 1893 and, a year later, the even more scandalous *Green Carnation*. The latter was published anonymously and, by seeming to reveal all of the secrets Wilde had so carefully managed to hold in dynamic tension, it proved perilously infectious. The book was an immediate success, running through several printings in a matter of months while scandalizing not only the wider public but Wilde's own circle of friends, who were outraged by its portraits of Douglas, Queensbury, and others. Like many romans à clef, its success depends less on plot or style than on an aesthetics of detail similar to "the petty realities of everyday life" Freud describes in his preface to "The Ratman." Its protagonist, Lord Reggie Hastings, is plainly modeled on Alfred Douglas, just as the witty and provocative dandy, Esmé Amarinth, so closely resembles Wilde that Frank Harris called it a "sort of photograph of Oscar," which "on all sides [was] referred to as confirming the worst suspicions."[48] Unlike *Dorian Gray*, the open secrets at the book's core are explicitly sexual, as Lord Reggie uses his green carnation to help seduce his fiancée's young son, urging him to "love" the flower that has "the supreme merit of being perfectly unnatural."[49] Eventually, the terrified fiancée breaks the engagement, much to the relief of Esmé, who tells the younger man he is again free to live "your marvelous scarlet life" and teach "the London tradesmen the exact value of your supreme aristocracy" (210). As the novel closes, Esmé relaxes in a railway carriage, smoking a "gold-tipped cigarette" while declaring "there is only one sanity in all the world, and that is to be artistically insane" (210).

Speculation about the author's identity was rampant and rumors suggested the portrait was so intimate and so exact that it must have been drawn by one of Wilde's closest intimates.[50] Indeed, although some suggested that it might have been penned by the best-selling Marie Corelli, others suspected Wilde himself may have been the anonymous author. As Neil McKenna notes in his biography, however, Wilde and his friends immediately sought to distance themselves from the book, since it threatened to infect and thereby shatter the "hypostatic tension" underlying both *Dorian Gray* and his popular plays. The roman à clef's structural tension between fact and fiction slips in *The Green Carnation*, transforming an otherwise vitally empty secret into the constitutive secret of homosexual desire. That is, the genre Wilde so effectively used to queer the binary opposition between fact and fiction quickly exceeded his control, becoming a narrowly proscribed queer narrative, its fictional secret reduced to the dangerous fact of homosexuality. Aware of the potential damage this book could do to all of his works by retroactively constellating them around the singular secret of same-sex love, Wilde promptly wrote to the *Pall Mall Gazette*: "Kindly allow me to contradict, in the most emphatic manner, the suggestion, made in your issue of Thursday last, and since then copied in many other newspapers, that I am the author of *The Green Carnation*. I invented that magnificent flower. But with the middle-class and mediocre book that usurps its strangely beautiful name I have, I need hardly say, nothing whatsoever to do. The flower is a work of art. The book is not."[51] Even as Wilde tries to maintain the ambiguity of his own emblem, he seeks to fall back on the very concept of aesthetic autonomy his works undermine by decrying the text as vulgar and unaesthetic. Significant damage, however, had already been done, as the genre's deconstructive potential gave way to its pragmatic social life. As McKenna notes, *The Green Carnation* only further inflamed the wrath of Douglas's father, and theater audiences began to turn on Wilde himself. The revelation that the book had, in fact, been written by Robert Hichens, who knew the principals only slightly, did nothing to diminish the reconstitution of Wilde's work around the central, organizing secret of homosexuality.[52]

The publication of *The Green Carnation* may not have actually precipitated the disastrous set of decisions that eventually led Wilde to the dock, but it clearly contributed to these events. As McKenna notes, the book's publication was extremely risky, and its publisher, William Heinemann, sought legal advice, fearing that he might be named in a libel suit by Wilde or Douglas (305). As we will see in the next two chapters, the relationship between libel and the roman à clef is complicated; it may well be that Wilde decided not to bring a case because it might only have further contributed to the suspicions already cast on his own work. The book and the damage it had done were still fresh, however, when Queensbury left his infamous card addressed to "Oscar Wilde posing as a somdomite [sic]" with a porter at the Albemarle Club in February 1895. This, of course, prompted Wilde (after being urged on by Douglas) to swear out a complaint of criminal libel against Queensbury, leading to the latter's arrest on March 2. This trial has been analyzed and treated in great detail by a wide array of critics, biographers, and theorists,[53] but following the publication of the complete transcript as *Irish Peacock and Scarlet Marques: The Real Trial of Oscar Wilde*, it has become clear just how powerfully the proceedings turned on the fictional status of *Dorian Gray*. This is largely a consequence of that infamous card accusing Wilde of "posing," a term that, in its emphasis on public performance, implies its own troubling disruption of the fact–fiction divide. To prove the truth of the libel in his defense, Queensbury had to establish conclusively not that Wilde had committed homosexual acts, but that he had created a public persona for himself as a "sodomite." Thus throughout the trial Carson cross-examines Wilde about the contents of his work, seeking to transform texts like *Dorian Gray* not into open confessions but into duplicitous romans à clef that deliberately yet openly conceal the secret of homosexuality.

This legal strategy first emerges when the defense enters into evidence the 1896 issue of an Oxford magazine titled *The Chameleon* containing "Phrases and Philosophies for the Use of the Young." Carson focuses his questions on a story from the same issue entitled "The Priest and the Acolyte" by John Edgar Bloxham that deals with an erotic relationship between a priest and a young man. After sparring over the potential immorality of the story, Carson asks "I think you would admit, Mr Wilde, that anyone who was connected with or who would allow himself publicly to approve of that article would be posing as a sodomite?"[54] Wilde denies this, but in doing so resorts to the very same defense he had publicly deployed against *The Green Carnation*, alleging that the story in question is in "very bad literary taste" (72). When pressed further, he reprises his response to the *Scots Observer*, telling Carson that "he who has found the sin has brought it" before insisting that he cannot be held responsible for the "misinterpretation of my work [by] the ignorant, the illiterate, the foolish" (78, 81). Hewing closely to the logic of the roman à clef, he refuses to acknowledge that the text possesses any central fact or secret, eventually frustrating Carson by telling him "you must remember that novels and life are different things" (103). Almost immediately, however, Wilde then invokes this same logic to include not just *Dorian Gray*, but several potentially damaging letters he had written Douglas and other young men. In discussing a phrase about "red rose-leaf lips" in one such letter, for example, he asserts a desire only to make a "beautiful thing" and thus "cannot answer any question" about morality or propriety "apart from art" (105). Wilde extends the "conditional fictionality" of his work to this letter in an attempt to disrupt Caron's line of questioning by undermining the supposed transparency of juridical evidence. As Wilde earlier told the court, "I rarely think that anything I write is true . . . not true in the actual sense of correspondence to actual facts of life" (74). Witty rejoinders like these were often met with laughter according to the transcript, but they become the most serious part of Wilde's own defense since they typically manage to graft fiction onto fact. As a result, the court's search for a unified, even organic sense of truth is temporarily replaced by the ambiguously open secrets at the heart of *Dorian Gray* that *The Green Carnation* had so dangerously filled.

In pursuing this strategy, Wilde sought not just to win his case against Queensbury, but also to reclaim some control over the roman à clef—the genre on which his own success was founded—by insisting on its instability. This may, in fact, help explain why he brought the case in the first place, despite warnings from friends like Harris that the defense could easily counter "clever talk about your books" by bringing up "a string of witnesses that will put art and literature out of the question."[55] Wilde treated his work as more than just "clever talk"; it was instead an acutely probative critique of aesthetic autonomy and novelistic realism. To the extent that the narrowly conceived libel in this trial turned on the word "posing," the author of *Dorian Gray* could thus continue to exploit the deep structural ambiguities so essential to the "prison house of realism," holding fiction at a conditional and therefore critical remove from reality. Thus, when

Edward Carson begins his opening remarks for the defense, he has to deploy a logic as convoluted as his syntax:

> Lord Queensbury took care in all his letters . . . to persistently state that he did not accuse Mr Wilde of the actual felony [of sodomy]—that would be a matter which would subject Mr Wilde to very serious consequences if it were true—but of 'posing as a sodomite' and I think you will say that really meant that Mr Wilde, by his acts and writings, was putting himself in that position that people might naturally and reasonably infer from the writings and the course of life he was adopting, that he, Mr Wilde, was either in sympathy with, or addicted to, immoral and sodomitic acts. (255)

Carson here clearly runs afoul of the roman à clef's structural contradictions as he struggles first to separate fact from fiction by alleging Wilde is not actually accused of being a sodomite, only to then collapse the two by arguing that the book may be used as evidence to indict the life.

Ultimately, however, libel laws exist essentially to demarcate and police a stark divide between fact and fiction. Carson's arguments thus succeed precisely at the moment he abandons "the question of the literature involved in this case" and shifts his emphasis from the ambiguities of "posing" to Wilde's sexual acts. As Carson threatens to introduce witnesses like Charles Parker and Alfonso Conway, the deconstructive powers of the roman à clef begin to fail as the text congeals around the constitutive secret of homosexuality. Rather than a book capable of queering the boundaries between fiction and fact, *Dorian Gray* suddenly becomes—like Hichens's *The Green Carnation*—a queer book founded less on a generative doubt than on a crippling "perversion." Aware that these witnesses could lead to Wilde's own criminal prosecution, his attorney abruptly sought to conclude the case by either withdrawing the charge or submitting to a verdict of "not guilty." In doing so, he too adopts Carson's tortured logic about Wilde's work, asking that the verdict itself have "reference, if to a part of the particulars at all, then to that part of the particulars which is connected with the publication of *Dorian Gray* and the publication of *The Chameleon*" (281). That is, he seeks here to return these texts precisely to the "prison-house of realism," rendering them mere fictions that do not actually impinge upon the facts of their author's life. As a "self-mastering mutilation," the roman à clef abruptly becomes less an extension of narrative power for Wilde than a dangerous threat to his personal freedom and individual integrity. The genre, in short, may introduce new kinds of knowledge and identities, but it also threatens constantly to fix those identities in broken, partial, or mutilated forms.

Later, in *De Profundis,* Wilde lamented "the hideous trap in which I . . . allowed myself to be caught"; critics now justifiably claim that the libel trial and its aftermath played a key role both in establishing homosexuality as an identity and in transforming it into a deeply constitutive secret.[56] *Dorian Gray* and its author's own daring performance on the stand, however, did more than help delimit an emergent homosexual identity. They also queered the boundary between history and the novel and, in the process, began to expose a series of faults in the legal and aesthetic dispensation on which the realist novel had been staked since its emergence in the eighteenth century. As literature became increasingly entangled with the open secret of its own potential historicity, the roman à clef once again began to operate as a creative counter-form to the novel. Wilde and Freud energetically seized upon it, and, though working from opposite sides of the fact–fiction divide, both successfully exploited its ability to generate new kinds of pleasure and knowledge. These same writers, however, also both eventually abandoned the form, finding—as others too would later discover—that it depends upon an unpredictable and even treacherous skepticism when routed through the networks of an expanding celebrity culture. The energies they helped unleash reactivated legal, aesthetic, and moral debates that resonated throughout the early decades of the twentieth century. As history and the novel began once more sliding into one another, authors, publishers, critics, and even law courts struggled to define the roman à clef's limits by seeking new ways to answer the question, "How much of this story is true?" As the next two chapters will show, this was as much a legal challenge as an aesthetic one, its implications extending from the monumental works of James Joyce to a British system of libel law that, until reformed, had all but declared fiction itself illegal. Despite the collapse of Wilde's own libel suit, in fact, the arguments over the precise fictional (or factual) status of a text like *Dorian Gray* formed a vital strand of this emergent modernism.

4. Libel
Policing the Laws of Fiction

And though no perfect likeness they can trace;
Yet each pretends to know the Copied Face.
These, with false glosses feed their own ill-nature,
And turn to Libel, what was meant a Satire.

—William Congreve, *The Way of the World*

In 1924, Osbert Sitwell published *Triple Fugue*, a small and delicately crafted collection of short stories offering thinly veiled satiric portraits of the snobbish London literary coteries through which he and his siblings moved. Among those savaged were Ottoline Morrell, Aldous Huxley, and Edmund Gosse, all of whom were suitably outraged. In a letter to Arnold Bennett, Sitwell emphasized the roman à clef's distinctive "aesthetics of detail," suggesting that it be treated as a scandalous "Book of Characters" structured less by plot than by "anecdote."[1] Fictional facades seem only lightly to conceal their historical originals. In the foreword to the title story Sitwell even cultivates the roman à clef's wanton infectiousness by hinting that "a student of social life" might see the text as a kind of "detective game" to be played "for his own amusement."[2] Although such a coy introduction certainly generates some ironic distance between Sitwell and these stories of social intrigue, it insists that the reader simultaneously savor the scandalous concoction of gossip, celebrity, and fiction. The initial reviews of the text looked dimly on such pleasures, typically echoing *The Spectator's* lament that it was symptomatic of "the biographical element in modern literature [which] threatens to become a menace."[3] *The Outlook* carefully avoided engaging directly in any of the detective work Sitwell's text invites, and regretted that this otherwise "decorative" prose stylist "preferred the annoyance of his enemies to the case of unicorns."[4] *The Times Literary Supplement* described the text's distaste for its own characters, noting the "dislike, contempt, or ridicule" with which they were portrayed.[5] More than just a snide indictment, however, this telling passage from the *TLS* gestures to the legal rather than to the aesthetic risks Sitwell took with these stories. This is because the phrase used by the unsigned reviewer echoes almost precisely one of the most famous definitions of libel in British jurisprudence as articulated by Baron Parke in the 1840 case of *Parmiter v. Coupland*: the expression in a relatively permanent medium of language meant to bring someone into "hatred, contempt, or ridicule."[6] Sitwell, this review suggests, has done more than violate the rules of literary decorum; he may, in fact, have crossed the thin but nevertheless dangerous boundary that legally separates fact from fiction and thereby exposed himself to civil and even criminal penalties. Here the roman à clef's anarchic skepticism becomes a legal rather than simply an aesthetic problem, and its consequences for cultural production in the first half of the twentieth century were enormous.

We have become all too accustomed to the dull legal boilerplate that appears in the front matter of most modern fictional works and dryly disavows any kind of connection to the real world and its inhabitants. Typically, it reads something like this: "This is a work of fiction. The characters, incidents, and dialogues are products of the author's imagination and are not to be construed as real. Any resemblance to actual events or persons, living of dead, is entirely coincidental."[7] The closer a novel comes to containing some element of historical or biographical truth, the more prominent such disclaimers become, their heightened visibility ironically reassuring the reader that there may indeed be some outrageously scandalous facts for a well-trained social detective to extract.[8] In *Triple Fugue* Sitwell extends his satire to include the often rank hypocrisy of this thin legal assertion of fiction's complete autonomy, going to far as to indict what Aaron Jaffe calls his own "imprimatur" as a modernist writer.[9] That is, he tests the aesthetic as well as the legal structures underwriting his authorial autonomy as the "sovereign site for artistic consciousness."[10] To do so, he appends his own mock disclaimer on the recto of the contents page: "In humbly presenting the following tales of the Old and New Worlds I should at the same time wish to warn my readers that any character failing to recognise himself will immediately be prosecuted for libel."[11] Sitwell here returns his fiction to the novel's origins in the eighteenth century when, as we have seen, such texts were prefaced by disclaimers that asserted their factual rather than fictional origins. By daring his readers to recognize themselves—indeed threatening them with legal action if they fail to see the ways they have been obliquely named yet directly indicted—Sitwell attempts to satirize and thereby disrupt the modern novel's trajectory toward a facile aesthetic autonomy that coyly effaces its direct investment in the markets for economic profit and personal prestige.

When his second volume of equally satiric stories, *Dumb Animal*, appeared in 1930, however, the limits of this critique became plainly, indeed painfully, evident. The collection's final story, "Happy Endings," describes a boy's education at a military academy just before the First World War and is clearly based upon Sitwell's own experiences at Ludgrove. The satire takes aim at drunken masters, hopeless students, and a hypocritical headmaster—a "tiresome, rather harmful old man" who urges the boys to sacrifice themselves to the Empire from behind the safety of his large desk.[12] The dull routine of the school is only broken by the garden and other splashes of decoration created by the headmaster's "Madame-Bovary-wife" who "had been compelled to indulge her romantic imagination, walking among these flowers which she alone loved here, seeing herself in a hundred other positions than the one she occupied, and with far more actuality, until her mind had begun a little to suffer."[13] The story concludes with news of her son's death in the war followed by her own mental breakdown. After chaining herself to the Prime Minister's residence with a sign reading, "Votes for Jesus," she is confined to a metal institution, her mind shattered by wartime carnage and home-front hypocrisy. Like much of Sitwell's work, this was tepidly received by the critics, and the various luminaries who had been savaged again refused to pick up the gauntlet. In drawing so closely on his own school experiences, however, Sitwell found himself unexpectedly named in a libel suit brought by Mrs. Welch, the real-life original of the headmaster's wife, who had herself suffered a painful breakdown during the war. Learning of the writ issued against him, Sitwell became suddenly evasive about his own techniques, writing of Mrs. Welch in a letter to Violet Hammersley, "I hardly know her," then glibly trying to seek refuge in a kind of Wildean epigram by claiming that "probably the character is, as always with imaginative writing, exactly as she is."[14] This reflexive defense, that life must be imitating art, merely conceals the fact, as Sitwell revealed in a subsequent letter to his agent, that he was a good deal more concerned about the financial damage a libel suit could do than his cheeky disclaimer in *Triple Fugue* suggests. Rather than worrying about the status of his authorial imprimatur, in other words, he is far more anxious that a public libel trial might draw enough publicity to the story that Mrs. Welch would be followed by a large number of former masters and students who might also seek disastrous claims for damages.[15] In the end, the affair was quietly settled by the destruction of the 600 copies remaining in stock and the payment of £500 in damages to Mrs. Welch plus costs.

Nor was this Sitwell's last encounter with the libel courts: he would famously return as a plaintiff, in 1939, winning a suit against a literary critic who claimed that "oblivion" had claimed him and his siblings "and they are remembered with a kindly, if slightly cynical, smile."[16] Two years earlier he had narrowly avoided a far more serious libel charge when his poem "Rat Week," a particularly nasty satire of King Edward VIII and Wallis Simpson, was pirated and published in *Cavalcade*.[17] Sitwell's critical assault on the conventions of fictional autonomy and his subsequent entanglements with such lawsuits are, in fact, symptomatic of the increasingly complicated legal circumstances that confronted writers in the early twentieth century. Our understanding of the intersection between law and literature in this period, however, has been severely distorted by an almost obsessive focus on the famous obscenity trials of *Ulysses* and *Lady Chatterley's Lover*, both of which have become part of a liberal romance of art's ever-expanding freedom. These now iconic texts have assumed a status that exceeds their considerable artistic merit precisely because they fit so well into a progressive historical narrative that couples sexual liberation to artistic innovation.[18] Indeed, early editions of both novels were regularly prefaced by the legal decisions that sanctioned them as works of art, redeeming the authorial imprimatur by transmuting it into the coin of contemporary liberal humanism.

The Sitwell libel case, however, provides an important counter-narrative to this swelling romance, one that reveals the complex ways his attempts to renegotiate the news/novel divide were constrained by a body of law that was itself in radical flux throughout the early twentieth century. This period of legal and aesthetic instability begins roughly with Whistler's legendary 1878 performance in the witness box when he won a farthing in damages from an elderly John Ruskin, who had condemned *Nocturne in Black and Gold*, writing, "I have seen, and heard, much of Cockney impudence before now, but never expected to hear a coxcomb ask two hundred guineas for flinging a pot of paint in the public's face."[19] As Ruskin's defense attorney argued in outraged defense of his client, "no artist could attain fame except through criticism" and Whistler expertly manipulated the proceedings to heighten his celebrity through this *succès de scandal*.[20] Whistler's exploits, in turn, likely played a key role in Oscar Wilde's subsequent decision to name the marquis of Queensbury in his own disastrous libel suit. The roughly four decades between Whistler's trial and the beginning of the Second World War correspond closely with the rise of aesthetic modernism, and mark a simultaneous boom in the production of romans à clef. Feeding on the rapidly expanding culture of mass-mediated celebrity, such texts placed increasing strain on the law's power to adjudicate cases of libel. Indeed, these same four decades also saw the rapid expansion of defamation law into the realm of art and literature, as individuals who discovered their unauthorized likenesses in books, film, and other ostensibly fictional media turned to the courts for redress. To the degree that modernism itself might be seen, in part, as an experiment in the roman à clef's resurgent possibilities, then relatively strict temporal boundaries can be drawn around it, beginning with the widely influential Aretmus Jones case of 1909 and concluding with a sweeping reform of libel laws initiated in 1939 and finally enacted as part of the Defamation Act in 1952. Rather than the kind of absolute victory achieved in the more famous obscenity trials of the 1920s and 30s, however, libel cases generated a series of jarring and often complicated negotiations between literature and the law that sharply delimited the horizons of modernism's possibility.

This chapter tracks the history of libel law as it evolved over the opening decades of the twentieth century in order to reveal the ways in which literary modernism failed in what Pierre Bourdieu calls its "conquest of autonomy."[21] It examines, instead of a narrative of liberation, the often bitterly fought contest between the roman à clef's attempt to subsume the real world and the state's attempt to police a strict boundary between fact and fiction. Modernism's sudden return to the roman à clef as part of its campaign against Victorian realism led—particularly in Britain—not to aesthetic autonomization, but to a turbulent encounter between literature and the law. The next chapter will focus narrowly on two of the period's most scandalous and iconic writers, James Joyce and Wyndham Lewis, both of whom structured some of their innovative narrative experiments around the disruptive ambiguities of the roman à clef. Joyce's *Ulysses* and Lewis's *Apes of God*, in fact, may have been two of the most libelous texts written in the early twentieth century, when the genre became useful for carrying out often nasty campaigns of literary assassination. Although their schemes for revenge (both grand and petty) can now only be gleaned from biographies and annotations, they nevertheless had profound and often quite damaging consequences for those who found their lives appropriated by works that often passed as pure fictions. Richard Best, for example, who appears in the "Scylla and Charybdis" episode of *Ulysses,* struggled for decades against the portrait Joyce had drawn—one that eventually overwhelmed his otherwise distinguished career as the Director of the National Library of Ireland. When approached by a reporter who wanted to interview him as part of a segment on *Ulysses,* in fact, he could only respond with what must have become a practiced indignation at the book's unique power over his life: "I am not a character in fiction; I am a living being."[22] Defamation law exists precisely to cordon reality off from fiction by affording a private individual like Best some protection from the misappropriation of his or her name and biography.

As we will see, modernism's experiments with the roman à clef cannot be easily accommodated to the ongoing conquest of aesthetic autonomy in which art gains its freedom from social and legal constraint. Instead, this infectious genre becomes so potent a site of narrative experiment in the early twentieth century precisely because it can arrest this historical drift toward isolation, abstraction, and obscurity. Ironically, just as the laws of obscenity that had constrained aesthetic production began to lose their force, libel laws came even more powerfully into effect, insisting that the novel hew to its presumed autonomy and thus surrender any claim to social utility. Joyce and Lewis illustrate the kind of strategies modernist writers pursued in attempting to resist their own evolving autonomy by engaging the laws of libel directly, provoking those very suits that Osbert Sitwell teasingly courted in the disclaimer at the opening of *Triple Fugue*. Though neither proved successful when their works were eventually called to legal account, their scandalous conflation of fact and fiction in the roman à clef provocatively reveals both the limits of modernism's autonomy and the steep cost such freedom could exact.

"Whatever a Man Publishes He Publishes at His Peril"

The concept of defamation as a civil and sometimes even criminal wrong has a complicated history that reaches back into nearly every known system of Western law.[23] At its core, it seeks to regulate the flow of information in civil society by protecting an individual's right to his or her reputation against publicly circulated lies and insults. Francis Holt in his 1812 study, *The Law of Libel*, traces the offense back to ancient times, locating precedents in Sumerian, Greek, and Roman law before concluding that "an injury . . . which affects [someone] in character" is the "next greatest injury" after direct physical harm.[24] In the fifth century B.C.E., Roman law codified the crime of *famosus libellus*, decreeing it so vile as to be punishable by death; and under the *Lex Talonis* of the Anglo-Saxons, a man judged guilty of defamation would have his tongue cut from his head.[25] W. Blake Odgers—whose massive 1881 *Digest of the Law of Libel and Slander* was considered authoritative on British defamation law until the middle of the twentieth century—maintains that "every man has a right to have his good name unimpaired" and that this is "a *jus a rem*, a right absolute and good against all the world."[26] The written word, because it could be so widely and persistently disseminated, was considered a particular threat to this fundamental right, and within British legal history the first laws of libel emerged almost simultaneously with the arrival of the printing press. As Holt argues, writing itself "no sooner commenced than the abuse [of libel] grew up with it, and therefore in legal intendment, as explained by constant practice, the law to restrain it."[27] Defamation law, in effect, serves to curtail the limits of free expression by protecting individuals from print's ability to convey often anonymous and damaging lies.[28]

By 1662 defamation laws had become so well established in England that a book called *Sheppard on Slander* appeared in London describing "thousands" of such cases. The earliest reference to this particular aspect of English law appears in 1275 when "*scandalum magnatum*"—the deliberate dissemination of insults to peers of the realm—was forbidden as part of an attempt to control seditious statements about noble families. British jurisprudence gradually evolved laws regarding four distinct modes of libel: defamation, blasphemy, obscenity, and sedition.[29] Each covers a particular aspect of written expression and, until the nineteenth century, effectively provided the legal framework that governed the flow of printed information while affording special protection to the Crown, the Church, and the nobility. Thus, until the Reform Act of 1832, it was a generally held principle (in stark contrast to American law) that a libel directed against a public person was considered more dangerous than one directed against a private individual.[30] Furthermore, until 1946, libel trials were conducted exclusively by so-called "special juries" drawn by statute exclusively from the ranks of "bankers, merchants, occupiers of private houses of a substantial rateable value, and esquires,"[31] on the presumption that only men who possessed good names could truly weigh the cost of a plaintiff's potential loss. The laws governing defamation in Britain are thus largely rooted in an attempt to protect the state, its agents, and its leading institutions from publicly circulated criticism.

This tradition of regulating speech by emphasizing the importance of an individual's public reputation also accounts for the odd bifurcation of British libel law into two distinct strands: one civil and the other criminal. This chapter focuses largely on the former (called the "tort" of libel), but the crime of libel too has played an important role in modernism's legal history. The case that ultimately destroyed Oscar Wilde, after all, was *Regina v. John Douglas*—that is, a criminal case brought by the state against a defendant whose alleged crime was so grievous that it threatened a breach of the peace. This particular body of law originated in the fifteenth century when the Star Chamber pursued such prosecutions in order to curtail violent duels among the upper classes. These special, nonecclesiastical courts defined libel as the publication in writing of a statement that might damage someone's good name, *regardless of its basis in fact*. Such publication could take the form not only of an article or of a book but of a private letter, a hastily scribbled note, or even a personal diary entry. Unlike civil law, which requires that a libel be published to a third person other than the author or the object of the defamation, criminal law sought to regulate all forms of written and printed matter.

The civil and criminal laws are otherwise similar with one crucial exception: in a criminal case the truth of a libel cannot generally serve as a defense. As Sir Edward, a Star Chamber judge, definitively wrote in the 1609 *De Libellis Famosus:* "It is not material whether the libel be true, or whether the party against whom it is made, be of good or ill-fame; for in a settled state of Government the party grieved ought to complain for every injury done him in an ordinary course of law, and not by any means to revenge himself, either by the odious course of libelling, or otherwise."[32] Until 1793, in fact, juries were permitted only to judge whether or not the document already deemed libelous by a judge had been written or published by the defendant in a case. That is, the matter of interpretation lay beyond legal debate since these insults had the potential to do such terrible damage. Throughout the early nineteenth century, criminal libel charges were thus regularly used to allow an individual to preserve potentially embarrassing or scandalous secrets. Because the author of such information was not allowed to enter any evidence about the truth of his or her statement, the mere fact of jotting it down opened the door to arrest, imprisonment, and suppression. Newspapers and magazines could also be indicted, even if they merely printed verbatim transcripts of trials or government meetings in which the libel was mentioned. Ironically, the considerable protections afforded a plaintiff in such cases meant, as one member of Parliament noted in 1843, that "the prosecution by indictment [that is, criminal libel] is practically an admission of the truth of the libel."[33] In an effort to relax these laws somewhat, the Libel Act of 1843 created a crucial exception, allowing defendants to plead guilty with special justification provided that they could prove *both* that the libel was true and that it had been deliberately published in the public interest. This is the exception that eventually landed Wilde in the dock himself, since it offered the only available line of defense to Queensbury at his 1895 trial. Indeed, Wilde was by no means the first plaintiff who had been deliberately provoked into bringing a libel charge precisely so that the truth of the defamation could be proved in open court.[34]

By the twentieth century, criminal prosecutions had become quite rare, in part because an 1884 case, *Regina v. Labouchère,* made it much more difficult to secure such indictments without prior approval from a government prosecutor. These reforms, however, did little to curtail a growing barrage of civil suits launched in response to the mass media's rapid expansion as information began to flow more freely through the public sphere. Unlike the criminal law, the civil tort of libel developed initially from the Ecclesiastical Courts and, like all torts, it governs that area of law not otherwise covered by criminal statute or formal contracts. Typically, libel cases are complicated and extremely expensive affairs both to prosecute and to defend, as Edith Sitwell's solicitor reminded her after Peter Ustinov produced a *drame à clef* entitled *No Sign of the Dove* satirizing her and her siblings: "Libel actions, as no one knows better than yourself and Osbert, are wearing things to stage and bring to fruition; wear and tear on nerves, anxieties, time occupied, and a whole host of other irritations are their inescapable accompaniment."[35] The damages awarded by a jury can be quite excessive, though because they are meant to recompense the plaintiff only for the damage done to his or her reputation, they may also be entirely symbolic—like the single farthing awarded to Whistler. Furthermore, because this area of law is so complicated by the patchwork of precedents and Parliamentary reforms stretching back to the seventeenth century, such cases can be incredibly expensive to wage. Very often, the costs alone will exceed even the most significant damages, and unless these expenses are also awarded to the plaintiff even a victory can prove pyrrhic.

The difficulty posed by such suits is further compounded by the fact that the truth can serve as a defense in civil actions, and modern libel trials typically turn precisely on a defendant's attempt to demonstrate the veracity of his or her claims. Indeed, libel law is nearly unique in this regard, for once a judge has decided as a matter of law that a particular piece of writing might be capable of defamatory interpretation then three legal presumptions follow: "The defendant was presumed to have published in malice, the words were presumed to be false, and the plaintiff was presumed to have suffered damages."[36] Unlike a criminal trial, in other words, in which a defendant is presumed innocent, in a libel suit he or she is instead presumed guilty and must assume the full burden of proof. That is, it must be conclusively demonstrated to a jury that the defendant's comments were, in fact, true and that they were not published in a malicious attempt to damage the plaintiff's business or personal reputation. Thus, as the Sitwells' attorney argued, there is more to be weighed than just the defense of one's reputation in filing a writ for libel, since it has the potential to open the most unsavory details of one's life to very public scrutiny.

Despite these difficulties, however, the tort of libel nevertheless plays a vital role in regulating the public sphere. As James Scarlett argues in *Cooper v. Wakley* (1828), "every man in England is at liberty to publish what he pleases," but such freedom "would become the source of the most bitter tyranny that ever an unhappy country laboured under, unless in those instances in which that freedom is abused some constitutional tribunal did exist to correct it."[37] At its core, then, the civil tort of defamation provides a legal forum where truth can be separated from fiction and where those who use the mass media's power to disseminate lies can be called publicly to account. As Lennard Davis demonstrates in *Factual Fictions,* libel laws played a vital institutionalizing role in the novel's rise during the eighteenth century, effectively creating a set of legal definitions designed to separate political discourse from fictional invention. A series of Parliamentary laws and legal decisions beginning with *Queen v. Hart* (1711) and culminating with Fox's Libel Act (1792) "made it more difficult for narratives to rest in some grey area between fact and fiction. Those narratives that bore too close a resemblance to the world, that were too factual, ran the risk of being legally actionable; those narratives that clearly asserted their fictionality and that bore little resemblance to the world were unharmed."[38] This legal distinction between fact and fiction created the consensus upon which the growing autonomy of the nineteenth-century aesthetic sphere was staked, consequently forcing, as Davis concludes, "writers who wished to write about the world away from such overtly political modes as the one offered by the newspaper and toward a more protected form of writing" such as the novel (100). This consensus, however, began to collapse at the end of the nineteenth century as writers used the roman à clef to extend their work into that long-suppressed and potentially anarchic "grey area." As a consequence, the laws of libel entered a new period of instability and flux as writers experimented with an infectious and "conditional fictionality" capable of breaking down the legal boundary between the novel and the news. Indeed, as Eric Barendt argues, libel does not simply regulate the production of literature, it effectively becomes a part of "the law *of* literature" every bit as significant as copyright.[39] Just as copyright provides the structures of ownership governing the dissemination of printed matter in a capitalist society, so too the tort of defamation—by legally separating fact from fiction—provides the framework through which a particular piece of writing is presumed to be pure invention and thus without financial, legal, and moral consequence for living individuals. Despite that fact that libel thus essentially constitutes the law of fiction, however, its importance in shaping modern literary production has been almost entirely ignored.

"It Does Not Signify What the Writer Meant"

This critical gap in our institutional histories of modernism is all the more striking because the rules of evidence in a defamation case effectively transform the courtroom into an impromptu literature seminar where jurors weigh alternative interpretations of a particular text.[40] Libel trails are so expensive to wage, in part, because a complex body of law has developed since the seventeenth century governing quite narrowly the kind of evidence that can be introduced, the methods of argumentation that are permitted, and the standards of reason and good judgment by which a final, definitive interpretation can be produced. The most important such principle—and certainly the one with the most far-reaching consequences—explicitly rules the intentions of an author entirely inadmissible in a jury's attempt to determine the meaning of a potentially defamatory text. "The question," according to the 1885 decision *Bolton v. O'Brien,* "is not what the defendant, in his own mind, intended by [his] language, but what was the meaning and inference that would be naturally drawn by reasonable and intelligent persons."[41] Long before William Wimsatt founded modern literary criticism on the cornerstone of the intentional fallacy, in other words, British and American libel courts had already been struggling to build a mode of interpretive practice based on the absence of an authorial guarantee.[42] The final arbiters of a text thus are the members of the jury themselves who constitute a community of ideal readers, a representative public sphere in which meaning can be debated and adjudicated. This is the central principle governing defamation cases, and its effects came into full force in 1852 when it was judged that no court of appeal could ever reverse or undo a jury's judgment about the meaning of a text. "After a verdict for the plaintiff," Odgers writes, "the defendant can no longer argue that it does not sufficiently appear to whom the words relate."[43] Appeals, in other words, can only be based on points of law or courtroom procedure since the meaning of a text is entirely a matter of fact and as such can only be settled by a jury.

As we will see in a moment, this empowerment of the jury as ideal readers and the complete invalidation of authorial intention had far-reaching consequences for novelists in the early decades of the twentieth century and eventually prompted some of the key reforms set in place by the 1952 Defamation Act.[44] There is, however, a second crucial component of libel law regulating the kind of interpretations admissible in court, one of particular importance to the roman à clef's resurgence and the extreme skepticism it deploys to thrust art into the mass-mediated public sphere. The deliberate encoding of real people and events within an apparent fiction, after all, means that even the most insulting and pernicious libels may well be invisible to anyone but those who possess, or even simply believe themselves to possess, the proper interpretive key. Thus, the same narrative mechanism that generates the roman à clef's anarchic uncertainties simultaneously affords its authors a vital degree of legal protection, since a defendant may always simply claim that allegedly defamatory works do not refer to the plaintiff. In the 1848 case of *Le Fanu and another v. Malcolmson,* however, the British courts found such a defense insufficient, noting that "whether a man is called by one name, or whether he is called by another, or whether he is described by a pretended description of a class to which he is known to belong, if those who look on know well who is aimed at, the very same injury is inflicted, the very same thing is in fact done, as would be done if his name and Christian name were ten times repeated."[45] In the absence of authorial intention, however, proving such "conditional fictionality" means not only that a single text must be capable of multiple interpretations, but that additional, contextual knowledge is required by the jury.

In filing a libel suit, a plaintiff introduces such material as part of what is called the "colloquium": a thick collection of documents describing the text's reception based upon witness depositions, letters, and other such supporting materials. "It is not essential," Peter Carter-Ruck writes in his modern study of libel, "that there should be anything in the words complained of to connect them with the plaintiff if, by reason of facts and matters known to persons to whom the words were published, such persons would understand the words to refer to the plaintiff."[46] The colloquium thus typically provides statements from witnesses who claim that they have recognized a portrait of the plaintiff in the text and descriptions of the way in which it has damaged or altered their opinion of the person. These materials, however, cannot by themselves prove definitive, for British courts have also held that even when two interpretations of a passage are possible, juries are under no obligation to decide that the defamatory one holds sway. They should not, as Odgers writes, "dwell on isolated passages," but instead "consider the whole of the circumstances of the case, the occasion of publication, the relationship between the parties, &c."[47] Like good scholars, in effect, jurors are asked not only to ignore the intentions of an author, but to form an interpretation of the text based upon close reading of individual passages—supported by the wealth of historical context provided in the colloquium—while nevertheless balancing such local reading with a global view of the text itself. Sounding very much like a philologist rather than a lawyer, Odgers writes that within a text the "insinuation may be direct, and the allusion obscure . . . the language may be ironical, figurative, or allegorical," but in the end "if there is meaning in the words at all the Court will find it out, even though it be disguised in a riddle or in hieroglyphics."[48] Libel courts have thus developed their own modes of textual interpretation that are surprisingly congruent with those used by contemporary literary critics. Furthermore, these legal procedures operate explicitly to enforce a particular kind of aesthetic autonomization: judges and juries weigh ambiguous texts in order to adjudicate their status as either fact *or* fiction, thereby arresting the roman à clef's destabilizing interruption of these categories.

The sudden expansion of a mass-mediated celebrity culture at the end of the nineteenth century, however, placed new pressures on the social and legal conventions that helped establish the news/novel opposition so essential to the realist novel's consolidation. The sudden increase in literacy rates following the Education Act of 1872,[49] coupled with improvements in printing technology like the introduction of bitonal printing, for example, meant that a wider array of reading materials became cheaply available to an audience of widely diverse tastes and interests.[50] The 1881 Newspaper and Libel Registration Act also had a particularly profound effect on cultural production, limiting the legal liability of newspapers in defamation cases and thus laying the foundation for the New Journalism. The legislation itself had been designed to moderate one of the more extreme consequences of common law precedents, which held that each publication of a libel was a new and unique offense. Thus a newspaper or magazine, for example, could not report directly on many legal proceedings (including libel and divorce cases) or even on some government meetings and Parliamentary debates for fear of deliberately (or even unintentionally) publishing a libelous statement. The reform legislation granted properly registered newspapers that met specific conditions the freedom to cover such events and simultaneously required that the Director of Public Prosecutions first issue a formal indictment before allowing any criminal libel case to be filed against such periodicals.[51] This new provision did serve to reduce cases of criminal libel, but it produced a consequent jump in civil suits as an array of new tabloids began to trade on the newly opened market for scandal and gossip. Henry Labouchère, in particular, proved adept at exploiting these new legal provisions, wielding his scandal-ridden newspaper *Truth* as a political weapon while proudly displaying an overflowing box of legal writs outside his office door.

Relaxed libel laws were one of many institutional factors that contributed to the expansion of celebrity culture in the nineteenth and twentieth centuries, but the near simultaneous rise of new media forms, including photographs, film, radio, and tabloid journalism, created new legal problems. Strictly defined, the term "libel" refers only to written documents and was sharply distinguished from slander, a spoken form of defamation that, because it could be uttered in the heat of the moment and could not survive this initial articulation, was presumed to be far less damaging. The cinema and other such modes of mechanical reproduction, however, bedeviled this founding distinction since they granted once seemingly ephemeral expressions a new permanence. It was not until the passage of the 1952 Libel Act that defamation protections were definitively extended to any medium other than speech. Some of the most influential libel trials of the early twentieth century, in fact, turn precisely on media other than print, such as the precedent-setting 1934 case of *Youssoupoff v. Metro-Goldwyn-Mayer Pictures Ltd.* In this widely followed test of defamation law's extension to film, a jury initially awarded the astounding sum of £25,000 in damages to an aggrieved plaintiff following the release of *Rasputin, the Mad Monk*, a 1932 film about the start of the Russian revolution. This cinematic adaptation luridly suggests not only that one of the Romanov princesses was seduced by Rasputin, but that her brother helped kill him out of a desire for revenge. Prince Youssoupoff, a member of the Russian royal family living in exile when the film appeared, was generally assumed to have taken part in the assassination, though there was little evidence tying him directly to the act. In making the film, the producers carefully chose actors who looked nothing like the Russian royals and took the added precaution of changing the family name to Chegodieff. The ensuing libel trial turned precisely around these changes as the solicitor for the defense argued that "the Producer was obviously playing fast and loose with history." As a consequence, he concluded, the film should be seen entirely as a fiction in which it would be "rather ridiculous to try to assign a historical counterpart to every character."[52] The film's producers thus tried to inject a critical degree of skepticism by turning it into something like a roman à clef, hoping its ambiguity would afford a degree of legal protection—despite the movie's quite obvious references to real people and events. The fact that the case focused on royal scandal and touched on the film industry meant that it drew a great deal of attention from the popular press; it was also closely watched by cultural producers and legal theorists who correctly saw it as a watershed case within the burgeoning field of entertainment law. The outcome, after all, would have far-reaching consequences for any writer or producer who sought to cross the line between fact and fiction in a still rapidly evolving medium. A series of appeals consistently supported the claims of the plaintiffs and, though the case was finally settled out of court, it effectively set a clear boundary around the production of fictional narratives. Although the dead have no rights in common law—and thus cannot be libeled—the deliberate attempt to disguise real events as fiction was finally judged defamatory and carried in this case a particularly large financial penalty sure to discourage other similar attempts.[53] As we will see, the same principles structured the field of literary production as well, where cases brought against the works of both Joyce and Lewis were also decided in favor of the plaintiffs, effectively rendering illegal some of modernism's most daring experiments with the roman à clef.

Even more significant for writers of all sorts, however, was the 1909 case of *E. Hulton and Co. v. Jones*. It upset the legal foundations of the novel by exposing the pervasive infectiousness of the roman à clef within a mass-mediated culture. The case began when the Paris correspondent for the *Sunday Chronicle* wrote an article on "Motor-Mad Dieppe" about the social scene surrounding the city's auto races in 1908. Adding a spicy flourish to the piece, the author introduced a fictional playboy named Artemus Jones, a normally quiet and conservative man who, when in France, becomes "the life and soul of a gay little band that haunts the Casino and turns night into day, besides betraying a most unholy delight in the society of female butterflies."[54] Though plainly an invention, as the publishers of the *Sunday Chronicle* would doggedly argue, a real man named Artemus Jones, who was otherwise unknown to the author, claimed that the piece was a scurrilous libel and sought legal redress even after a formal (albeit somewhat sarcastic) apology had been printed.[55] After Jones introduced witnesses who claimed that they had indeed confused him with the character in the article, the entire burden of proof fell on the paper, which contended that the portrait was entirely fictional and had no connection to a real individual. Because statements of intention were inadmissible, however, the paper could not mount much of a defense and the jury took only fifteen minutes to return a guilty verdict and award damages of £1,705.

It quickly became clear that this decision had enormous consequences for the suddenly collapsing news/novel divide, since writers and publishers alike were held liable when readers confused fact with fiction. The initial verdict traced a complicated path through the appellate courts, but the initial ruling was finally upheld by the Law Lords, despite its widely acknowledged threat to all forms of print culture. Lord Goddard, writing as a member of the Court of Appeal, noted that the decision "added a terror to authorship" and could alter fundamentally the field of literary production.[56] The bar against authorial intention, after all, so empowered individual readers that even the most obvious fictions could be interpreted as factual descriptions since the final power of adjudication always lay with the whims of a jury. As Barendt argues in his attempt to introduce some reform, this power was so extensive that once a plaintiff claimed some reasonable connection with an apparently fictional character then "the author of a fiction has no defence."[57] After all, since the work on its face claims to be a fiction, the defendant could not then resort to the standard defense against a libel claim by asserting that the publication was true. The law, in effect, simply could not accommodate the concept of "conditional fictionality," and as a consequence it insisted that juries make rigid distinctions between fiction and fact. At the same time, it acknowledged that fictions could reach deeply into the public sphere in ways entirely unrecognized and unintended by their creators.

In the course of the appeals following the initial jury verdict, British jurists quickly began to develop the concept of "unintentional libel" to describe precisely those cases in which fact becomes accidentally or contingently infected with fiction. This did not free writers, printers, or publishers from libel suits, but it did at least limit their financial liability—provided they made a good-faith effort to renounce any inadvertent intrusion into the public sphere. Contracts thus increasingly required authors to warrant that they had not committed libel and were willing to indemnify the publishing houses against lawsuits. Similarly, the now standard legal disclaimers guaranteeing the novel's fictional nature became widespread. These statements in themselves provided no direct defense against libel but did evince a genuine attempt to regulate a text's reception and thus mitigate the roman à clef's anarchic powers. Ironically, as Sitwell's own satiric version demonstrates, they often served only to make readers even more curious about the possible scandalous secrets a seemingly fictional work might encode.[58] The relatively stable boundary between fact and fiction that had emerged in the eighteenth century thus came under increasing legal pressure from the rapidly expanding institutions of a mass-mediated culture of celebrity. New consumers of printed texts, furthermore, could not be counted on to sustain what Barendt describes as the consensual view of fiction, which holds that "readers can, or at least should be able to, distinguish works of fiction from factual reporting, and that, therefore, they are most unlikely to identify characters in the former with real people whom they know and whom they know of."[59] As chapter 1 argues, however, this is far from an obvious or common-sense assumption and is instead merely one contingent mode of reading that was only tenuously consolidated in nineteenth-century realism. In the early decades of the twentieth century writers and readers alike strained this consensus as the roman à clef began to proliferate within the formal and informal institutions of a mass-mediated culture.

Because the law invested ordinary readers empanelled as part of a jury with so much power, libel cases instantiate the kinds of interpretive regimes operating beyond those sanctioned by trained authors and critics; and we discover in them a far riskier literary field, where fact and fiction are deeply intertwined. The concept of unintentional libel as articulated in the Artemus Jones case, in particular, reveals the extent to which the novel could and did impinge on the historical world—even in those cases where authors did not intend for it to do so. By confusing fact and fiction in ways individual authors and publishers could neither intend nor anticipate, readers themselves resisted the conditions of aesthetic autonomization while exposing the still anarchic skepticism supposedly arrested by the novel's rise. Faced with this crisis, libel law frantically struggled to isolate fictional works from the real world by holding individuals financially accountable for their instability, thereby enforcing a stark division between fact and fiction. Throughout the early twentieth century, however, the law was pushed to increasingly absurd and untenable conclusions. The Youssoupoff case, after all, made it basically impossible to create historical fictions while any of the actors were still alive and the Jones case meant that nearly every novel ran some risk of creating a character that might be confused with a real person. By the late 1930s, however, this trend began to abate as the implications of such precedents were narrowed. In the 1938 case of *Canning v. William Collins and Co. Ltd.*, for example, a stockbroker sued a publisher for unintentionally using his name in a satiric novel entitled *People in Cages*. As in the Jones case, the plaintiff introduced witnesses claiming they had mistaken the fictional character for a real man named Mr. Canning, but judge and jury alike were convinced by the defense's rhetorical claim during cross-examination that such a claim was "utterly and absolutely ridiculous, that this is a perfectly inoffensive novel with one character in it that does not bear the slightest resemblance to you except that the authoress has called him Captain John Canning."[60] A quick decision was returned in favor of the defense (though it was partially premised on the idea that a stockbroker's "good name" had little intrinsic value). The growing unease with the reach of libel law into the realm of fiction evident in this decision culminated that same year in the appointment of a special commission to reform the law. Though adjourned during the war, it eventually recommended a lengthy series of changes designed to accommodate mass mediation and new media forms, most of which were passed as part of the 1952 Libel Act.

That the period roughly between the Artemus Jones (1908) and Canning (1938) cases coincides with the rise and consolidation of literary modernism is by no means coincidental. Far from conquering autonomy, as Bourdieu contends, the modern novel's status as a discrete aesthetic object came under intense pressure as the boundary between fiction and fact became increasingly blurred within the mass-mediated cultural marketplace. The sheer contingency upon which the Artemus Jones case turned dramatically revealed just how inadequate the laws governing the circulation of printed information in Britain had become. The readers empanelled as a jury, as well as a series of appellate judges, all held steadfastly to legal and moral concepts initially articulated in the late eighteenth century that imposed an absolute divide between history and the novel. That the author of "Motor-Mad Dieppe" knew nothing of the historical Artemus Jones was finally deemed immaterial, since the text itself—if only by sheer accident—had damaged his reputation. Only thirty years later, however, when Canning filed a case based almost exactly upon the same set of circumstances, an entirely different decision emerged; the jury implicitly acknowledged that fiction could impinge upon the public sphere without necessarily doing the kind of damage libel law intends to redress. In the narrow gap between these two decisions, literary modernism flourished, in part, by using the roman à clef to explore this same set of legal and epistemological contradictions.

Aware that nearly any text could land them in costly legal troubles, printers and publishers became increasingly concerned about libel just as authors like Woolf, Joyce, Lewis, Lawrence, and many others began to experiment with risky assaults on the critical and legal bars separating fact from fiction. A number of these writers eventually ran afoul of the law. Lawrence's *Women in Love*, for example, faced a number of potential libel suits, and his letters and manuscripts reveal deft attempts to skirt these charges. George Orwell similarly faced such accusations,[61] as did Evelyn Waugh who, like Sitwell, deliberately provoked them in the typescript preface to *Vile Bodies*, which he decided not to publish: "BRIGHT YOUNG PEOPLE AND OTHERS KINDLY NOTE THAT ALL CHARACTERS ARE WHOLLY IMAGINARY (AND YOU GET FAR TOO MUCH PUBLICITY ALREADY WHOEVER YOU ARE)."[62] Rich though the period may be with such cases, however, the next chapter abjures cataloging them in order to focus instead on the symptomatic struggles of James Joyce and Wyndham Lewis. Though we typically think of them as the "Men of 1914," their modernism is shaped not simply by narrative experimentation and aesthetic difficulty, but by a direct and provocative engagement with libel as "the law of literature." By writing deliberately defamatory works lightly cloaked in the roman à clef's "conditional fictionality," they exploited the genre's potential to disrupt the legal, moral, and aesthetic compromises that underwrote the novel's rise in the eighteenth century. Like the laws of obscenity and copyright that Joyce and Lewis also incorporated and critiqued in their works, so too does defamation play a vital role in their exploration of the limits of fiction and the legality of literature.

Appendix: A Brief Digest of British and Irish Libel Law

> "Fox's" Libel Act (1792): This legislation conferred on a jury the responsibility to determine whether or not a text was libelous. Previously, this decision rested entirely with the judge, leaving the jury to decide only if the text had been created and/or published by the defendant.

Parmiter v. Coupland (1840): This British decision framed what would become one of the most famous and widely cited definitions of libel: "a publication without justification or lawful excuse which is calculated to injure the reputation of another by exposing him to hatred, contempt or ridicule."

Libel Act (1843): This act, which would later play an instrumental role in Wilde's downfall, sought to limit the use of criminal libel charges merely to suppress embarrassing information. It held that in a criminal case, the truth of libel could be used as grounds for a plea of justification, provided that the libel had been deliberately published in the public interest.

White v. Tyrell (1856): This British ruling held that authorial intention was entirely inadmissible in a libel case. See *Bolton v. O'Brien*.

Newspaper and Libel Registration Act (1881): This reform legislation granted properly registered newspapers limited immunity to print libelous statements read out in court, in Parliament, and in other government forums.

Bolton v. O'Brien (1885): An Irish decision that mirrors *Whyte v. Tyrell* in ruling authorial intention inadmissible: "The question is not what the defendant, in his own mind, intended by [his] language, but what was the meaning and inference that would naturally be drawn by reasonable and intelligent persons."

E. Hulton and Co. v. Jones (1909): Described as a "terror to authorship," this landmark case established that authors, publishers, and printers may be sued even for unintentional libel.

Youssoupoff v. Metro-Goldwyn-Mayer Pictures Ltd. (1934): A precedent-setting case in entertainment law, it extended to cinema the libel protections that had initially been reserved for print media.

Canning v. William Collins and Co. Ltd. (1938): In its particulars, this case is almost exactly parallel to *E. Hulton and Co. v. Jones*, but it reached the opposite conclusion and created a legal exception for unintentional libel.

Porter Committee (1939): The House of Commons appointed this special committee to recommend reforms of defamation law.

Its work was delayed during the war and its report was not published until 1948.

Defamation Act (1952): This legislation instituted reforms proposed by the Porter Committee, extending defamation law to cover new media forms, creating a "fair use" exception, loosening some restrictions on newspapers, and codifying the principle of "unintentional libel."

5. The Novel at the Bar
Joyce, Lewis, and Libel

In a well-known 1922 photograph, James Joyce appears seated in Sylvia Beach's Shakespeare and Company bookstore at 12 rue de l'Odéon on the bohemian Left Bank of the Seine. He is nattily dressed, sporting a bow tie, a neatly trimmed goatee, and slicked hair, all of which lends him a distinctly bourgeois air of elegance and sophistication. The black patch covering his left eye, however, warns us that something is amiss, as does the alarmingly large poster on the wall behind him: a reproduction of the April 1, 1922, *Sporting Times,* proclaiming "The Scandal of 'Ulysses'" in towering black letters. In the foreground, Joyce and Beach appear to be studiously examining ledger books and order slips for the text, which is denounced in the paper behind them as the production of "a perverted lunatic who has made a specialty of the literature of the latrine."[1] The poster plainly hovers there in this meticulously framed photograph as an advertisement, attempting to lure cultural tourists as well the Parisian avant-garde into the store where they could obtain a very expensive copy of the book that outraged American and British censors were destroying at their borders. In buying a copy of *Ulysses,* early readers also bought a little bit of this titillating scandal. The photograph of Joyce and Beach, in fact, has become iconic precisely because we have never really stopped proclaiming the scandal of *Ulysses* in the classroom, in literary scholarship, and in the popular press. This was true when Samuel Roth published not one but two pirated editions in the United States, and it remained true when the Collectors Publications edition appeared containing forty-three pages of advertisements for pornographic books and magazines.[2]

As a scandalous object, *Ulysses* has been regularly cast as the hero of a modern morality tale, tilting brilliantly at narrow-minded censors and anti-vice crusaders who dared suppress so bold a portrait of human sexuality. Joyce, Katherine Mullin argues, actually anticipated this role for himself, becoming a subtle "agent provocateur" who responded to Victorian prudery "through the creative appropriation of prevailing debates about art, morality, and sexuality."[3] At the heart of this scandalous encounter, of course, lies the text's blunt treatment of sex, ranging from Leopold Bloom's masturbatory encounter with Gerty McDowell on Sandymount Strand in the "Nausicaa" episode, through the sadomasochistic fantasies in "Circe," to Molly Bloom's nighttime thoughts in "Penelope," the section Joyce himself described as "probably more obscene than any preceding episode."[4] Judge John Woolsey's decision to lift the American ban on *Ulysses* in 1933 further emphasized the importance of sexuality in the book's suppression. He struggled to determine whether *Ulysses* was an obscene text that, according to the legal definitions then in place, might "stir the sex impulses or lead to sexually impure and lustful thoughts."[5] His famous conclusion that the "net effect" of the book "was only that of a somewhat tragic and powerful commentary on the inner lives of men and women" at once freed *Ulysses* from the grip of the government censor and transformed it into an icon of liberal humanism, free speech, and aesthetic integrity. The issues of censorship and outrage adjudicated in this case appeared to confirm the continuing autonomization of the aesthetic sphere around which the idea of a "high modernism" gradually coalesced. Joyce's book became a scandal because it jumped this expanding gap between art and the law, temporarily exposing both the contradiction and the distance between these two kinds of judgment. Indeed, scandal in this case might best be defined as the precipitate of the encounter between law and literature that is produced by the unexpected conflict between these two otherwise independent spheres of thought and assessment. When seen this way, then the "scandal of *Ulysses*" must be extended to include not only obscenity, but Joyce's potentially illegal and deliberately libelous experiments with the roman à clef.

Like Joyce, Wyndham Lewis too cultivated this same generative conflict: a mode of experimentation that provides a new way of linking their agonistic modernism. Where Joyce embraced "silence, exile, and cunning," however, Lewis declared himself the "Enemy," using his vast and multifaceted talents to wage a more direct—and ultimately unsuccessful—assault on the institutional structures underwriting art's claim to autonomy. Augustus John called his sometime friend and onetime protégé a "new Machiavelli" who treated art as if it were a battle in "an arena, where various insurrectionary forces struggled to outwit each other in the game of artistic power politics."[6] Libel became one of Lewis's most powerful weapons, and he modeled his own early career, in part, on James McNeil Whistler, the gadfly artist who composed an autobiography entitled *The Gentle Art of Making Enemies* and signed his work with a barbed butterfly. Lewis too possessed a barb, but lacked the graces of a social butterfly. Instead, he made a regular habit of turning abruptly on even his closest friends—often by brutally folding them into his romans à clef. "Being in solitary schism, with no obligations at the moment towards party or individual colleague" he wrote in the first issue of his little magazine, *The Enemy,* "I can resume my opinion of the society I have just left, and its characteristics which might else remain without serious unpartisan criticism."[7] Locked in a one-sided battle with literary London—from Bloomsbury to Fleet Street—he cultivated such hostility in order to expose what he believed to be the hypocrisy and petty snobbery of an aesthetic sphere that cloaked itself in the claims of radical autonomy only in order to preserve antiquated structures of social prestige.

Lewis drew deliberately on the roman à clef's anarchic powers to savage the realist novel by extending fiction into the historical world. In a letter to Ford Madox Ford, he expressed open hostility toward "You fellows [who] try to efface yourselves; to make people think there isn't any author and that they're living in the affairs you ... adumbrate, isn't that your word? ... What balls! What rot! ... What's the good of being an author if you don't get any fun out of it; ... Efface yourself! ... Bilge!"[8] Modernist impersonality, for Lewis, was a sham, an archaic appendage of the genteel nineteenth century that both concealed the "arena" in which art was actually waged and demeaned the pleasures readers derived from texts that rendered unstable the distinction between fact and fiction. He rebuts Ford's narrow aestheticism and deliberately courts scandal by libelously developing his own art of extreme skepticism. He even taunts the very readers who activated and sustained such pleasures, as this passage from an abandoned introduction to *Blasting and Bombardiering* indicates: "I am about to gossip. I am going to be exceedingly 'personal' about certain persons. But this is not at all because I wish to be. It is because of *you* that I descend to these picturesque details. Quite at the start it is far better that I should lay the blame where it is due—namely at your door—for anything that is of too familiar a nature that may be uttered in these pages."[9] Nowhere was such scandal-mongering more effectively or brutally executed than in Lewis's massive 1930 novel *The Apes of God.* Intended as a critical response to Joyce's *Ulysses,* it engages in many of the same narrative experiments in the roman à clef. Though this book narrowly managed to avoid a libel suit, it would be the last of Lewis's major novels to do so. Throughout the following decade, the libel laws Joyce eventually managed to elude increasingly restricted Lewis's own parallel experiments with the roman à clef, conspiring with the hegemonic aesthetic of modernist impersonality to marginalize his most daring experiments at the boundary between fact and fiction. By recalibrating the major works of Joyce and Lewis around their engagement with the roman à clef, this chapter recovers the assault both writers launched on the law of libel, setting the canny strategies of one against the increasingly frantic struggles of the other. Their strategic resistance, as we will see, defines the core component of an alternatively conceived node of modernist resistance to Victorian morality, the realist novel, and Eliotic impersonality. Yet it also delimits the legality of such writing while challenging our liberal narratives of modernism's ever-expanding freedom.

James Joyce

"The Passage Complained of Is a Malicious and Deliberate Libel upon Me"

Our hagiographic studies of Joyce have focused too long and too narrowly on the comfortingly liberal narrative of his victory over Victorian prudery and state censorship. This has led us to ignore or simply neglect the far more subtle mechanisms of repression structuring the aesthetic field. There remains, after all, one additional scandal that has been largely overlooked, yet which shapes *Ulysses* even more profoundly than either sexuality or intellectual property. It pervades the book from its opening to its closing pages and has troubled generations of critics who have developed somewhat torturous intellectual arguments to evade its most troubling implications. Hugh Kenner alludes to it when he describes Joyce's decision to abandon the convention of the initialed dash when writing about real people and events, a practice that dates back to the very rise of the novel. "In the year 19—, in the city of D—," Kenner writes, "that would have been the decorous way to go about it."[10] As he notes, the French printers who initially set *Ulysses* cared so little for this little English nicety that Joyce was able to indulge in "a very orgy . . . of naming." This use of real names and places, in fact, accounts for some of the peculiar pleasures of Joyce's text, encouraging readers not only to track references to real people and places in the 1904 *Thom's Directory* but to follow the fictional paths of Bloom and Stephen minute by minute and step by step as they make their way through Dublin. Joyce famously declared *Ulysses* so accurate that "if the city one day suddenly disappeared from the earth, it could be reconstructed out of my book."[11] There is a danger, however, in such precision, for this particular orgy—like the one in Bella Cohen's brothel—runs a very real legal risk of suppression, not for obscenity, but for libel. In *Finnegans Wake* Joyce alludes to this directly when his "Shem the Penman," in writing "his usylessly unreadable Blue Book of Eccles . . . scrabbled and scratched and scriobbled and skrevened nameless shamelessness about everybody he ever met."[12] Just as Joyce deliberately provoked the encounter between law and literature when writing about both obscenity and copyright, so too did he engage the civil statutes of libel that sought to regulate the novel's engagement with fact. Indeed, because Joyce published his work privately in Paris—far from the sanctions of the British libel courts—the legal risks and consequences of his writing remained largely invisible, emerging only when *Ulysses* was successfully sued for libel in 1955.

Joyce first became entangled in the webs of British defamation law when, in 1912, he returned to his native city in what would quickly prove a disastrous effort to force the publication of *Dubliners*. Six years earlier the book had already run afoul of censorious printers unwilling to take the risk of being singled out by the city's Vigilance Society, and after repeated negotiations about possible revisions, Grant Richards had declined to publish it. Having secured a new contract from George Roberts of Maunsel and Company, Joyce found himself again confronted with a bewildering array of editorial objections, this time focused initially on the crude language of the characters in "Ivy Day in the Committee Room" who refer to Queen Victoria at one point as a "bloody old bitch."[13] After moderating this passage somewhat—just as he had done in similar negotiations about obscenity with Richards—Joyce confronted what seemed an even more quixotic demand: that in the same story he remove all references to King Edward VII. Roberts feared that such passages, which described the deceased monarch as "fond of his glass of grog and . . . a bit of a rake,"[14] might provoke a charge of criminal libel since, as Joyce's own solicitor advised him, the description "could be taken as offensive . . . to the late King."[15] This is certainly not the kind of legal difficulty we most often associate with Joyce's work, and to a modern reader this passage's threat has become essentially illegible. Nevertheless, libel continued to menace the negotiations with Maunsel as the firm's solicitors grew ever more concerned about the absence of those decorous dashes Kenner describes. The genuine threat of a libel suit by the Crown in this case was likely quite small, and Joyce, in an effort to dispel Roberts's concerns, actually wrote a letter to George V explaining his situation and asking that the monarch "inform me where in his view the passage (certain allusions made by a person of the story in the idiom of his social class) should be withheld from publication as offensive to the memory of his father."[16] Not surprisingly, the king's secretary refused to offer an opinion in the case, leaving Joyce few options as a book that once ran afoul of obscenity laws now foundered on the threat of a libel charge.

Joyce was understandably apoplectic and wrote an open letter to the press decrying "the present condition of authorship in England and Ireland" while citing specifically the passage Roberts wanted to change.[17] As the letter notes, Grant Richards had not raised any objections to the description of the king in 1906, and by publishing the extract in the paper, Joyce strategically hoped to allay any concerns about its legal status. *Sinn Féin*, in which the letter appeared, did print the passage, though the *Northern Whig*—a far less nationalist paper—declined to do so, no doubt because its editor too was concerned about his potential liability. Joyce likely did not realize that following the passage of the Newspaper Libel and Registration Act in 1881, periodicals had a far greater license to publish such material since they were merely reporting news rather than themselves making libelous claims. The situation for Richards, however, was far more delicate since libel law in both Great Britain and Ireland allowed for the possibility of both civil suits and even criminal prosecution for author, publisher, and printer alike. As Holt notes in *The Law of Libel*: "The offence of libel and slander is proportionately more criminal as it presumes to reach persons to whom special veneration is due. The diminution of their credit is a public mischief, and the state itself suffers in their becoming the objects of scorn; not only themselves are vilified and degraded, but the great affairs which they conduct are obstructed, and the justice they administer is thereby disparaged."[18] It seems unlikely that by 1911 the Crown would undertake the prosecution of such a libel case, but Ellmann suggests rather vaguely that some kind of informal pressure may nevertheless have been brought to bear upon the firm by Lady Aberdeen, the Lord Lieutenant's wife.[19] In fact, at a stormy 1912 meeting in Dublin, Roberts demanded that all mentions of the king be deleted from the collection. Joyce immediately consulted a solicitor, George Lidwell, who obligingly wrote to Roberts, carefully reserving judgment on the question of obscenity, while effectively minimizing the threat of a libel prosecution brought by the Crown. "I have read . . . 'Ivy Day in the Committee Room,'" he writes, "and I think that beyond the questionable taste of the language (which is a matter entirely for the author) in referring to the memory of the last two reigning Sovereigns of these Realms, the vulgar expressions put into the mouths of the Characters in the dialogue are not likely to be taken very serious notice of by the Advisors of the Crown."[20] The letter proved to be of little use, in large part because Roberts was receiving his own legal advice from Maunsel's London office, which proved even more wary than its Dublin agent.

At the same August 1912 meeting in which Roberts demanded changes in "Ivy Day," he thus—on the advice of his London solicitors—made an even more far-reaching request, one so broad that it would eventually sink the entire project and again leave Joyce without a publisher for his stories. This time his concern lay not with the Crown but with the Dubliners whom Joyce dissects in his stories. No doubt well aware of the Artemus Jones case and its implications, he requested that all of the real public houses mentioned in "Counterparts" be given fictitious names, before expanding this demand to include the alteration or deletion of every real person and place of business mentioned by name in any of the stories. He sought, in short, to remove any trace of the roman à clef by limiting Joyce's distinctive use of detail as well as the text's "conditional fictionality." Roberts was furthermore advised by the London office that Joyce himself should now back the publication by securing large sureties against a potential suit.[21] Should this fail, the editor was then advised to sue the author for deliberately breaking his publishing contact by providing a text he knew to be libelous. Thomas Kettle, the solicitor to whom Joyce first (unsuccessfully) turned for help, had already advised him that the book might indeed be brought to court, and we have seen that even Lidwell qualified his opinion carefully and focused it narrowly only on "Ivy Day." On August 23, 1912, Joyce made a frantic attempt to save *Dubliners*, offering to drive Roberts to the various businesses mentioned in order to secure permission directly to use their names. Joyce was desperate, as what initially appeared to be a relatively minor quibble about the direct mention of King Edward VII expanded rapidly into a wide-reaching series of demands not only to suppress a key element of the text's innovative style, but to indemnify the house upon its publication. Though negotiations with Roberts would continue for another week or so, it had become clear that Maunsel would not publish the book, and on September 11, the printer—according to Joyce's now disputed claim—finally destroyed the sheets for fear that he too might be named in a libel suit.

Dubliners would, of course, appear nearly two years later without any such editorial objections. In 1912, however, the "nicely polished looking-glass" Joyce hoped to hold up to his native city finally proved too accurate in its fidelity, its intricate details rendering suddenly hazy the increasingly unstable bar between fact and fiction.[22] Roberts and Maunsel, after all, were correct: by using real names and places of business, the stories did run the very real risk of incurring any number of potentially very damaging lawsuits. When Joyce forswears the dash—describing directly "the ten o'clock slow train from Kingstown" in "A Painful Case" and naming real pubs like "O'Neill's," "Davy Byrne's," and "the Scotch House" in "Counterparts"—he potentially casts these businesses and their owners into the kind of "hatred, ridicule, and contempt" that defines the tort of libel.[23] In his incredulous letters to Nora, Joyce writes of his attempts to find some kind of compromise and he assures Roberts that though "a railroad co. is mentioned once," it is immediately "exonerated from all blame by two witnesses, jury and coroner." In the public houses, he further contends, "nothing happens. People drink."[24] Attempting to resolve the risk of libel, in other words, Joyce argues that the text is not defamatory, but is instead merely an accurate representation of the city of Dublin and some of its well-known institutions. Rather than feeling damaged, he desperately concludes, "the publicans would be glad of the advertisement."[25] Joyce, in effect, contends that he does not mean to libel anyone and adduces such intentions as proof against any finding of defamation.

As we have already seen, however, his intentions were entirely irrelevant in court, and though he may have believed, for example, that the railway company in "A Painful Case" had been exonerated by the overt description of events in the story, Maunsel's solicitors were rightly concerned that the subtle play of irony and the shifting instability of the story might introduce a reasonable interpretation that the company had been negligent in its actions. Similarly, the publicans in "Counterparts" could contend that far from an advertisement, the story in fact harmed their ability to conduct business by falsely asserting that they allowed the profligate consumption of alcohol. I do not mean, of course, to introduce these readings as particularly convincing, but cautious writers and printers had long sought to avoid the risk and considerable cost of a trial by carefully excising the mention of real people and places either by introducing fictional names or resorting to the conventional Victorian dash.

The eventual publication of *Dubliners* in 1914 might seem to vindicate Joyce's arguments, and it does suggest that in a world on the brink of war less attention was being paid to the publication of potentially libelous short stories. The absence of that secretive dash, in fact, has by now come to seem an integral part of a distinctly Joycean aesthetic in which fictional events are deeply and perhaps inextricably embedded in the historical realities of Edwardian Dublin.[26] According to his brother Stanislaus, when Joyce began work on the novel that would eventually become *A Portrait of the Artist as a Young Man*, he initiated an even more aggressive assault on the constraints imposed by the restrictions of libel law: "Jim is beginning his novel, as he usually begins things, half in anger.... It is to be almost autobiographical, and naturally as it comes from Jim, satirical. He is putting a large number of his acquaintances into it, and those Jesuits he has known. I don't think they will like themselves in it."[27] *Portrait, Ulysses,* and *Finnegans Wake* all make use of this same technique, and generations of critics have devoted considerable effort to revealing—inadvertently perhaps—that Joyce indulged in an essentially unprecedented campaign of libel that nevertheless remains relatively illegible to those unfamiliar with turn-of-the-century Dublin. Herbert Gorman, in an early biography written under Joyce's own careful guidance, notes the frustrating inability of many readers "to crack the hard nuts of certain paragraphs containing comments on actual personalities" and concludes that an intimate knowledge of Dublin "might heighten one's enjoyment, for the scandalous aspects of [*Ulysses*] would then be more greatly emphasized."[28] The extensive guides and annotations that now provide maps indicating the precise location of Davy Byrne's and references to real figures only further reinforce the importance of this telling aesthetics of detail for the book.

Joyce used the roman à clef to invade not only the city's outhouses and whorehouses, but its historical realities as well. In doing so, he forged a distinctly modernist aesthetic that sought to rupture realism's autonomy by breaking down the tenuous legal distinction between novels and news. The risks he initially incurred have now largely dissipated. In American jurisprudence, the First Amendment's broad protection of free speech has significantly constrained the reach of libel, and the civil laws in Britain state that the dead cannot be libeled. Unlike the potent sexuality, which still has the power to rankle and even shock some readers when they come across it, the dense web of names and the multifold acts of revenge pervading Joyce's works have increasingly become mere scholarly arcana rather than the stuff of legal wrangling and public scandal. But the first time *Ulysses* actually entered a British or Irish court of law, the case involved neither Gerty and her thighs nor Molly and her masturbation. Instead, Reuben J. Dodd filed a suit for libel.[29] In the "Hades" episode, Martin Cunningham tells a story about Dodd's alleged attempt to commit suicide by jumping into the Liffey and his father's miserly offer of a florin to the boatman who saved his son's life. In 1954, the BBC broadcast a reading of *Ulysses* featuring this episode and Dodd promptly secured from the High Court of Dublin a summons on the broadcaster claiming damages for defamation. In his affidavit, Dodd spells out his complaint clearly, hewing to the legal requirement that the passage be shown to have intentionally aimed to harm his reputation and his business: "James Joyce, the author, whom I knew as a schoolmate, had a personal dislike for me because of what he alleged my father did to his father. And so, when he wrote his book 'Ulysses,' in or about the year 1904, he made some disparaging references, including moneylending transactions, to a Mr. Reuben J. Dodd. . . . The passage complained of is a malicious and deliberate libel upon me and its dissemination by the B.B.C. exposes me to personal humiliation and injury. The whole incident described was a malicious falsehood and, in particular, that I attempted to commit suicide."[30] Dodd essentially won his case by securing a substantive out-of-court settlement. The BBC's decision to withdraw demonstrates that even more than thirty years after its initial publication Joyce's text continued to generate not only scandal but a very real risk for publishers, printers, and broadcasters who might find themselves subject to any number of suits. After all, Dodd is but one of the hundreds of real people mentioned in the text, many of whom might also reasonably claim that Joyce deliberately sought to bring them into "hatred, contempt, and ridicule." In using the roman à clef to reach from fiction into the world of fact, Joyce expands the scandal of his libelous writings to provoke a collision between a seemingly autonomous aesthetic sphere and the web of legal constraints structuring its development.

"The Disguise I Fear Is Thin"

Given his own abrupt introduction to defamation law, there can be little doubt that Joyce knew what he was doing when he began to fill *Ulysses* with a staggering array of very precise information about his native city. Unlike the stories in *Dubliners*, which mention only a few public houses and a railway company, *Ulysses* invokes a vast array of names ranging from individuals to businesses to commercial products. Just as he began *Portrait* "half in anger," so too Joyce seems to make it explicit in the early pages of *Ulysses* that this is a libelous book out to settle some old scores. Atop the Martello tower, Buck Mulligan mocks the sullen and solipsistic Stephen Dedalus before suddenly declaring, "it's not fair to tease you like that Kinch, is it?" In the ebb and flow of Stephen's consciousness, this jovial apology is treated as an act of self-defense: "Parried again," he thinks, realizing that Mulligan "fears the lancet of my art as I fear that of his. The cold steel pen."[31] We read this, of course, just as Joyce himself is spearing Oliver Gogarty with that very pen, exacting the revenge Mulligan may have feared but nevertheless failed to escape. Proving the legal principle that libel does indeed have the ability to displace fact with fiction, the historical Gogarty struggled against this satiric portrait for the rest of his very distinguished life. Indeed, *Ulysses* haunted his very grave and though his glowing obituary described his fury about the fact that "posterity would remember him as Buck Mulligan," it nevertheless carried an attention-grabbing subhead that reads: "Author and Wit was Prototype of Character in 'Ulysses.'"[32] As Claire Culleton argues, the book's "conditional fictionality" is more than just an innovative technique, it is also "the ultimate revenge, in that it condemns a real person to caricatured fabrication."[33]

Gogarty was by no means the only one to recognize his potentially libelous portrait: according to Ellmann, when the book first appeared "a tremor went through quite a few of [Joyce's] countrymen, who feared the part he might have assigned to them."[34] George Bernard Shaw wrote in the 1921 preface to *Immaturity* that "James Joyce in his *Ulysses* has described, with a fidelity so ruthless that the book is hardly bearable, the life that Dublin offers to its young men," an opinion he simultaneously conveyed to Sylvia Beach when he called the book "hideously real."[35] Although the sheets had been printed privately in France, Joyce nevertheless took care to employ some pseudonyms in order to deflect his most serious legal risks. Gogarty, therefore, appears as Mulligan; Joyce is partially figured as Stephen; the Englishman Trench is concealed behind the pseudonym Haines; and the villainous Michael Cusak becomes the anonymous Citizen. There are other such alterations, but these three seem specifically intended to help elude the potentially most damaging libel suits by at least partially obscuring both Joyce's maliciousness and the historical antecedents of some of the work's most treacherous characters. To bring a libel suit, after all, Trench or Gogarty would first have to admit that they recognized themselves in their supposedly fictional portraits in order to convince a court they had been defamed. This, in turn, would not only grant Joyce and his work a certain degree of publicity, but would simultaneously offer the opportunity for this famously aggrieved author to defend himself by trying to prove that the portraits in *Ulysses* were more or less accurate.

Despite the possible appeal of such publicity, however, Joyce remained concerned about the risks he had run. In a brief note appended to his 1967 essay, "James Joyce's Sentimentality," Clive Hart suggests that Joyce had "a still more cogent reason" for avoiding Dublin after 1922 than the romance of exile—namely, "the certainty of disastrous libel actions if he returned."[36] The decision to remain out of reach of the British courts afforded him an important bulwark, though it also appears that he did take some additional steps. A research note Richard Ellmann did not incorporate into his biography describes a conversation with A. J. Leventhal, who recalls that as late as 1921 Joyce, explicitly concerned about the threat of libel, asked if any Blooms still resided in Dublin. Leventhal assured him that they had departed, apparently convincing Joyce that he could use the name of the most clearly fictional character in *Ulysses* without undue risk.[37] If Bloom had some sort of clear historical antecedent, of course, or even if some tenuous connection could be drawn to a living person, then the grounds for a defamation suit would have been quite strong, particularly since the text delves so deeply into his sexual habits and private thoughts.

These textual precautions only emphasize the importance of libel law to *Ulysses* and the book's critique of the legal constraints delimiting literary realism. In his own attempt to disrupt the intentional fallacy, William Empson argues that rather than developing techniques (such as David Hayman's "Arranger") for distancing the author from the text and thus affirming the supremacy of fiction, we should instead realize "that Joyce is always present in the book—rather oppressively so, like a judge in court."[38] Empson's metaphor is more literal than he perhaps realizes, because *Ulysses* puts its readers in the strangely juridical position of serving as those jurors who, according to the tort of libel, are alone empowered to determine whether or not a particular character has a historical antecedent and whether or not he or she has been defamed. This begins, as I have already suggested, when the novel itself begins atop the Martello tower, but it continues throughout the text in myriad ways. It emerges almost comically, for example, in the conundrum of the famous "man in the mackintosh," an unnamed character who flits mysteriously in and out of the text. Scholars have struggled for decades to arrive at possible historical correlates for this character, a quest forever stymied by a stubborn anonymity that at once embodies and satirizes our search for the real facts behind this conditional fiction. Sebastian Knowles, in his study of gamesmanship in *Ulysses*, argues that the book "is built on the equals sign," a figure that describes not only the parallel paths taken by Bloom and Stephen but our own attempt to locate equivalences for the characters themselves.[39] Bloom himself thematizes our search for the history behind the fiction when, after masturbating on the beach, he strolls to the tide's edge and uses a stick to write in the sand "I. . . . AM. A." (U 13.1258, 1264). The sentence remains incomplete, and any number of serious studies have attempted to infer the conclusion of this elliptical phrase. Joyce, however, deliberately provokes here our inability to know who Bloom actually is—a mystery Joyce quite legalistically preserved as his conversation with Leventhal indicates. The extreme skepticism so distinctive of the roman à clef is dramatically compounded with the aesthetics of detail in the "Circe" episode, where names, identities, and descriptions shift so rapidly and so fantastically that identification becomes an endlessly mutating puzzle. As hypothetical members of the jury, we are left with a paralyzing doubt that might exonerate Joyce precisely because the boundary between fiction and fact cannot be fixed.

The scandal of libel, however, is more than just an implicit component of the book's deeply interwoven symbolic structures, since it also constitutes an explicit part of the plot itself. It is there at the Martello tower and emerges later in the day when Bloom runs into Josie Breen who complains of her eccentric husband, Dennis: "He's a caution to rattlesnakes. He's in there now with his lawbooks finding out the law of libel" (U 8.229–230). Bloom quickly learns that Dennis received an anonymous postcard reading "U.P." or perhaps "U.p.: up" (8.257, 258).[40] Like the man in the mackintosh, this card too has troubled any number of readers who not only have difficulty making sense of it, but who struggle to discover a meaning so defamatory as to occasion the suit Breen intends to file "for ten thousand pounds" in damages (8.263–4). Richard Ellmann argues that the card implies some sort of erectile dysfunction, while others suggest that it is a reference to Dickens's *Oliver Twist*, in which the letters U.P. are used to signal an old woman's death. Alternatively, it may simply indicate that the somewhat dotty Breen is mentally ill, the two letters signifying that, like weak whisky, he is "under proof."[41] All of these readings seem more or less feasible, which means that any case for libel—even if the person who sent the card could be identified—would likely fail. The case, after all, would turn narrowly on the meaning of the card, and a jury would be asked to determine a particular interpretation that was clearly defamatory. The multiple possibilities, however, make it unlikely that a clear finding of fact could be determined. The roman à clef's conditional relation to truth, in other words, which cannot be legally grounded in authorial intention, essentially serves as a potential defense against any charge of libel. Like much of the rest of *Ulysses*, this card can be multiply interpreted and contested, with definitive meaning held in permanent abeyance. The book's potentially defamatory scandals, therefore, can be at least partially deflected by its difficulty, as the roman à clef's anarchism serves simultaneously as a testament to its aesthetic power and a possible barrier to its prosecution.

Breen, in pursuing his unlikely suit, seeks out the services of John Henry Menton, a real Dublin solicitor with offices on Bachelor's Walk. Like many characters in the text, Menton too appears amidst the fantasies and nightmares of "Circe," where Bloom—accosted by the watch and asked for his name—first identifies himself as "Dr. Bloom, Leopold, dental surgeon" (15.721), the name of another real Dublin figure in 1904. In what amounts to a skillful act of deception, Bloom gives his name yet fails to properly identify himself. He then identifies his solicitors as "Messrs John Henry Menton, 27 Bachelor's Walk" (15.730). This encounter with the guards, furthermore, is immediately preceded by an imagined conversation with Josie Breen, who expresses her mock horror at finding Bloom in Nighttown. Flirting with her, Bloom grows suddenly alarmed when she mentions his name: "Not so loud my name. Whatever do you think of me? Don't give me away. Walls have ears" (15.398–399). Anxious about being caught in a potentially scandalous position, Bloom attempts to conceal his identity behind layers of confusion and misdirection, subtly evoking the hint of libel. Just as a jury must decide on a defamatory interpretation of a passage, so too must they agree that the plaintiff in the case is actually the person described in the text. In suits involving nonfictional texts, this is rarely an issue, but it typically constitutes the core of any action involving a roman à clef. In a potentially libelous passage describing Bloom's trip to a bordello, Joyce thus evokes the apparatus of defamation law, introducing once again the Breens and their solicitor, Menton, as Bloom employs pseudonyms and borrowed names to elude detection. Joyce already knew from Leventhal that Dr. Bloom no longer lived in Dublin in 1922, but for his readers this moment would have effectively summarized one of the text's most pressing questions: Who is the historical antecedent of Leopold Bloom? Were he real, after all, he would be the most defamed character in the text and his identification would no doubt spark a major scandal. We now recognize him as one of the few characters in the book without a direct historical antecedent,[42] but this moment of confusion and misdirection in "Circe" both obscures his identity and promises to reveal it. As a result, we are sent stumbling into a thicket of historical and fictional antecedents that exemplify the roman à clef's anarchic power to activate the kind of skepticism barely suppressed by the realist novel.

Throughout *Ulysses,* Joyce deliberately and provocatively invokes this genre to probe the boundary between fact and fiction, thereby pitting legal and aesthetic modes of interpretation against one another in a scandalous yet creative conflict. The pleasure and frustration of this practice is nowhere more evident than in the "Scylla and Charybdis" episode, in which more real names are invoked than anywhere else in the text. As the scene opens in the National Library, we are immediately confronted with John Eglinton, the editor of *Dana* and a well-known man of letters. His name can be tracked through various guides, revealing the details of his quite real and very accomplished life; yet we also learn that he is not John Eglinton, that this is merely a pseudonym he used (his real name was William McGee). Furthermore, he is asking Stephen Dedalus—a pseudonym for James Joyce in 1904[43]— about his plans to write a book comically entitled *The Sorrows of Satan,* the title of a wildly popular novel written by Marie Corelli—a pseudonym for Mary MacKay, who thought she was the reincarnation of William Shakespeare. As if this roster of displaced names is not confusing enough, the conversation is shared by Æ, the mystically initialed name taken by the writer and spiritualist George Russell. Finally, Dedalus, feeling the "elder's gall" behind Eglinton's question about his novel, merely smiles and then thinks of a fragment from a poem originally written by Oliver St. John Gogarty, which Buck Mulligan later recites when he appears. This most learned episode, in which scholarly sources are bandied about against the background of a vast cultural archive, thus begins amidst a welter of names and identities that disrupts any attempt to define the text's fictional limits. By the end of the episode, this confusion is explicit as "MAGEEGLINJOHN" asks Stephen, "What's in a name?" (9.901–2). What indeed? As the narrative suggests, even Eglinton's own identity is a conditional fiction, and one could only wonder what a jury might do were it asked to consider this text in a libel suit. If Joyce defamed Eglinton, does that mean that he also defamed Magee? Does a pseudonym have the same right to a good name that a real person has? Noting their propensity to change names and to adopt distinct public personas, Stephen calls the writers gathered in the library "cypherjugglers" (9.411)—itself an entirely apt way to describe the roman à clef's manipulation of details. Even more than the nightmare of "Circe," this episode mixes fact with fiction, preventing us from simply accepting the text as pure invention even as it insists on its historical veracity.

Amid this misdirection, "Scylla and Charybdis" features Stephen's long-awaited theory of Shakespeare's plays, itself a dazzling yet defamatory attempt to deduce historical fact from otherwise apparently fictional works. Mingling textual and documentary evidence, Stephen extracts all manner of libelous gossip from the plays, prompting Æ to depart and dismiss such talk as "prying into the family life of a great man," for information that is "interesting only to the parish clerk" (9.181, 184). In an episode already mired in a complex assortment of names and pseudonyms, however, we cannot depart with the snobbish poet and are left instead with what appears to be something like Hamlet's instructions to the players—that is, an encoded and ambiguously satirical set of instructions from the author himself about how we might go about reading *Ulysses* as a roman à clef.[44] Just as Stephen instructs his listeners in how to draw fact from fiction, so too we as readers (and perhaps even jurors) are asked to listen to these instructions and apply them not to Shakespeare's plays, but to *Ulysses* itself.[45]

Stephen crucially contends that the Bard played the ghost in *Hamlet*, talking to an incarnation of his own dead son, Hamnet, about the infidelity of Anne Hathaway. Rocked by tragedy, however, he can do more than speak to this other version of himself in an act of painful revelation. "His beaver is up," Stephen notes of the ghost, suggesting that when Shakespeare walked on the stage, his own face was visible to the audience as he related this tale of murder and adultery, making fiction "consubstantial" with fact just as the ghost itself is "the son consubstantial with the father" (9.481). The conditional qualities of this fiction drives Stephen's theory just as it drives our own attempts to read *Ulysses*, mired as we are in the text's deliberate and provocative refusal to abide by the laws of libel and defamation. Even this reading, however, becomes ironic, as Stephen ends his performance by telling Eglinton that while he does not believe his theory, he is nevertheless willing to sell it for a guinea. This mocking conclusion again suggests the way we too might read *Ulysses:* neither as fact nor fiction but as an elaborate edifice of gossip and defamation—a distinctly modernist experiment in rejuvenating the roman à clef. "You are a delusion" Eglinton finally tells Stephen (9.1064). This constitutes the core of Joyce's assault on the legal limits of fiction: Stephen is indeed a delusion, a fantasy like the ghost of Hamlet's father that both appears to speak the truth and yet critically refuses to validate that knowledge.

"Scylla and Charybdis" concludes with Buck Mulligan revealing his own satirical rendition of the proceedings in the library, a "national immorality in three orgasms," which mocks all this theorizing as mere intellectual onanism. He reads it to Stephen, telling him that "the disguise, I fear, is thin" (9.1178), thus rehearsing in his own little drama the same kind of lightly veiled and deeply libelous attacks Stephen finds in Shakespeare, and that we too can tentatively find in *Ulysses.* The disguise is indeed thin, since we do know that this is both Buck Mulligan's play and Oliver Gogarty's, just as this is both Stephen's Dublin and Joyce's own. Rather than concealing its engagement with historical reality as Victorian novelists typically did by decorously avoiding the names of real people, Joyce uses the roman à clef to destabilize the autonomy of art and the increasingly fraught legal institutions designed to maintain a critical distance between fiction and fact. This deliberate and potent confusion constitutes one of the most remarkable and original aspects of Joyce's writing, though it has been largely obscured by the text's epic legal entanglements with obscenity laws and, over the course of time, the gradual diminution of its ability to bring living people into "hatred, ridicule, and contempt." It nevertheless constituted a vital aspect of the book's scandal. Joyce recorded "nameless shamelessness about everybody he ever met" and in so doing at once courted libel suits and crucially revealed the fragility of the legal assumptions about the novel on which they would have depended.

As he learned from his attorney when trying to bring *Dubliners* into print, even his own intention could not constitute a defense, nor could it legally guarantee the meaning of any particular passage. In *Ulysses,* therefore, Joyce created a work that is blatantly libelous yet seeks to elude that charge in its misdirected names, its aesthetic difficulty, and its deconstructive ironies. As the Dodd trial later revealed, this defense proved insufficient and justified Joyce's own decision to remain in exile, safe from the sanctions of British and Irish courts. In a 1909 meeting, after their friendship had collapsed, Gogarty told Joyce, "I don't care a damn what you say of me so long as it is literature."[46] Joyce took him at his word, and in the process attempted to undermine the concept of literature as it had taken shape in the eighteenth century, exposing the limits of its imagined autonomy while simultaneously challenging the law's ability to delimit the nature and structure of art. Long after

Woolsey's decision and the novel's ascension in the canon, this remains one of the scandals of *Ulysses* we have yet fully to confront.

Wyndham Lewis

"Remove from Satire Its Moralism"

Despite the fact that his work deals everywhere in libel, Joyce himself entered a courtroom as part of a defamation action only once—after he sued an English consular agent named Henry Carr in a Swiss court. The dispute arose from a feud between the two men regarding a semi-professional performance in wartime Zurich of Oscar Wilde's *The Importance of Being Earnest*. Joyce had served as the production's business agent, and when he showed up to collect a disputed debt, Carr threatened him with violence and called him a swindler. The legal proceedings were protracted and the British embassy sought deliberately to hinder them, so that by the time of the trial Joyce was forced to withdraw his claim and pay court costs of 120 francs.[47] Though frustrating, this was little more than a minor inconvenience and Joyce—according to form—exacted his revenge by giving the name "Private Carr" to the solider who assaults Stephen Dedalus in "Circe." Like the author of *Ulysses,* Wyndham Lewis too often waged rather than merely wrote fiction, brandishing his pen in a campaign of cultural critique and petty revenge. But, where Joyce largely managed to evade the limits of libel law, Lewis found his own similar experiments stymied and suppressed by the paradoxical British laws governing defamation in the wake of the Artemus Jones case. Between 1913 and 1938, Lewis was directly involved in at least six direct or threatened actions for libel, almost all of which were lost when nervous editors agreed to settlements. Two books, *The Doom of Youth* and *Filibusters in Barbary,* were withdrawn from publication, while the type for a third—*The Roaring Queen*—was broken up at the proof stage. In drawing so explicitly on the conventions of the roman à clef, Lewis too lodged his work at the scandalous boundary between fact and fiction, where a deliberately formulated skepticism collided with the legal constraints governing the novel. Unlike Joyce's work, which gained a certain degree of freedom through its author's self-imposed exile, Lewis's troubled career more clearly exemplifies the ways in which the law constrained other kinds of experiments with the roman à clef by seeking to regulate its uncanny social life.

Lewis's onetime publisher, Rupert Grayson, who was himself brutally satirized in *Snooty Baronet,* remembered Lewis wielding the same "cold steel pen"

Stephen describes atop the Martello Tower and with equally hostile intentions: "He employed his usual weapon, a pen sharpened to a dagger point with which he etched my likeness . . ., cutting lines jagged and deeper than scars and poisoned with acidic brilliance."[48] Unlike Joyce, who leavened *Ulysses* with humanism and sentimentality, Lewis sought to "remove from Satire its moralism" by deploying the roman à clef as a cruel and alienating counter-form to the novel.[49] This radical critique, which spans most of Lewis's major works, reaches its climax in the *Apes of God*, only to be increasingly diminished by a series of defamation suits of the sort Joyce generally managed to avoid (until after his death). Lewis's career, therefore, offers a compelling example of the ways in which the laws of libel shaped early twentieth century literature by constraining a particularly caustic mode of narrative experimentation with the roman à clef that finally revealed the precise limits of modernism's imagined autonomy.

Lewis infamously thrived on the carefully constructed image of himself as "The Enemy," a cunning provocateur who, as his biographer Jeffrey Meyers notes, "protected his privacy at the same time that he courted publicity, for he moved about in a furtive manner, as if in constant expectation of arrest, yet wore conspicuous and flamboyant hats and capes that instantly drew attention to himself."[50] Such contradictions form the very core of the aesthetic flaunted by Lewis, who sought to inhabit the world of art and letters in order to reveal its fatuous claims to autonomy. Indeed, one of his earliest and perhaps best known works of fiction, the 1918 *Tarr*,[51] used the formula of the *Bildungsroman* to turn a coldly dispassionate eye upon himself even as it mocked the genre's bourgeois solipsism. Like Joyce's *Portrait* and D. H. Lawrence's *Sons and Lovers*, it focuses on the rising consciousness of an aesthetically sensitive artist.[52] Yet the dynamic subjectivity of characters like Stephen Dedalus and Paul Morrell, as Paul Peppis argues, becomes in Lewis's work "a repetitive, torturous vortex of conflicting forces" so that the central characters can only "strive to adopt an identity they wish were authentic in hopes that by performing that pseudo-self it might somehow become real."[53] In *Tarr*, there is neither authenticity nor epiphany, only an endless and chaotic jumble of social and psychic forces that coalesce as publicly staged identities. Just as Lewis guarded his own private life with paranoid intensity yet ostentatiously staged that privacy, so too the characters in this early work find themselves always already implicated in the very structures they seek to escape. Rather than providing some glimmer of authenticity or redemption, the world of art becomes little more than another capital marketplace where identity is ceaselessly commodified and even the most private moments are weighed in the public scales of profit and loss.

Such a critique of authenticity is by no means entirely unique to Lewis, and even Joyce's *Portrait* is now typically read as an ironic critique of the *Bildungsroman* it once seemed to exemplify. The "new secondhand clothes" Stephen's mother lays out for him at the end of the book symbolize the recycled and thus inauthentic nature of his own romantic pursuit of exile in bohemian Paris. Unlike Joyce, however, who generally managed to remain always on the edges of the bohemian world—even when he finally moved to its Parisian heart in 1920—Lewis was throughout his career deeply embedded in the vicious and competitive world of coterie modernism that he otherwise endlessly savaged in his works. His first encounter with libel law, in fact, found him on the offensive in 1913 after he broke with Roger Fry's Omega Workshop. Though the details of this particular scandal remain somewhat murky, Lewis believed that Fry had stolen a commission from him to design a "Futurist room" for the Ideal Home Exhibition sponsored by the *Daily Mail*. Lewis responded by first securing the services of a solicitor from the offices of Fry, Vandercom, and Co. and then publishing a circular to the friends and clients of the Omega Workshop. The letter was plainly meant to provoke Fry into naming Lewis in a defamation suit, asserting first that he had taken the commission "by a shabby trick" and that he had furthermore deliberately misled the organizer of an exhibition about the availability of another artist's work.[54] It then concludes by condemning the Omega Workshop as a crass, bourgeois attempt to appropriate the energy of a radical art movement: "This enterprise seemed to promise, in the opportunities afforded it by support from the most intellectual quarters, emancipation from the middleman-shark. But a new form of fish in the troubled waters of Art has been revealed in the meantime, the Pecksniff shark, a timid but voracious journalistic monster, unscrupulous, smooth-tongued and, owing chiefly to its weakness, mischievous."[55] Lewis condemns Fry and his cohort for their alleged obsession with commercial gain and their ability to manipulate the press in order to puff themselves at the expense of others. As Bloomsbury immediately realized, however, Lewis too was playing "Pecksniff shark," hoping to provoke a defamation suit that would serve primarily to advertise his own work and reputation. Vanessa Bell wrote to Fry explicitly to warn him that Lewis may have been setting just such a snare, and that what he "would really like would be an action for libel."[56] No response to Lewis's broadside would, in fact, be published and, despite continued provocations, the legal gambit reached its conclusion when his solicitors sent a bill along with a note regretting that the circular had "failed to arise Roger Fry."[57]

Following this break with Bloomsbury, Lewis formed his own alternative coterie of artists and writers, first creating the Rebel Art Center, then organizing the

Vorticist movement and editing the two remarkable volumes of *Blast*. Such projects, however, were short-lived, not only eclipsed by the First World War but driven into obscurity by Lewis's own hostility toward the very kind of organizations he sought to create. The larger trajectory of his career, in fact, consistently reiterates the paradox of the private man in the gaudy costume, for though he embedded himself deeply in bohemian life, he nevertheless ceaselessly critiqued its institutionalization. After cursing "snobbery" and the "fear of ridicule" in the first issue of *Blast*, for example, he then embraces the savagery of a modern art movement inextricably entangled in the mechanisms of mass-mediation and celebrity that were themselves rapidly expanding their reach during the first decades of the twentieth century.[58] "This enormous, jangling, journalistic, fairy desert of modern life," he writes, serves the modern artist "as Nature did more technically primitive man."[59] Rather than a refuge from the commercial world, he contends bohemia is merely one of its many commercial outgrowths, its organization and institutions fully penetrated by advertisement, competition, and self-promotion. In order fully to critique the "journalistic" world of modernity, in effect, Lewis refuses to exempt himself from critique, becoming the very sort of "Pecksniff-shark" that he once condemned. This is what he means when he writes of a satire without morals: an assault upon the very institutions that have made his own work possible, one so insistent and pervasive that it condemns both reader and writer alike. Unwilling to claim any sort of moral highground, Lewis instead becomes the Enemy—even to himself.

This self-critical impulse pervades his work, but finds its most powerful expression in the massive 1930 roman à clef, *Apes of God*. The title refers to the vast number of "New Bohemians": the "gossip-mad, vulgar, pseudo-artist, good-timers" who, the text claims, are "more damaging for the very reason that they are identified in the mind of the public with art and intelligence."[60] In a series of brutal sketches, the narrative traces the journey of an idiotic young man, Dan Boleyn, through this treacherous world of "restlessness, insecurity and defamation" in which art is never more than a veiled attempt to secure fame or exact revenge on one's enemies. The text itself is extraordinarily long and densely packed, its loosely organized chapters brutally targeting almost the entire panorama of modern aesthetic production. Boleyn himself conjures the generic codes of the *Bildungsroman*, and he spends a good deal of the narrative treasuring his supposed genius while suffering a bewildering array of humiliations. Bloomsbury, psychoanalysis, sexology, homosexuality, Proust, and literary coteries are all savagely attacked, and the book concludes with Dan's pointless death in the 1926 General Strike.

The most remarkable aspect of *Apes of God*, however, is its dogged manipulation of the roman à clef's anarchism. Writing in *The New Review*, Ezra Pound lightly dismissed this aspect of the work, suggesting that "in eighty years no one will care a kuss whether Mr X, Y or Z of the book was 'taken from' Mssrs Puffun, Guffin or Mungo."[61] As Pound so often did, he attempts here to remake this book into something he finds more suitable, even at the cost of doing great damage to the underlying text. Thus, the review huffily separates *Apes from God* from the taint of the roman à clef in an attempt to counter the more popular perception of the book, summarized by an anonymous reviewer for the *Evening News:* "Just what it is all about I cannot say, for I have not the key. Mr. Lewis hates widely and well. I assume that there are many portraits in this book, but they are portraits, for the most part, of those whom I do not know.... I should have preferred ... less mysteriousness in the matter of identification."[62] The more snobbish reviewer for *Everyman* is equally explicit, calling the book nothing more than a portrait collection of "the people you read about day by day in the popular Press."[63] Despite Pound's defensive lament, *Apes of God* remains most strikingly vibrant now for the same reason in did in 1930: it draws on the structural ambiguity of the roman à clef to undermine the legal and aesthetic compromise underwriting the realist novel.

Rather than a set of broadly drawn stereotypes, *Apes of Gods* manipulates the finest descriptive details to single out real individuals, attacking them personally while simultaneously using them to allegorize the hypocrisy underwriting the entire aesthetic field of production. Of a piece with the circular letter mailed in 1913, the book was carefully designed to provoke a libel suit. Though Lewis did not retain a firm of solicitors in advance of its publication, he still managed the text's circulation very carefully. Two short extracts were published in Eliot's *New Criterion,* but they focused narrowly on parts of the book that did not contain any portraiture. In 1924, Lewis offered Eliot a third extract from the climatic chapter entitled "Lord Osmund's Lenten Party," which harshly describes the Sitwell family's obsessive pursuit of celebrity as well as their *"professional* wistful juvenility" (393). When Eliot received some portion of this in the *New Criterion* offices, however, he asked Lewis to delete one explicit—if relatively innocent—reference to Bloomsbury, while also suggesting that the fictional names "Lord Osmund" and "Stillwell" should be more radically altered in order to avoid legal action. Even though these changes were quickly made, Eliot continued to equivocate, and by 1925 Lewis began to lose patience, withholding another piece he had already submitted while warning that "should any of these fragments find their way into other hands before they appear in book-form, I shall regard it as treachery rather than a harmless trick, or as the inadvertence of a harassed man."[64] Lewis had good reason to be worried, particularly if he were indeed hoping to provoke a defamation suit. One of the basic principles of British law is that an act must first be committed before it can be enjoined. Thus, Lewis could not be named in a suit until and unless he actually published the work. As we have already seen in chapter 3, however, publication itself is defined simply as writing a defamatory statement and sharing it with a third party. Thus, were a manuscript copy of the section into find its way into the Sitwells' hands before it had been published, they would be free to sue Lewis for libel before the text had even gone to print, effectively short-circuiting any attempt to profit from the chapter's publication. In the end, Eliot declined to publish the piece, though Osbert Sitwell did get wind of the larger project, warning Lewis in a 1929 letter not to "get onto a frail biographical track in your new book, as it would be extremely tiresome to make us either self-conscious or quarrelsome."[65]

Lewis, of course, was perfectly aware of the risks he ran in writing this kind of text, and by 1930 the consequences of the Artemus Jones case had rippled throughout the publishing industry. Merely changing a few names in the final text—Finnian Shaw for Sitwell, for example, or Matthew Plunkett for Lytton Strachey—afforded him little legal protection, particularly when the veneer of fiction was so lightly applied. A plaintiff would have little difficulty in filing a colloquium demonstrating that many readers would draw quick and clear connections between the Sitwells and the Finnian Shaws. Both families consisted of two brothers and a sister, a caretaker, and a cranky old father, all of whom shared an ancient manor house and hosted magnificent parties frequently described in the pages of gossip columns. Many of the other portraits, furthermore, are equally pointed. The Strachey character, for example, is a tall yet awkward gay man, the "fairy giant of a Bloomsbury pantomime" (81), who is fascinated by psychoanalysis and carries on an awkward romantic relationship with a diminutive woman, herself a dead ringer for Dora Carrington.

Perhaps the most striking aspect of the book is its methodical—even manic— delineation of external detail, so that the characters assume the kind of concrete nastiness evident in some of Lewis's most striking paintings. "No book has ever been written," he proudly wrote, "that has paid more attention to the *outside* of people. In it their shells or pelts, and the language of their bodily movements, comes first, not last."[66] Hugh Kenner calls this "puppet-fiction,"[67] and a number of critics emphasize what a radical departure it was from the stream of consciousness and interior monologues Joyce and Woolf both had so skillfully developed. Particularly when read against Lewis's condemnation in *Blasting and Bombardiering* of "time consciousness," these portraits depend on a comedy that arises from "the observations of a *thing* behaving like a person."[68] That is, by refusing to provide any kind of narrative access to individual consciousness, Lewis engages in a philosophical assault on the world, his objective aesthetic deliberately reducing what Vincent Sherry calls "the pretense of human superiority" to a mere "animal's humorous impersonation of free and thinking humanity."[69] This widely accepted description of Lewis's aesthetic, however, obscures the fact that such objectivity inevitably produces texts shot through with the roman à clef's distinctive aesthetic of detail. The focus on the external body, after all, makes it easy for select readers to identify the real people moving through an apparent work of fiction, particularly since their features and habits are described with such telling detail. Lewis's objective aesthetic, therefore, draws its critical energy not just from a philosophical resistance to Joycean stream of consciousness, but from a much more scandalous deployment of the roman à clef as well.

Apes of God relishes its own unstable and potentially disruptive social life. It begins with a framing narrative focused on an aged gossip columnist and reaches its climax at the Finnian Shaw costume ball where the participants arrive in fancy dress as characters from fiction, "human cryptograms . . . vegetative, secretive—grown from spores, without true seed, stamen-and-pistilless" (355). The text, in other words, thematizes its own identity as a roman à clef, generating characters who are themselves lightly disguised as literary figures while indulging "gluttonously [in] gossip" and "stale personal allusion" (354). Lady Fredigonde Follett, the "Gossip-Star" who opens the book, wonders, as Stephen Dedalus does in the National Library, "*What's in a name?*" (15, italics in original). This is the very question that drives the roman à clef and, as the Artemus Jones case made clear, it is also a crucial element in determining the nature and extent of a libel. As Follett realizes, however, names are particularly slippery things: "*Bolts from the blue they flop down on men and women from nowhere, in their cradles, on each anonymous noodle—all of us worse luck have to be a Something! Seeing how at random names fall upon the heads to be accommodated with tags, descriptive whatnots—the shower of Violets, the downpour of Jacks, Joans, Peters, Toms—what reference can there be?*" (15). Positioned as an introduction to the text, this passage asks readers to consider precisely the question of names. Although it does not offer an explicit key, it suggests that the names Lewis uses are indeed somewhat haphazardly assigned and thus invites readers to look tentatively beyond them to the brutal descriptions that offer a much more precise reference to an individual's personality and identity than terms like "Jack" or "Violet" could. And yet, in a passage that could easily have been drawn from a treatise on libel, Follett also recognizes that "*we survive by* words . . . things *perish*" (15, italics in original). Defamation law rests upon precisely this assumption—that printed words, in particular, have the power to do a unique and lasting kind of damage. Lewis thus frames *Apes of God* as a gossip-driven roman à clef that exploits the random and unstable nature of names in order to relate unpleasant truths about the real people he describes.

Such ambivalence is, of course, essential to the genre's infectious ability to reinject a destabilizing skepticism into the news/novel divide. This opening narrative, in fact, only heightens the reader's appetite for scandal by assuring him or her that real damage has been done. Mark Perrino argues that Lewis modulates such ambiguities quite carefully in order to afford himself some degree of protection: "With his external method Lewis portrayed people so objectively, literally as physical objects, that the images were painfully embarrassing, yet he included enough fantasy to allow him to claim that the characters did not derive from particular individuals."[70] There is unquestionably a degree of satiric excess in the book, and it may indeed afford Lewis some small degree of plausible deniability; but it is consistently shadowed by the text's dogged insistence that it is indeed a roman à clef—that its fictions are actually facts. Indeed, in the gossip-driven world Dan explores, people are endlessly concerned not only about their own reputations but about how they might appear to others. Guiding Dan through this maze of performativity, deception, and deceit is Horace Zagreus, a darkly satiric Virgil who provides insights into the petty habits of the bohemian Apes. He sets Dan a variety of odd assignments, arranging for him to move through the parties, salons, and studios of London while requiring the dim-witted young man to write up his often bizarre experiences—ranging from posing nude for a lesbian painter to observing another artist's collection of whips.

Each chapter unfolds in roughly the same fashion as Dan goes on one of these visits and uncomprehendingly observes the hypocrisy of a fully institutionalized bohemian subculture. Even the roman à clef, it emerges in a chapter entitled "Chez Lionel Kein, Esq.," is an essential part of this deeply corrupted art world, precisely because it was used so regularly even by otherwise ardent defenders of art's impersonality and autonomy. Lewis modeled Lionel Kein, around whom this chapter congeals, on Sidney Shiff, Proust's English translator and a well-known man of letters. After listening to Kein and his wife praise *À la recherche du temps perdu* as the greatest of literary works, Zagreus anticipates Edmund Wilson by noting that Proust wrote a roman à clef rather than a novel. Furthermore, he emphasizes that those who insist on the work's supreme aesthetic value obscure its darker satiric ends. "How is it that no one ever sees himself in the public mirror—in official Fiction?" he asks. "People feel themselves under the special protection of the author when they read a satire on their circle. . . . It is always the *other fellows* (never them) that their accredited romancer is depicting, for their sport" (255). Cutting through what he imagines to be vacuous rhetoric about literary aesthetics, Zagreus contends that these "new bohemians" miss the point of work by Proust and others. Believing themselves safely ensconced in the author's coterie, they see only the brutal portraits of others and fail to acknowledge the indictments leveled against themselves.

Throughout the chapter Zagreus spells out the consequences of this conditional mode of writing and reading, which he contends is becoming ever more damaging and widespread. Modernist impersonality, in particular, degenerates into mere strategic misdirection, becoming "a wonderful patent behind which the individual can indulge in a riot of personal egotism" (260). Far from a marginal or archaic genre, he contends, the roman à clef has become the very essence of a new mode of writing that disrupts the novel's complacent autonomy: "*Fiction*, as we call it, is indeed no misnomer, since it is generally an untruthful picture. In its high-brow forms it is in fact the *private news-sheet,* the big 'Gossip'-book—the expansion of a Society newspaper-paragraph—of the Reigning Order. And the Reigning Order is the people with the pelf and the circle of those they patronize, and today it is the High Bohemia of the Ritzes and Rivieras. And the 'great novels' of this time are *dramatised social news-sheets* of that particular Social World" (262, emphasis in original). Within a celebrity-obsessed culture, Zagreus contends, the divide between news and novels collapses as readers come to believe they can unlock most any text to reveal the real people populating the gossipy social columns of the burgeoning popular press. Furthermore, the infectious consequences of this confusion radiate into reality itself, so that people begin to confuse themselves with characters in books. Bohemia is thus filled with empty and mechanical beings in search of an author to write them fully into being: "they have all been written about in their own or their friend's books—upon that you may rely. But what of Fiction? It is a Fiction as dependent upon reality—*such a poor reality and so unreal*—that they are neither flesh nor fowl—they are *fictional mongrel facts*" (293, emphasis in original). Like Joyce's term "cypherjugglers," this aptly describes the revived roman à clef, and for Zagreus it becomes the definitive genre of a rapidly decaying modernity in which reality has collapsed into the celebrity apparatus of the popular media. Indeed, before he is finally thrown out of the Kein's flat, he concludes that the couple constitutes perhaps the poorest class of modern bohemians, "*the people who have never been able to become fiction,*" precisely because no one has ever bothered (until now) to write about them (294, emphasis in original).

The ironies of this particularly pointed critique of modernist aesthetic production abound, since Lewis himself deploys the roman à clef in order to critique its disastrous predominance. Gossip, innuendo, and celebrity scandal drive *Apes of God* just as powerfully as they do the works Zagreus condemns, introducing into the text a bewildering hypocrisy that seems to undermine some of its most eloquent moments. Critics like Perrino who seek to redeem Lewis for a more Eliotic modernism misunderstand this aspect of the book when they contend that Lewis attempts to "obscure the most effective aspect of the novel (especially to his contemporary audience), the insulting portrayal of actual people [and] that these protests constitute a *covert* denial of the novel's personal dimension, a denial that ironically attests to some measure of guilt."[71] There is nothing ironic about Lewis's sense of guilt; he self-consciously condemns himself, his text, and his readers in *Apes of God*. This satire without morality, as he describes it, does not allow for the creation of a position of superiority or impersonality outside of the text. Instead, like the idiotic Dan, we too are led through the warrens of London's new bohemia and invited—even required—to indulge our desires to read reality into the book as if it were a "private news-sheet," ferreting out the lightly disguised figures behind its fictional façade.

Zagreus himself initially appears to be Lewis's alter-ego, his manifestos and proclamations echoing closely many of the author's own positions on the maniacal cult of youth, the naked pursuit of publicity, and the dissolution of bohemia. This character's homosexuality, however, as well as his predilection for devious pranks more closely associates him with Horace de Vere Cole, a marginal member of the Bloomsbury coterie who participated in the 1910 Dreadnought Hoax by disguising himself as an African dignitary to sneak aboard a British warship. Furthermore, Zagreus himself articulates very few original ideas over the course of the narrative and instead opens and closes many of the chapters by "broadcasting" the theories of a shadowy and mysterious figure named Pierpoint. Indeed, Zagreus increasingly seems to be simply an older version of the hopelessly misguided Dan: having himself once received Pierpoint's "Encyclical" describing the apery of the new bohemians, he now passes it on to younger, sexually attractive men in order to serve as their guide and mentor. By the midpoint of the Finnian Shaws' party, the other characters (as well as the reader) grow tired of these secondhand lectures: "Ratner realized that Horace was preparing to 'broadcast' or to try out a new Pierpoint Record, and that he might begin at any moment now. He resigned himself to listen to the ubiquitous loud-speaker, with the hated voice of Pierpoint starring" (449). The guide who brings us into the world of the "apes," in other words, is himself revealed to be nothing more than a kind of empty, mechanical puppet who recites someone else's words. Even this mysterious off-stage voice, however, is deeply submerged in the same culture of gossip and celebrity it otherwise condemns, creating its own coterie that transforms Pierpoint into a media star. His incisive critiques are, therefore, less ironic than they are self-condemning, and the whole mass of *Apes of God* engages in this reflexive mode of satire that does not allow for a moral position outside of itself. Within the pervasive institutions of celebrity culture, the novel's autonomy inevitably gives way, in Lewis's book, to the roman à clef's "conditional fictionality." Without a position to occupy outside of this system, author, reader, and characters alike all become the very apes the text condemns, left to wander this narrative warren in which fact and fiction are irremediably entangled.

Lewis's risky narrative experiment deliberately challenges the idealized autonomy of the aesthetic sphere, revealing a hypocritical pursuit of fame and fortune at the heart of modernism by itself mordantly seeking such rewards. Like *Ulysses*, *Apes of God* is a wildly libelous book. Eliot was aware of this, and finally declined to publish the extract satirizing the Sitwells. Lewis's editor at Chatto and Windus also grew alarmed at the risk the firm would run in producing the book and wrote to ask for extensive revisions to conceal or even remove any association between the seemingly fictional characters and real individuals. Lewis's response is strikingly disingenuous, drawing on what has become the well-worn claim that he is merely describing broad types rather than actual people:

> As to your believing that you detect a likeness in some of the personages to people in real life, in that you are mistaken. I have here and there used things, it is true, that might suggest some connection. But the cases you choose [Lionel and Isabel Kein] are not ones I could, I am afraid, remove from my picture. If the bodies I describe fit in the morning suits of real people and they thrust themselves in and lay claim to them, however much the clothes fitted I should not countenance the wearing of such mis-fits by any of my characters, to all of whom I supply suits from *my own* store.[72]

As we have seen, the Kein chapter openly invites readers to see it as a libelous roman à clef, subject to the same infectious instability pervading the entire literary field. Indeed, even as he disavows any intentional attempt to mix fiction and fact, Lewis still snidely allows that any number of people might deliberately misrecognize themselves in the text, seeking out an author able finally to write them into stardom. Legally, of course, Lewis's stated intentions carry no weight, but he may be trying to invoke another defense against libel—namely that groups cannot be defamed and individuals who feel themselves libeled must prove that they alone suffered harm. Thus, authors are free to write about artists or bohemians in general, provided they do not single out a particular individual by name or description. For Lewis, who sees all humans as devoid of individuality, such a defense may have made a certain kind of philosophical and even critical sense, but, given the narrow description of the Keins and their friends, such reasoning could not gain any sort of legal traction.

Not surprisingly, Chatto and Windus voided their contract after Lewis failed to make the invasive changes they requested. Furthermore, word of the book had already begun to circulate throughout London, and Osbert Sitwell's letter warning Lewis off was likely accompanied by similar admonitions issued to other interested publishers. The book had the potential to generate a great deal of scandal-driven publicity, but the legal risks proved insurmountable. In the end, Lewis followed the same strategy Joyce had, using a private imprint—the Arthur Press—to publish a limited edition of 750 copies complete with illustrations and priced at a fabulously expensive three pounds.[73] Initially, no legal action was taken, despite the fact that a number of reviewers clearly identified it as a roman à clef, with Naomi Richardson in *Time and Tide* noting that those singled out include "the Sitwell family—also probably a good many others of his [Lewis's] contemporaries whom I am not gossip-column-ape enough to recognize."[74] Seizing on the decision by Ellis Roberts of *The New Statesman* to reject a positive review written by Roy Campbell, Lewis cobbled together a pamphlet entitled *Satire and Fiction,* which all but dared the figures he had named to sue him for libel. This broadsheet contains a copy of Roberts's rejection letter, a piece by Lewis in defense of satire, and a short but provocative essay by Campbell. The latter section begins by claiming that "an electrical atmosphere pervaded all of London" after the publication of *Apes of God,* and that Lewis himself had been viciously libeled in "anonymous letters of the most violent sort."[75] A number of those satirized in the book had indeed mailed Lewis a postcard reading "GREETINGS TO TARZAN FROM A GATHERING OF THE APES" and signed the names assigned to them in the book. Richard Wyndham, one of Lewis's ardent supporters, who was nevertheless drawn as a particularly ridiculous ape, used the personal columns of *The Times* to offer some of Lewis's most important paintings—including *Kermesse* and *Plan for War*—for sale at ridiculously low prices.

In *Satire and Fiction,* Campbell treats these private acts of revenge derisively, noting that though the perpetrators see themselves in Lewis's apes, they nevertheless lack the courage to reply openly: "What is interesting to observe is the *manner* in which the satrised of to-day behave, in contrast to that of their classical counterparts. At least it can be said that today they are far more *anonymous!* It is in that respect chiefly that they differ. In nothing have they the courage to appear *openly* and *publicly*."[76] By first noting that these figures yearn for celebrity and then taunting them for their anonymity, the pamphlet throws down a gauntlet, daring the objects of Lewis's satire to abandon their anonymity and sue him for libel.[77] As the reviews of the book clearly indicated, any number of real people recognized themselves as Apes; Campbell's essay relishes relating the story of Edith Sitwell glimpsing "Mr. Lewis's advancing sombrero in a Bayswater street" and suffering a "seizure" before her friends could revive her with an "old-fashioned remedy of Arquebuscade Water."[78] Legal action, however, would require a plaintiff to file a colloquium, providing a judge and jury very precise information about how and why he or she might be identified with one of the book's brutally satiric portraits. Furthermore, at trial Lewis himself would be given a very public forum in which to vent his spleen, and even if he should be found guilty, the plaintiff would likely secure little in the way of damages and Lewis's reputation as the "Enemy" would be all the more highly burnished.

In the end, no one took up Lewis's implicit challenge and the book remained something of an oddity—a "cubist telephone book"—in which the boundary between fact and fiction had been powerfully breached despite the injunctions of British defamation law.[79] More than any other author aside from Joyce, Lewis manipulated the conventions of the roman à clef to launch an assault on the institutions of the modern novel by provocatively testing the very limits of its presumed autonomy.[80] By making himself an object of his own "satire without morals," furthermore, Lewis mined the realist novel's foundations by extending the roman à clef's reach into the public sphere. A deliberately defamatory book, *Apes of God* sought to destabilize the troubling nexus between art, morality, and the law in order to disrupt the institutions that had long underwritten the novel as a form. It ultimately failed to produce the kind of legal action that would have proved its own argument about the cultural sphere, yet it also marked the limits of Lewis's probing experiments with the roman à clef. As he sought to extend his formal innovations with the genre throughout the next decade, he encountered increasing legal resistance that finally foreclosed this mode of experimentation by setting profoundly disabling limits on the modernist roman à clef.

"Vexatious Laws Abound"

After completing work on *Ulysses* in 1922, Joyce's interest in the roman à clef's possibilities increasingly gave way to an obsessive fascination with language. For most of the rest of his life he labored to construct the astonishing densities of *Finnegans Wake*, a text that effectively abandons normative codes of plot, genre, and character (though it does not shy away from its own distinctive style of portraiture). Lewis, however, continued throughout the 1930s to pursue the implications of *Apes of God,* pushing even harder to extend the roman à clef's critical potential as a counter-form to the novel. Tyrus Miller, in *Late Modernism,* links Lewis to a larger group of writers in this same period who rejected the Joycean ecstasy of language and instead presented "unlovely allegories of a world's end" in which "subject and object, figure and ground, character and setting are only weakly counterposed or even partly intermingled."[81] For Lewis, as we have seen, this results in texts without a grounding morality—often vicious yet always conditional fictions that fold together the novel and the autobiography in a coldly measured, self-consuming satire. Miller calls this new kind of work a "generalized mimetism," and it is characterized by "role-playing, contagious imitation, 'rhythmic' forms of association, anthropomorphic 'animation' of the object-world, [and] ritualized behavior."[82] Lewis and other later modernists, in other words, saw the infection of fiction with fact as part of what they imagined to be the larger disaster of modernity itself.

This aesthetic mimetism Miller usefully identifies carries considerable legal risks, since by deliberately blurring the boundary between fiction and history, it threatens to violate one of the central legal structures on which the news/novel divide rested. Throughout the 1930s, in fact, Lewis increasingly ran afoul of both the formal and informal mechanisms of libel law; by the time he published *Blasting and Bombardiering* in 1937, he had become uncomfortably aware of the limits imposed upon his compositional strategies. "You quite realize," he advises his readers in the text's introduction, "that there are limits to the truthfulness in which I may indulge I hope? Vexatious laws abound."[83] He refers here explicitly to the laws of libel, which bedevil his desire to create an anarchic alternative to the novel. In an earlier version of the same document, he is equally explicit about the legal absurdities that led him to deploy the roman à clef's conditional facts and fictions: "That is the danger with me—I have to guard against my tendency never to do things by halves. For then I might after all not find myself lying cosily side by side with Mr. Priestly or Miss Baum upon the railway bookstall, but squatting cheek by jowl with some embezzler in one of His Majesty's jails."[84] While Lewis perhaps overestimates the jeopardy in which he might place himself (since a criminal libel charge would be almost impossible to secure in most cases), he nevertheless acknowledges that defamation law sharply delimits his innovative critique of the novel.

The final version of the book's preface actually provides a kind of recipe for the roman à clef, contending that almost everyone of some notoriety already acts as if they had become characters in a novel: "Every 'great man' to-day knows that he is living potentially a life of fiction. Sooner or later he will find himself the centre of a romance, and afford some person incapable of true invention the opportunity of stealing the laurels of the fictionist."[85] To someone unfamiliar with Lewis's work, of course, this may look like the sniping of a literary purist disgusted by a lack of artistic originality. Almost all of his own major texts, however, are romans à clef, attempts to reveal the ways in which "great men" have always already become emplotted and thus fictionalized machines. As we have come to expect, Lewis thus indicts himself along with the rest of the literary world, but he also acknowledges that his experiment with genre has become hopelessly frustrated by those "vexatious laws." *Blasting and Bombardiering,* perhaps one of his now most widely read books, thus marks the end of his most innovative work, as he abandons the ambiguity and complexity so carefully cultivated in *Apes of God* and instead produces a conventional memoir hewing judiciously to the distinction between fact and fiction.

Lewis's caution in *Blasting and Bombardiering* is the hard-learned lesson gained from a series of bitter encounters with the law that began shortly after the publication of a somewhat similar book in 1932 entitled *The Doom of Youth.* Once again taking up the mantle of "the Enemy," he launches an assault in this text upon what he believes to be an infatuation with youth pervading modern culture—an obsession that effectively infantilizes art by creating the "*Age-snob*" who cares for nothing other than a certain naïve vivacity.[86] In many ways, this argument simply reiterates themes from *Apes of God,* in which Zagreus celebrates Dan's "genius," despite the fact that he is little more than an idiotic, albeit attractive, young man. Without the ambiguous protection afforded by the roman à clef, however, Lewis's satire became essentially indistinguishable from defamation, and two libel actions followed. Both emerged from a single chapter, "Winn and Waugh," which critiques "*Youngergenerationconsciousness,*" treating Alec Waugh's popular memoir, *Loom of Youth,* as a particularly egregious case of this malady. The editors at Chatto and Windus had already considered the legal risks posed by Lewis's book, warning that he may have gone too far in his description of Michael Arlen: "We speak with no precise knowledge of the working of the law of libel, but we are inclined to think that the effect of calling him 'this dismal asiatic caricature of a *rastaqouère*' and 'this tawdry gentleman who has filched the christian name of an archangel' would be to send him hot-foot to his solicitor. . . . [T]here is no point in putting one's head in the noose."[87] This is the same kind of gamble Lewis had freely made in *Apes of God*—indeed the essential pleasure of both texts resides in watching him take such enormous risks by exploiting the generic conventions of the very artists and writers he attacks. In *Doom of Youth,* however, ambiguity gives way to journalistic critique, and Lewis moderated the passage on Arlen in order to protect himself.

Shortly after the book appeared, however, Chatto received a letter from Godfrey Winn's solicitors warning that they intended to seek legal redress for a passage describing their client as a "salaried revolutionary agent" exploiting his youth to cover a lack of talent while shamelessly arousing "the envy and hatred of everybody for everybody else" (105).[88] Lewis promptly shot back a letter on June 26 telling the attorneys that Winn "regarded it as his mission to 'stop me' from writing books of the type of Apes of God."[89] Despite such combativeness, however, the editors at Chatto had already agreed that the passage was indeed libelous and proposed a series of alterations to be pasted into the remaining copies of the book and included in any subsequent editions. By then, however, Alec Waugh had threatened a second libel suit based on a series of passages that seemed to identify him as a homosexual. The grounds for such a claim were somewhat thin, emerging from Lewis's assertion that in "the strange case of Mr. Waugh . . . all the feminine, maternal attributes were thwarted" and that "the homosexual is, of course, an imitation-woman." (112, 206). Like Winn, Waugh demanded through his solicitors that the book be suppressed: "We are instructed to call upon you unconditionally and immediately to withdraw the book from circulation . . . and to publish a full and unqualified apology to Mr Waugh in terms approved by us in *The New Statesman and Nation, The Observer, The Sunday Times,* and *The Times Literary Supplement.*"[90] An outraged Lewis could not believe that of all the potentially damaging passages in the book, Waugh had settled on one that likely did not even contain a direct or even indirect imputation of homosexuality. Even were a libel trial to proceed, therefore, it would turn not on Lewis's indictment of the novelist's writing or careerism, but on the much narrower charge that he had sex with men. Waugh may have cannily been attempting to avoid just this kind of trial. His request for an immediate injunction on further sales of the text was defeated when a judge ruled that the allegation of homosexuality could not be pursued because the words did not apply to the plaintiff. Despite this initial victory, however, Chatto and Windus, as well as booksellers throughout London, remained concerned about other pending charges and the matter was not finally settled until 1933 when both plaintiffs agreed to withdraw. During the course of the proceedings, however, Lewis lost the support of his publisher and generated substantial legal costs that could not be recovered. *Doom of Youth* was finally pulped in 1934, having ignominiously sold only a few hundred copies.

This book, which in many ways simply advanced the same kind of satirical critiques launched in *Apes of God,* was a personal and financial disaster for Lewis. Without even the limited protection afforded by the roman à clef, Lewis found himself effectively without a defense. Winn and Waugh even managed to bring Lewis's relationship with Chatto and Windus to an end over this matter. Though he managed to find another publisher—Grayson and Grayson—this arrangement too was destroyed by another libel suit.[91] This time the case involved his 1932 travel book, *Filibusters in Barbary*, which details a trip taken to North Africa. Unlike *Doom of Youth*, the text carefully avoids naming a British agent whom Lewis found particularly distasteful, but it nevertheless provides a damning description of him as a "queer middle-aged middle-class Bulldog Drummond of an ex-temporary Major" who bribes corrupt French officials and engages "in every lawless activity under their noses on the grounds that [he is a] Briton."[92] By withholding the man's name, the book occupies a kind of middle-ground between the direct claims of nonfiction and the coy allusiveness of the roman à clef. There is no clear or obvious key to be distributed, nor does the man indicted have the kind of celebrity status that might make it easy to recognize him as many readers did the characters in *Apes of God*.

Lewis and his publishers, however, received a solicitor's letter in 1933 informing them that Major Thomas McFie claimed to have recognized his portrait: "It is manifest from a most careful perusal of this book that it is permeated with libelous matter of a most serious character concerning our Client, and we shall be glad to hear from you not later than next Wednesday morning what proposition you have put forward to compensate our client on a liberal basis before proceedings are instituted."[93] As we have seen, Lewis often courted such suits, hoping to bring his targets fully into the open and force them to defend themselves under oath against his claims. This constituted, in fact, a vital part of his critique of celebrity culture and the institutionalization of bohemia in *Apes of God*. McFie, however, did not belong to this world, and once again Lewis published these statements as part of a clearly nonfictional work. His target in *Filibusters in Barbary* would likely be unembarrassed by a trial, and the matter did, in fact, move promptly into court in early 1934 where a portion of the colloquium was read into the record: "In the Book there are descriptions which are capable of being understood to refer to Mr MacFie, and which were so understood, and they are in fact grossly defamatory of him and hold him up to the greatest ridicule. It accuses him of defying the French Authorities and activities such as engaging in contraband traffic and smuggling arms and such like."[94] Grayson and Grayson could mount little in the way of an effective defense and immediately agreed to pay £250 in damages and withdraw the book from circulation.

Lewis's initially successful attempts to develop the roman à clef's critical and aesthetic potential had, only three years after the publication of *Apes of God*, become increasingly frustrated by the courts. One book had been officially withdrawn from publication and another pulped after the threat of additional legal action kept it too out of circulation. In the process, Lewis destroyed his relationship with two London publishers who had taken considerable risks on his behalf and even covered his mounting legal costs. His sense of frustration and betrayal is evident in the book he began after finishing *Apes of God*. Also structured as a roman à clef, *The Roaring Quean; Foul Play's a Jewel* caustically indicts the systems of patronage and celebrity he felt drove the production of British literary culture. As was the case with *Apes of God*, many of Lewis's targets were lightly disguised, but his focus on physical detail made it easy to recognize portraits of Arnold Bennett, Virginia Woolf, Nancy Cunard, and Victor Gollancz.[95] Once again, Lewis used the genre's "conditional fictionality" and its infectiousness to expose the ways in which seemingly autonomous works of art actually functioned as profitable nodes within systems of mass-mediated celebrity and social capital. The generic conventions he employed in the text, however, afforded him little legal protection as the boundary between news and novels once again imposed itself through the mechanism of libel.

The first version of *The Roaring Quean* was submitted to Chatto and Windus in 1930 and rejected almost immediately. "The piece seems too risky for Chatto to do," his editor wrote. "Too many heads are cracked, and the result would be that the wounded would take it out of us."[96] A private edition proved too expensive, and Lewis did not have the money to mount a legal defense, nor could he locate a private sponsor as he had for the *Apes of God*. As a result, the manuscript languished until Cape agreed to publish it in 1935. As had been the case with Joyce's *Dubliners*, the text was set into proof and then shown to the company's legal advisors for an opinion—a decision likely motivated by Lewis's other legal difficulties, including Waugh's then unresolved suit over *Doom of Youth*. "I am exceedingly sorry," Lewis's new editor soon wrote, "that the final conclusion come to by our solicitor is that he must advise us not to publish the book."[97] As he and Campbell had done in *Satire and Fiction*, Lewis tried to plead for the fictional and satirical qualities of the text, arguing that it dealt primarily in mechanical stereotypes rather than actual individuals, and that although he attacked "the Bloomsbury principle" there was "no caricature of any *individual Bloomsbury*."[98] Seeking the cover he believed the roman à clef afforded, Lewis further pressed his point by noting that such a charge was merely indicative of the very gossip-ridden publishing world he sought to critique: "In any satire there is almost always the possibility—indeed almost the probability that someone or other (either with a grudge against the author, or with a keen business sense and desire to turn an honest penny) will come forward and claim financial compensation for an alleged libel."[99] The defense Lewis tries to mount here, as we have seen, would have had no standing in the course of a defamation trial. After all, the very fact that someone may come forward implicitly acknowledges that the legal interpretation of the text lies with the reader and not the author—no matter what his professed or documented intentions might be. Lewis appears to misunderstand this crucial element of libel law, and his own experiment with the roman à clef founders on this interpretive failure.

By using the roman à clef to extend fiction into the public sphere, Joyce and Lewis alike sought to contest the legal, moral, and aesthetic foundations on which the realist novel had rested since the eighteenth century. They all too successfully reactivated the genre's latent powers, and in the process found themselves entangled in legal structures designed to hold skepticism about fiction's simulation of reality in check. This constitutes, in fact, a key element of modernism's assault on nineteenth-century realism, albeit one that does not comport well with our liberal humanist narrative of the period's artistic and social revolutions. This part of modernism's rise and consolidation, after all, cannot be recuperated into the kind of heroic liberation and truth-telling associated with the obscenity trials of *Ulysses* and *Lady Chatterley's Lover*. Joyce, after all, largely abandoned his experiments with the roman à clef after 1922, likely well aware that suits such as the one eventually brought by Dodd would inevitably limit his work by imposing on it severe legal and financial risks. For Lewis, the consequences of his own experiments in a "satire without morals" were even more dire, essentially bringing his potentially most creative period to an end amidst a welter of lawsuits and crippling judgments. By rereading the works of both these writers through the lens of defamation, we reveal a far more complex relationship between law and literature, uncovering not a steady march to truth but an array of both overt and subtle mechanisms for negotiating fiction's limits. The roman à clef reveals the operation of this field of force that both produced and constrained modernism's experimental attempts to challenge the terms of its own autonomization.

6. The Coterie as Commodity
Huxley, Lawrence, Rhys, and the Business of Revenge

The experiments Joyce and Lewis conducted at the interface between modernism, libel law, and the roman à clef were often extraordinary, but they were by no means unique. Narratives of all kinds throughout the early twentieth century began to put so much pressure on the news/novel divide that the publishing industry as a whole took notice. In the June 1931 issue of *The Bookman,* Hugh Ross Williamson devoted his monthly editorial column to the resurgent skepticism provoked by the roman à clef and the scandalous reading habits it cultivated. In a series of paragraphs with headings such as "Honest at a Discount" and "Drawing from Life," he laments the increasing "affinity of history to fiction" as well as the wide popularity of a "modern school of historians who contrive to make [biography] more entertaining than the legitimate novel."[1] He imagines ominous consequences for both the novel and history as each begins to blur into the other and thus surrender its own autonomous and unique claims to truth. "A great number of novels today," he continues, "are of course *romans à clef,* and now that so many authors are also reviewers of each other's work, this game has become a sort of family pastime."[2] A magazine devoted precisely to the business of authorship and publishing, *The Bookman* was very much a part of this same family, and no matter how serious the editor's concerns, his reviews and advertising columns were nonetheless filled with references to the sort of works he critiques.

In this same essay, in fact, he tackles one of the most famous cases of the day: the publication in 1930 of Somerset Maugham's *Cakes and Ale,* a roman à clef that seemed to lay bare the secret life and loves of Thomas Hardy. Maugham himself vehemently denied he had done any such thing, seeking, no doubt, to protect himself from a libel suit threatened by Hugh Walpole, who is savagely portrayed in the book as the manipulative opportunist Alroy Kear.[3] The scandal, however, was well publicized and in 1931 Elinor Mordaunt (writing under the pseudonym "A. Riposte") published a roman à clef of her own, entitled *Gin and Bitters,* which cast an equally caustic eye upon Maugham himself. Fearful of a libel suit herself, Mordaunt published the book in the United States, where William Soskin, writing for *The New York Evening Post,* pointed out the book's "propagandist purpose."[4] After describing this expanding literary quarrel, *The Bookman* closes its editorial by lamenting the "astounding egoism" of writers: "An author's assumption that the foibles of his own little coterie must be of surpassing interest to the great reading public is surely unwarranted. Had not they been told, what percentage of readers of either 'Cakes and Ale' or 'Gin and Bitters' would have suspected an ulterior motive? Surely in both cases it would have been better to have refrained from comment and left the family circle to its game."[5] Surprisingly, Williamson appears entirely resigned to a conception of literary creativity in which fiction is, in fact, largely derived from real events. He seeks only to suppress these presumably vulgar origins and thus hush up the roman à clef's ambiguities by concealing them behind a shroud of authorial and critical silence.

As we have seen throughout *The Art of Scandal,* self-consciously experimental writers in the early twentieth century developed the roman à clef to forge new aesthetic and epistemological structures capable of reengaging their art with the public sphere. Readers themselves responded in often unexpected ways, helping revivify a genre the realist novel had supposedly suppressed. Both Williamson's editorial, and the scandal that occasioned it, furthermore suggest just how acute the crisis provoked by the roman à clef's resurgence had become. The grafting of fact onto fiction evident in the works of Wilde and Freud as well as in their reception had quickly expanded into a thoroughgoing critique of the realist novel and its institutions—a process we now associate with literary modernism. The pleasures of such scandalous innovation, however, have been partially defused not only by the Eliotic insistence on "impersonality," but by the constitutive fiction that modernism is staked on a "great divide" between elite and mass culture.[6] This essentially blunts the roman à clef's power, channeling critical attention away from the news/novel divide and toward matters of style, difficulty, and symbolism. Yet Adorno and Horkheimer in *The Dialectic of Enlightenment* instructively insist that the autonomy of modernist cultural production has always been an illusion: the outgrowth of a marketplace complex and diverse enough to afford the author, at least, a sense of "purposelessness" and "anonymity." The rise of what they call "the culture industry," however, changes this formulation so that "what is new is not that [art] is a commodity, but that today it deliberately admits it is one; that art renounces its own autonomy and proudly takes its place among consumption goods constitutes the charm of novelty."[7] The early twentieth century, in other words, is largely defined not by an autonomy that was itself only a vestigial illusion of the marketplace, but by a more direct engagement between producers and consumers made possible by the aggressive growth of a public sphere that dismantled and replaced Williamson's "family circle" of elite cultural producers. Ironically, as the marketplace for literary goods expanded exponentially in the early twentieth century, authors themselves increasingly lost that sense of "anonymity" Adorno and Horkheimer describe, finding themselves and their works entangled in a vast web of magazines, reviews, newspapers, and quarterlies, all of which sought to appeal to different segments of a highly differentiated reading public.

Ever since Bonnie Kime Scott's 1990 book, *The Gender of Modernism*, we have been aware of the complexity of modernist production; her diagram linking the various authors to one another reveals with startling clarity the dense web of relationships connecting early twentieth century artists, writers, and publishers.[8] What's missing from this diagram—and indeed from most critical analyses of modernism itself—is the even more intricate web of relationships and interconnections between modernist producers and their immediate consumers. In a 1924 essay entitled "The Patron and Crocus," Virginia Woolf, herself one of the densest points of intersection in Scott's diagram, examines precisely this part of the modernist equation. "For whom should we write?" she asks. Resorting to the language of "patronage," she notes that "the present supply of patrons is of unexampled and bewildering variety. There is the daily Press, the weekly Press, the monthly Press; the English public and the American public; the best-seller public and the worst-seller public; the highbrow public and the red-blood public; all now organized self-conscious entities capable through their various mouthpieces of making their needs known and their displeasure felt."[9] As owner with her husband Leonard of the increasingly successful Hogarth Press, Woolf knew exactly what she was talking about: by the early twentieth century the market for literary goods had become incredibly complex and she had proven adept at negotiating it. No longer governed by massive anthologies and three-volume novels circulated through lending libraries, this market became as highly fragmented as that for any other consumer good. Indeed, one way to think of modernism—as Woolf herself appears to suggest in this essay—is not as a shared set of aesthetic traits or thematic concerns, but as merely one segment of a diversified cultural marketplace. In other words, we should think of modernism not only as a site of production, but also as a mode and method of consumption as well.

Woolf, in fact, goes wrong in the essay only when she turns suddenly away from this penetrating insight and falls back upon the phantom "patron," a romanticized entity presumably capable of preserving genuine art in the face of mass culture. In doing so, she abruptly shifts her emphasis to the production side of the equation and then mystifies it, severing elite cultural goods from the mass-marketplace by appealing to the intimate connection between the producers and the consumers we now typically associate with modernism's coterie cultures. Both real and imaginative spaces, these sites often function in histories of the period as aesthetic utopias turned jealously inward upon themselves in order to cultivate the early twentieth century's greatest writers. This chapter will argue, however, that these coteries played a formative role in shaping what Aaron Jaffe provocatively calls the "modernist brand": the fully commodified image of an elite culture that markets itself precisely as a site of anticommercial aesthetic values.[10] After all, while physical spaces like Woolf's Bloomsbury, Ottoline Morrell's salon at Garsington Manor, the Left Bank of Paris, and the brownstones of Greenwich Village may have provided real points of contact for modernist producers, they also functioned as icons of imagined bohemian autonomy and sexual liberation. As such, they became lucrative profit centers for writers who regularly used the roman à clef in order to "sell out" their patrons to a diverse reading public eager both for the vicarious experiences and scandalous details of these salons. Inextricably embedded in the celebrity culture of modernity itself, these coteries and the romans à clef that flowed from them expose the active interface between elite production and mass consumption. In doing so, they simultaneously reveal the ways in which modernism, itself a constitutive part of Adorno and Horkheimer's "culture industry," aspires to the status of art and commodity simultaneously.

The widespread experimentation with the roman à clef in the early twentieth century and the genre's own provocative infectiousness are essential to understanding the ways modernism can be productively reconfigured not as the far shore of a "great divide," but as a carefully cultivated segment of the mass marketplace itself. The genre's often incisive critique of modernist claims to aesthetic autonomy, however, can quickly wither over time as its scandalous connection to a particular place and time fades. A book like D. H. Lawrence's *Women in Love*, for example, has generally been canonized as a work of high modernism, despite the fact that it contains in its pages a vengeful and rather easily recognized portrait of his onetime patron, Lady Ottoline Morrell. Similarly, Jean Rhys's early works, including *Quartet* and *After Leaving Mr. Mackenzie,* have, since their republication in the 1960s, been generally received as the autonomous novels of a forgotten woman writer rather than clever and lucrative acts of public reprisal against her former lover, Ford Madox Ford. For their contemporary audiences, however, such books provided an alluring glimpse into the celebrity culture of elite producers themselves, often succeeding in the marketplace precisely because they "sold out" the "family circle" and effectively transformed it into a cultural commodity. Elite producers, like Rhys and Lawrence, deployed the roman à clef's ambiguities to critique the presumption of aesthetic autonomy so essential to coterie culture while simultaneously working out their own relationship to the literary marketplace. It allowed them to trade successfully on their insider knowledge while disavowing the calculated instrumentality of their texts. The roman à clef, therefore, became an aesthetic crucible in which formal experimentation could be alloyed to a profitable engagement with commercial culture.

Such innovative practices, however, have long been ignored or suppressed, not only by the more general critical dismissal of the roman à clef, but by a distinctly gendered set of tropes that transfer such obsessions with the marketplace onto the abject figures of women. As Susan Stanford Friedman argues, high modernism itself is characterized by a doubled representation of women. On the one hand, "WOMAN" served as a signifier of what Alice Jardine calls "epistemological crisis," a crisis itself often structured, according to Rita Felski, around "her close association with consumerism and the marketplace."[11] On the other hand, this symbolic presence is paired with "the active *presence* of women as innovative and important figures in the formation of modernist poetics and practice."[12] In using the roman à clef to rethink the modernist marketplace, this chapter will focus on the link between gender and genre as it plays out in two key spaces structured by the conflict between woman as symbol and women as subjects: Ottoline Morrell's Garsington Manor and the bohemian Paris of Ford and Rhys. Morrell, as a self-styled patron of the arts, was instrumental in bringing together some of the most remarkable writers and thinkers of her generation; yet she was also the subject of blistering romans à clef written by men willing to sell her out for considerable social and economic profit. Jean Rhys's tragic novels focused on disturbingly masochistic images of women surrendering to abuse by men; yet she skillfully deploys the conventions of the roman à clef precisely to avoid the devastation of her own heroines by profitably seeking revenge on her own patron and supporter, Ford Madox Ford. Both of these women continue to remain lodged between their historical identities (one as a patron and the other as an author) and their fictional images (as literary "lionhunter" and perpetual victim). These ambiguities, furthermore, are themselves signs of a doubling that extends through both genre and gender to become a constitutive element of modernism's engagement with the mass marketplace.

Buying In, Selling Out: Ottoline Morrell

"I cannot describe Garsington," Virginia Woolf wrote in her diary after visiting the country estate of Lady Ottoline Morrell in June 1923,[13] though this did nothing to stop her from drawing a deft if devastating portrait of the place: "Thirty seven people to tea; a bunch of young men no bigger than asparagus; walking to & fro, round and round; compliments, attentions, & then this slippery mud—which is what interests me at the moment. A loathing overcomes me of human beings—their insincerity. Their vanity—A wearisome & rather defiling talk with Ott[oline Morrell] last night is the foundation of this complaint—& then the blend in one's own mind of suavity and sweetness with contempt & bitterness. Her egotism is so great."[14] Morrell is a larger-than-life figure from the early twentieth century, a woman who penned only a few chapters of a memoir but whose name and image intersect with a dazzling array of artists, thinkers, and writers. Half-sister to the Duke of Portland, she was wealthy, eccentric, and deeply connected to the worlds of art and aristocracy. She and her husband were ardent pacifists and effective political activists who turned Garsington Manor into a haven for conscientious objectors during the First World War, providing them with relatively easy national service work (and often studio space as well) on the estate's farms. The group of men and women drawn into her orbit arguably exceeded the luminosity even of Bloomsbury. They included Aldous Huxley, D. H. Lawrence, Duncan Grant, Lytton Strachey, W. B. Yeats, Mark Gertler, Siegfried Sassoon, John Middleton Murry, and Katherine Mansfield, as well as those who moved on the edges like Woolf and her sister Vanessa Bell, Maynard Keynes, and the Sitwell siblings. With the knowledge and presumably consent of her husband, Morrell carried on extensive love affairs with the bohemian painter Augustus John and the renowned philosopher Bertrand Russell. Her correspondence, housed at the Harry Ransom Humanities Research Center at the University of Texas in Austin, runs to some thirty-four boxes and contains intimate letters from nearly every significant writer and artist of note during her life. Philip Morrell, her husband, was a regular Liberal candidate for Parliament, and Ottoline occasionally joined him on the hustings, despite the objections of her conservative family.

Garsington Manor, in short, should have survived in our cultural histories as an "institution of modernism" every bit as potent as Bloomsbury, Shakespeare and

Company, or Gertrude Stein's apartment at 27 Rue de Fleurus. Indeed, Woolf's deeply ambivalent relationship with Morrell grew, in part, out of a competition between Bloomsbury and Garsington to become the center of British intellectual and aesthetic life after the war. What sets Morrell apart, however, is that the men and women who entered her coterie turned on her with startling regularity, selling out their friend and patron by retailing portraits of life at Garsington to a public eager for scandal and gossip. Painters, including Augustus John, Duncan Grant, and Simon Bussy, created striking yet often cruel portraits of her that they then featured prominently in exhibitions. Grant, for example, abandoned his typically warm Impressionist style of the period (evident, for example, in his portrait of Ka Cox) and instead fashioned a shocking caricature in a 1913 canvas suffused with a sickly green and black palette. He even attached a block of wood, collage style, to the already outsize chin, drawing further attention to it.[15] While some later critics have tried to rehabilitate this piece as somewhat sympathetic, Morrell herself was clearly unhappy with its portrayal of her and refused to purchase it even for the modest fee Grant proposed. That same green color, furthermore, was picked up later by Simon Bussy, who after a visit to Garsington in 1918 produced a woodcut on which he based a later portrait. Bussy was a close friend of Grant's, and his own portrait not only draws out the green background, but heightens the impression of a caricature by eliminating any sense of depth and matching a nose of now impossible dimensions to Morrell's chin.

Had these portraits circulated privately among the closed social circles of London's elite, they would remain mean-spirited curiosities akin to Woolf's often cruel letters and diary entries.[16] As portraits, however, they hung in public galleries and have long played a role in shaping popular perceptions of Morrell and Garsington. This became particularly apparent when Augustus John featured his portrait of Morrell at a major exhibition in 1920. This image too is a merciless rendering of his former patron and lover; as Michael Holroyd notes, its "eyes are rolled sideways in their sockets like those of a runaway horse and her mouth bared in a soundless scream."[17] Morrell dreaded the exhibition, and the press expressed a bemused sense of shock at the presumed outrage it represented. In a flippant interview with *The Weekly Dispatch,* John said that he had not wanted to be cruel "but it was the aspect he had been unfortunate enough to get."[18] Morrell herself saved a clipping from *Everyman* describing the portrait: "That curiously Elizabethan 'Lady Ottoline Morrell' is even more unpleasantly snake-like and snarling. It may puzzle one to imagine why society women should like to see themselves painted like this, even by Mr. John."[19] An even more sympathetic reviewer for *The Star* writes (in another clipping Morrell saved): "I have seen some of these women in the flesh, and can assure them—with whatever sympathy they deserve—that they are not so bad as they are painted. Lady Ottoline Morrell is something finer than this grotesque travesty of aristocratic, almost imbecile hauteur."[20] These are cruel images, made all the more so by the fact that Morrell had energetically promoted and supported the painters who created them. The images thus also contain—in addition to their artistic merits—an air of deliberate public revenge.[21] The fact that the newspaper reviewers seemed to recoil from them and even reassured their readers that Morrell was not, in fact, a monster, suggests an excess of cruelty in these works that had nothing to do with formal experimentation.

These paintings, in fact, helped to produce and sustain the image of Morrell herself as a so-called "lionhunter"—a wealthy society hostess who gathered great figures around her in a naked bid to display her own social power.[22] Such women have long been dismissed as inconsequential and (as Woolf writes of Morrell) egotistical figures who offer the pleasures of social engagement but also threaten to transform art and artists alike into social capital. Recent attempts to theorize the often gendered work of modernist cultural production have revealed the vital roles that women editors and publishers played in creating, marketing, and sustaining modernism.[23] The lionhunters, however, continue to function as they did for the modernists themselves: easy targets for satire embodying a crass commercialism to which the artists themselves may be drawn but from which they must shelter their genius. Lois Cucullu argues that modernism stakes its own "expert" authority on the "conversion of the Victorian domestic sphere into an aesthetic sphere," thus accruing to itself "responsibility for ensuring the quality of everyday life."[24] The writers and artists who participated in this appropriation became "cultural capitalists who used the marketplace to advance aesthetic innovations that carry with them new narratives of consciousness and identity."[25] Cucullu thus constructs a contest for authority between the Victorian matron and the modern artist, the latter using an evolving discourse of professionalism to accrue new kinds of power and authority. Such an account, however, neglects the lionhunters and their salons as sites where social power, professional authority, and the self-conscious commodification of the aesthetic sphere intersect in tantalizing and often contradictory ways. In these spaces the modernist producers often felt themselves to be fungible objects just as deliberately gathered and displayed (at lavish parties, on invitation cards, etc.) as an old painting or an antique chair. The lionhunters thus effectively focalize the intersection between art and the market while also putting intense pressure on the very concept of a professionalism that falters precisely to the degree the aesthetic sphere loses its claim to a self-regulating autonomy.

Lodged at the interface of art and commerce, the lionhunter has become an abject figure for the social and economic utility of aesthetics—an identification further heightened by a distinctly gendered discourse linking these women (as Cucullu implicitly does) either to an archaic Victorianism or to a profit-driven modernity. Such abjection, however, makes it difficult to explain why modernist writers themselves so insistently returned to these women, inserting often only lightly veiled images of them in their works. Morrell herself, perhaps the most accomplished and well-connected of lionhunters, appears in at least ten romans à clef in the 1920s, including D. H. Lawrence's *Women in Love* (as Hermione Roddice); Aldous Huxley's *Crome Yellow* (as Priscilla Wimbush), *Those Barren Leaves* (as Mrs. Aldwinkle) and *Point Counter Point* (as Mrs. Bidlake); Gilbert Cannan's *Pugs and Peacocks* (as Lady Rusholme); Walter Turner's *The Aesthetes* (as Lady Virginia Caraway); and Osbert Sitwell's *Triple Fugue* (as Lady Septugesima Goodley). She and her husband Philip may also have served as models for Clarissa and Richard Dalloway in Woolf's 1925 novel. Like those portraits by Grant, Bussy, and John, furthermore, these are almost all brutal satires that either pillory Morrell for her vanity or transform her into a grotesque threat to the nascent aesthetic consciousness of young—typically male—artists. As deliberate acts of revenge, these books appear to shatter any kind of pretense of aesthetic autonomy. After all, rather than professional productions staked on a romantic claim to creativity, they are instead deliberate bids for social and economic capital. Their authors sell out Morrell, turning on her with painful regularity to declare their independence from the world of cultural values she is made to represent while simultaneously capitalizing on the market for gossip about England's wealthy, aristocratic families. By exploiting the roman à clef's anarchic skepticism, however, these same writers conjure modernism's most potent and persistent myth of radical autonomy—that alchemical formulation Pierre Bourdieu calls "interested disinterestedness."[26] The genre's "conditional fictionality," in other words, grants the author a plausible deniability so that when Morrell does protest that she has been treated unfairly in a work of fiction, the charge can be turned back upon her as further proof of the very egotism and "interestedness" the book satirizes.

Morrell's correspondence is, in fact, filled with these kind of devious exchanges. Here, for example, is Virginia's Woolf's response to a letter from Philip Morrell claiming that he recognized himself in the character of Richard Dalloway:

> One thing interests me very much—that you should think yourself the dullest man in the book. I wonder what extraordinary complex this springs from? . . . There were originals for some of the people in Mrs. Dalloway: but

very far away—people I last saw 20 years ago & even then did not know well. These are the people I like to write about. But I'm so much interested by this revelation of what you think I think of you that perhaps one of these days I shall be tempted to break my rules and try to do you. But no—I couldn't.[27]

Woolf cleverly turns the allegation that she has written a roman à clef back upon Morrell himself, suggesting that his own insensitivity as a reader—and presumably his own vanity as well—are far more revealing than anything in the novel.

This not-so-subtle tone of condescension is equally evident in a 1921 letter from Huxley to Morrell following the publication of *Crome Yellow*. Like Woolf, he too concedes that the book has some vague historical referents, but that it is otherwise entirely fictional: "I cannot understand how anyone could suppose that this little marionette performance of mine was the picture of a real milieu:—it so obviously isn't. . . . My mistake . . . was to have borrowed the stage setting from Garsington. I am sorry; but it never for a moment occurred to me that anyone would have so little in imagination—or perhaps so much—as to read into a comedy of ideas a portrait of the life of the place in which it is laid."[28] Like Woolf, he turns the charge that the book is a roman à clef back upon Morrell, indelicately suggesting that she, her friends, and even the book's reviewers lack the proper "imagination" to understand that the text is entirely fiction. He then concludes by adopting the persona of a world-weary novelist desperate to withdraw into the very sort of autonomous space Garsington itself might have represented: "This incident is to me another proof of something I said in the book: we are all parallel straight lines determined only to meet at infinity. Real understanding is an impossibility. I write something which seems to me immediately and obviously comprehensible for what it is. You, running on your parallel, read into it meanings I never so much as dreamt of. Others, in their parallels, find other meanings and contemptuous portraits of people unknown to them. What is one to do or say?"[29] The obfuscation here is remarkable, though by no means unique, and that final rhetorical question suggests that the beleaguered writer can only resign himself to the vulgarity of a mass reading public so desperate for scandal that they would transform his "comedy" into a roman à clef. Morrell herself, however, is placed in a delicate situation: by insisting on the book's rather obvious references to her she would group herself with this mass public and thus be forced to acknowledge that Garsington had failed as a kind of haven for modern art. To "do or say" anything about the novel—by writing a letter to the reviewers or bringing a suit for libel—would be to acknowledge that she surrounded herself with "marionettes" and lived in the absurd world of Crome itself. Faced with such an impossible choice, Morrell remained silent.

Crome Yellow has now become a relatively obscure novel, in part because some of its comedy depends upon a reader's ability to recognize it as an exposé of real people and their petty squabbles.[30] Huxley, in his letter to Morrell, wrote that he found the experience of having even been suspected of writing a roman à clef so troubling that "Next time I write a puppet comedy of ideas I shall lay the scene a thousand mile away from England. That will, I hope, make impossible misunderstandings such as this."[31] He was, in a way, as good as his word, and his next novel, *Those Barren Leaves,* is set on the Italian coast, albeit on an expensive estate owned by a wealthy, aging Englishwoman named Lillian Aldwinkle who surrounds herself with artists, poets, and novelists. Like Morrell's Garsington, the "palace of Vezza" is an imposing if entirely artificial invention. Imagining herself a true heiress to the Italian Renaissance, Mrs. Aldwinkle seeks, as the narrative satirically notes, to make the otherwise obscure mansion "re-become what it had never been."[32] This fantastic attempt at patronage, however, is shot through with an avaricious desire to transform not only the arts but all of Italy itself into a commodity: "With the palace Mrs. Aldwinkle has purchased vast domains unmentioned in the contract. She had bought, to begin with, the Cybo Malaspina [the aristocratic family who once owned the house] and their history. . . . The whole peninsula and everything it contained were her property and her secret. She had bought its arts, its music, its melodious language, its literature, its wine and cooking, the beauty of its women and the virility of its Fascists" (19). Fully reified and thus cut off from both its own history and even its surrounding landscape, the house is shot through with intersecting flows of social, economic, and cultural capital. For Huxley, it also becomes the ideal site to challenge the news/novel divide in an effort to secure his own autonomy.

Mrs. Aldwinkle is a clear narrative double for Morrell, who is consequently portrayed in this text as neither patron nor friend, but as a self-deluded woman who surrounds herself in the "Saloon of the Ancestors" with the busts and portraits of the ducal family who once owned the house (21). Imagining herself to be both their spiritual and even real heir, she dreams of impossible and entirely anachronistic gatherings that once drew Galileo, Boccaccio, Dante, and Aquinas to the same house. Huxley, furthermore, does very little to conceal the actual figure behind his ostensibly fictional portrait and invites his readers to share in the gossipy dissection of a prominent social figure. Francis Chelifer, the apparent narrative double for Huxley himself, alludes directly to Morrell's celebrity: "I have begun to talk of Mrs. Aldwinkle and you do not know who Mrs. Aldwinkle is. Nor did I for that matter. . . . I knew no more, then, than her name; who does not? Mrs. Aldwinkle the salonnière, the hostess, the giver of literary parties, and agape of lions—is she not classical? A household word? A familiar quotation? Of course" (72). As a "lionhunter," she represents the naked commodification of aesthetic culture, and she gathers around herself an absurd congeries of sycophants who mouth platitudes about art while constantly jockeying for money and fame. Indeed, her oldest friend in the text, Mr. Cardan, is a master of witty conversation who has accomplished nothing and freely shares his theory of the "parasite."[33] Traveling from great house to great house, he has few resources of his own and thus spends a good deal of the book attempting to marry a mentally ill woman to secure the modest fortune she has inherited. His plans, however, fail when she eats a piece of rotten fish and dies an excruciating death. The house is further stocked by equally absurd characters, including a Labour MP trying desperately to radicalize a bored aristocrat; Mrs. Aldwinkle's niece, who is constantly being instructed by her aunt to fall in love and then break off the affairs; a best-selling woman novelist who pursues an affair with another guest so that she can transform it into material for a new book; and finally Chelifer himself, a modest poet who has happily taken a job as editor of the *Rabbit Fancier's Gazette*. Far from an intellectual hothouse or inspiring salon, in other words, the palace of Vezza is a "marionette performance" like *Crome Yellow* in which all the characters—lightly concealed behind with the roman à clef's "conditional fictionality"—try to turn their access to Mrs. Aldwinkle's famed coterie to their own social and economic advantage.

Like much of Huxley's early work, the satire in this novel is by turns gentle and biting, yet it is significantly leavened by long sections of drawing-room dialogue that do little to advance the plot or add psychological depth to the characters. The text's assault on Mrs. Aldwinkle, however, is unrelenting, and Huxley seems to take a sadistic pleasure in exposing her inanity while at the same time gesturing constantly to Morrell herself. Embodying the genre's obsessive interest in the finest and thus most revealing details, the character manically attempts to root out and then exhibit the most intimate details of her friends' lives. "Perpetually haunted by the fear that she was missing something," Mrs. Aldwinkle "didn't want her guests to lead independent existences out of her sight" (17). This desire, furthermore, remains unsated even at the book's end when, as the palace empties, she feels abandoned and depressed: "Mournfully she looked back over her life. Everybody, everything had always slipped away from her. She had always missed all the really important, exciting things; they had invariably happened, somehow, just round the corner, out of her sight. . . . Why had Cardan brought that horrible imbecile creature to die in front of her like that?" (286) This callous and solipsistic meditation on life and death suggests, on the one hand, that Mrs. Aldwinkle's acquisition of the palace of Vezzia was itself a failure because she ultimately could not purchase the friendship and allegiance she desires. As her guests leave, therefore, she confronts the emptiness of her salon and its crass connection to the brutal pursuit of capital, here gruesomely symbolized by the death of Mr. Cardan's would-be bride. On the other hand, this final image of the abandoned Mrs. Aldwinkle also reminds the knowing reader of Morrell's own sense of betrayal, symbolized not simply by the departure of the artists she once sheltered but by their campaigns against her in print and paint.

The text actually alludes regularly to those portraits by John and others. When Mrs. Aldwinkle first appears, she is, we are told, "an impressionist; it was the effect at a distance, the grand theatrical flourish that interested her" (16). This, in addition to the fact that she is described as a kind of collage, "built up of sections from different people," alludes to the Grant painting, a gesture heightened by the fact that she is constantly clad in green. Furthermore, we later discover that she imagines herself in these same terms: "She saw herself . . . looking like one of those wonderfully romantic figures who, in the paintings of Augustus John, stands poised in a meditative and passionate ecstasy against a cosmic background. She *saw* herself—a John down even to her flame-coloured tunic and emerald-green parasol. And at her feet, like Shelley, like Leander washed up on the sands of Abydos, lay the young poet, pale, naked and dead" (150). The "poet" here is Chelifer, who had been struck accidentally by Mrs. Aldwinkle's boat while he was swimming in the bay. The scene Huxley draws clearly alludes not only to that infamous John portrait of Morrell (which cast her as anything but a romantic figure) but to the clear threat so self-obsessed a lionhunter presents to the casually brutalized artist.

In *Those Barren Leaves,* Huxley manipulates the roman à clef's generic codes to critique not only Morrell herself, but the full commodification of aesthetic culture and the consequent collapse of literary patronage as an ideal. The book actually contains two meta-fictional surrogates for Huxley himself: Mary Thirplow, the best-selling novelist, and Francis Chelifer, the poet resigned to editing a magazine on rabbit care. Throughout the course of the novel, these two characters are pitted against one another as satiric embodiments of high and mass culture facing off across the "great divide." Like Mrs. Aldwinkle, Miss Thirplow treats the palace of Vezzia as a marketplace for symbolic capital where she trades on her fame while seeking out material for her latest book—itself a roman à clef. Her identity is highly theatrical and throughout the text she constantly changes her appearance, manner, and beliefs to suit any given situation and thus effect the kind of artificial intimacy that lets her pry into the secrets of others. Early on, for example, she appears as a worldly and sophisticated writer, entirely at home amidst the splendor of the Italian villa. When the handsome yet jaded Calamy appears, however, she begins a sudden and comic transformation into a meek woman writer utterly unconcerned with social advancement or professional success. Here she is during their first encounter, frantically stripping off her ornate jewelry while decrying the vanity of the very salon they both inhabit: "'The inanity of the lion hunters. The roaring of the lions!' It was unnecessary to do anything with her hands now; she had dropped them into her lap and took the opportunity to rid herself of the scarab and brilliants. And like the conjurer who makes patter to divert attention from the workings of his trick, she leaned forward and began to talk very rapidly and earnestly.... 'What rot the lions do roar! I suppose it's awfully innocent of me; but I always imagined that celebrated people must be more interesting than other people. They're not!'" (12–13). As this entirely affected performance continues, Miss Thirplow desperately stashes her rings and bracelets in the couch cushions while insisting on her own "genuineness" and expressing a fear "of losing my obscurity" (13). She laments both the absurdity of celebrity and expresses a profound relief that Calamy himself is so modest rather than "one of those people in the *Sketch*" (14).

This absurd critique of celebrity culture, however, is itself merely a ruse designed to entangle Calamy in an affair that might form the core of her next book. As their romance grows, she constantly experiments with her own personality in order to evoke varying reactions from her lover. These she records in a "secret note-book" from which she draws the plot and dialogue of her novels. This is, of course, a clear meta-fictional reference to *Those Barren Leaves*, itself the product of just such secret jottings that Huxley could often be seen taking down in Garsington's drawing room.[34] Even this diary, furthermore, is itself only a partial and not entirely honest record of her thoughts, since she "was always apprehensive that someone might find her secret note-book and read it" (217). As the author of a roman à clef, she is well aware of the power and profit of privacy, and is thus concerned that her most intimate thoughts might be transformed into profitable commodities. Even when her affair with Calamy is passionately consummated, her thoughts turn immediately to the rewards she can reap from the experience: "[She] couldn't help reflecting that there was, in all this, the stuff of a very deep digression in one of her novels. 'This thoughtful young writer...' would be quoted from the reviewers on the dust-cover of her next book" (283, ellipsis in original). When the affair finally concludes near the end of the novel, so too does Miss Thirplow's draft of her next best-seller: "She shut the book and put the cap on her fountain pen, feeling that she had done a good evening's work. Calamy was now safely laid down in pickle, waiting to be consumed whenever she should be short of fictional provisions" (293). The lady novelist here is as brutally satirized as the lion-hunting Miss Aldwinkle.

Huxley condemns both women for their close connection to a mass-mediated marketplace in which authenticity and art succumb to the naked manipulation of economic and symbolic capital.

These satiric portraits explicitly link women as the creators and brokers of modern aesthetic culture to a degraded marketplace, making them simultaneously the cause and symptom of a more general cultural decline. Miss Thirplow is deceptive and emotionally manipulative, while Miss Aldwinkle presides over a mock salon that barely conceals its endless pursuit of personal profit behind a snobbish façade of passion and "genuineness." Posed against these forces is Francis Chelifer, who seemingly represents the last redoubt of an autonomous highbrow art. He first appears in a section of the text entitled "Fragments from the Autobiography of Francis Chelifer," itself a counterpart to the suspect notebooks of Miss Thirplow. An aesthete and poet, he is resigned to the presumed decadence of a modern commercial culture that does not permit the "mental luxuries" afforded earlier writers (89). As editor of the *Rabbit Fancier's Gazette*, he is, in fact, lodged at the very core of an insipid, profit-driven media culture in which even amateur rabbit breeders command a wider readership than lovers of poetry. Sitting in his Fleet Street office writing these "fragments," he accedes to a dreary modernity: "An inveterate smell of printer's ink haunts the air. From the basement comes up the thudding and clanking of the presses; they are turning out the weekly two hundred thousand copies of the 'Woman's Fiction Budget.' We are at the heart, here, of our human universe. Come, then, let us frankly admit that we are citizens of this mean city, make the worst of it resolutely and not try to escape" (78). The connection between women and mass culture is again made clear, and Chelifer is entirely resigned to what Leah Price calls the "banalization of literacy."[35] He explicitly rejects the artificial autonomy promised by Miss Aldwinkle, ignoring her occasional invitations, and instead dedicates his "allegiance" to the proprietress of his seedy London boarding house: "Ah, those evenings at Lady Giblet's—I never miss a single one if I can help it. The vulgarity, ignorance and stupidity of the hostess, the incredible second-rateness of her mangy lions—these are surely unique. . . . And the conversations one hears within those marble halls—nowhere, surely, are pretensions separated from justifying facts by a vaster gulf. Nowhere can you hear the ignorant, the illogical, the incapable of thought talking so glibly about things of which they have not the slightest understanding" (73). Posed explicitly (if satirically) against the palace of Vezzia, the boarding house reveals the impossibly empty pretensions of Miss Aldwinkle's salon while simultaneously insulating Chelifer himself from even the illusion of a genuinely autonomous aesthetic space. The best, it seems, a modern poet can do is "make the worst" of things by seeking the security of ironic detachment.

This strategy collapses, however, when Chelifer takes a vacation to Italy and is nearly killed by Miss Aldwinkle's boat. Pulled from the sea, he finds himself trapped in the very salon he sought to avoid. "You're exactly the sort of person I want," his hostess tells him when he recovers, transforming him almost immediately into a kind of commodity like her villa (140). For Chelifer, the house becomes a prison and he is almost literally forced to write poetry under Miss Aldwinkle's supervision, all the while feeling that "there is no escape" (137). Unlike Miss Thirplow, who engages in a barely disguised economic exchange—in which she swaps her artistic aura for inside knowledge about her patron—Chelifer preserves an intense anxiety about his position. Lacking the ironic distance afforded by his embrace of London's mass-mediated modernity, he finds himself at once seduced and terrified by the promise of patronage. Seeking to become his muse as well as his lover, Mrs. Aldwinkle sets up a writing desk for him in a romantic grotto where he falls under her acquisitive gaze: "every ten minutes or so she would come tiptoeing into his retreat, smiling, as she imagined, like a sybil, her finger on her lips, to lay beside his permanently virgin sheet of paper a bunch of late-flowering roses" (153). This caricature of Morrell is, of course, every bit as brutal as the portraits by John and Bussy, the attempt at patronage rendered an absurd farce: "Mrs. Aldwinkle had tried to take possession of Chelifer; she had tried to make him as much her property as the view, or Italian art. He became at once the best living poet; but it followed as a corollary that she was his only interpreter" (150). As the narrative progresses, her advances become increasingly aggressive and the woman herself more ridiculous as all the alleged sins of the marketplace are heaped upon her.

At the diegetic level, Huxley's novel is exactly the same kind of wooden "marionette" theatre he constructs in *Crome Yellow*, albeit significantly lengthened by the sometimes pithy and sometimes dull philosophical abstractions most of the characters are made to parrot. Filled with dyspeptic satire, it pits two models of authorship against one another: the best-selling woman writer and the male poet resigned to obscurity and failure within a profit-driven modernity. Both are themselves critiqued throughout the book, deployed as part of an even more punishing attack on the patron who forces cultural producers into such absurd positions. What seems initially to be an idealistic refuge from the marketplace is instead its very apotheosis, as patronage of the arts gives way to the lionhunter's ruthless pursuit of symbolic capital. Chelifer's cool irony thus comes to provide the only apparent relief, allowing him to write his poetry to the rhythm of the printing presses turning out the *Woman's Fiction Budget*. Aesthetic autonomy resides, the text seems to claim, precisely in the ability to elude art's social and economic capitalization.

This would be the case, at any rate, if *Those Barren Leaves* wasn't itself a roman à clef. This book's real interest, after all, lies less in its dull plan and wooden characters than in its manipulation of genre to disrupt its own facile critique of the cultural marketplace. When read explicitly as a roman à clef, the entire logic of the narrative is disrupted, since Huxley himself seems to resemble not Francis Chelifer but Mary Thirplow. His "marionette theatre" then becomes a clear attempt to trade profitably on his own access to one of England's most exclusive salons. Like the best-selling novelist he skewers in the narrative, he too has laid his own friends "down in pickle."

On the one hand, it is possible to treat this as simple hypocrisy, though it becomes difficult to understand why Huxley so ferociously attacks the very patron who helped him launch his career. Morrell herself certainly felt maligned by the book and brought her friendship and correspondence with its author to an abrupt close. On the other hand, by attending to Huxley's manipulation of the roman à clef, we can see his own agonistic attempt to resolve the deep contradictions of modern authorship. Caught between the demands of art and the demands of profit, he chooses both: writing a novel lamenting the commercialization of aesthetics while simultaneously capitalizing on his access to Morrell to assure the book's scandalous success. By incorporating the figure of his own patron and even a meta-fictional portrait of himself, however, he insists on the complete interdependence of mass and elite culture. Patronage offers no refuge from the mass market because it is merely one segment of that very marketplace that effectively mystifies itself in the language of highbrow art and elite consumption. Everyone in *Those Barren Leaves* is perpetually selling one another out and there finally is no refuge from the marketplace—no idealized realm like the palace of Vezza or the headquarters of the *Rabbit Fancier's Gazette* where the arts are somehow purified of their inevitable connection to commerce. Even irony itself proves a facile self-delusion. As a roman à clef, the text does more than simply satirize a lionhunter or redeem the autonomous figure of the male modernist; instead, it also implicates Huxley, his reader, and his critics in a tangled web of capital exchanges. To succeed as a coterie writer, Huxley realizes, is not to escape the marketplace, but to be confined to only one narrow segment of it.

D. H. Lawrence: "Secondary Creativity"

In Huxley's romans à clef, Ottoline Morrell symbolizes less the marketplace itself—which pervades the entire diegetic and extra-diegetic world of the text—than the author's own seemingly contradictory relationship to its order and values. She thus bears a terrible burden, becoming the abject figure for the failure of aesthetic autonomy. This is true of almost every textual representation of Morrell and is nowhere more painfully evident than in D. H. Lawrence's *Women in Love*. Like *Ulysses*, its difficulties in the literary marketplace were legion, and were initially complicated by the fact that Lawrence broke the story of the Brangwen sisters into two lengthy texts.[36] The first, of these, *The Rainbow*, appeared in 1915 but was almost immediately suppressed for obscenity. Lawrence completed work on the sequel late in 1916, preparing two typescripts that were circulated among publishers and close friends. The paper rationing and generally depressed book markets of the First World War, however, made it impossible to place the text and it languished over the next three years. Martin Secker, who eventually published the book in England, no doubt expressed the views of many publishers when he wrote to his silent partner, the wildly successful novelist Compton Mackenzie, "I feel instinctively that anything to do with D. H. is rather dangerous" and "I am not prepared to invest £1500 in a *cause célèbre* to entertain the world of letters."[37] Secker may also have been aware that the book risked not only the threat of legal action for obscenity—though it would eventually pass the censor without difficulty—but also the potentially even more financially damaging risk of a libel suit from Morrell, who is cruelly figured in the text as Hermione Roddice. Secker and other publishers were no doubt right to be wary about the text; despite Lawrence's sometimes excessive defense of the book's imaginative autonomy, it draws heavily on his experiences both at the edge of bohemian London and in Morrell's salon at Garsington.

Lawrence first met Morrell in January 1915 and quickly became an intimate member of the inner circle, developing a passionate relationship with the woman he ecstatically addressed in a letter as "the priestess, the medium, the prophetess" who had become more than a mere "salon lady or lionhunter."[38] She (temporarily) embodied for him an almost sacred ideal of cultural autonomy far removed from the crass sensualism and commercialism of bohemian London: "It is rather splendid that you are a great lady. Don't abrogate one jot or tittle of your high birth: it is too valuable in this commercial-minded, mean world: and it *does* stand as well for what you really are."[39] Lawrence, in other words, had fully vested himself in the stark oppositions governing the traditional conception of modernism as an aesthetic deliberately opposed to the alleged vulgarities of the marketplace. Following the suppression of *The Rainbow*, of course, he may have had little option but to embrace this conception of patronage, and it was compounded by his own desire to establish a utopian community "like the Boccaccio place where they told all the *Decamerone*."[40] Like many others, Lawrence and his wife Frieda stayed at

Garsington, joining the various other pacifists and protestors who were offered shelter and support during the war. There he received the Morrells' strong support and Ottoline's husband twice raised questions about the prosecution of *The Rainbow* in the House of Commons. Lawrence also continued working during this time on the book that would eventually become *Women in Love*.

Garsington during this period was an exciting and vibrant place, packed with artists and intellectuals who shared an aversion to what seemed the pointless violence and destruction taking place across the Channel. There was, furthermore, a clear consciousness of place, a shared knowledge that Morrell had managed to assemble a salon where new and important work was being done. Partly in jest, Dora Carrington proposed in 1916 the creation of a newspaper entitled *The Garsington Chronicle* where those living on the estate could publish essays, poems, and pictures without fear of the censor. She drew up a fanciful prospectus, noting that anything libelous would be happily accepted and published anonymously.[41] There is clear reference in this plan to Lawrence's own trouble with official suppression and also an awareness that Garsington might be providing not only shelter from the world of politics but also source material for novels, poems, and plays. Indeed, at almost the same moment that Carrington urges the creation of an in-house gossip sheet, another of Morrell's guests, the painter Dorothy Brett, writes to insist on the preservation of her privacy: "*Please don't* show my letters to you to anyone. I should only be laughed at, because what is serious between two people is nearly always ridiculous to outsiders and although you and I understand each other and one's relations to each other, outsiders don't."[42] The consciousness of Garsington as a place, in other words, meant also a clear awareness of its value as a cultural commodity that could be retailed not only in the proposed *Garsington Chronicle,* but in the wider literary marketplace as well. Siegfried Sassoon, a guest at the estate while on leave in 1916, later wrote of his own sense that the house had become a piece of fungible capital and that Morrell "had yet to learn that the writers and artists whom she befriended were capable of proving ungrateful."[43] In that same year, in fact, the first of the Garsington romans à clef appeared: Gilbert Cannan's *Mendel*, in which Morrell is well disguised but nevertheless visible as Mary Tutness. The intimacy of the salon had been breached, and there was an immediate rush to profit from insider knowledge. Even Brett herself, who had urged Morrell to protect her privacy, boasted just after the publication of *Mendel* that she had "bought some more paper and a darling tab book to write my Garsington memoirs in!!"[44]

In Huxley's romans à clef we have already seen how the modernist salon could be transformed into just a segment of the marketplace it presumes to escape. If anything, Huxley may have underestimated the powerful flows of social, cultural, and economic capital moving through Garsington. With each new portrait and roman à clef, Morrell seemed to grow ever more absurd, her own striking idiosyncrasies nakedly marketed as open secrets to a scandal-hungry public. Lawrence's portrait in *Women in Love,* however, is far more brutal than most, in part because he rejects Huxley's satire and instead renders Morrell as the aggressive and even murderous Hermione Roddice, who is made to bear all the sins of a decadent world. She first appears in the book as a celebrity spectacle glimpsed at a wedding by the Brangwen sisters. The text, in fact, traces a fascinating narrative line as we are invited first to behold Hermione's greatness then critique it, as if we were watching a parade of modern celebrities strut down the red carpet. Thus she "came along, with her head held up, balancing an enormous flat hat of pale yellow velvet, on which were streaks of ostrich feather, natural and grey. She drifted forward as if scarcely conscious, her long blanched face lifted up, not to see the world."[45] A carefully detailed description of Hermione's clothes and appearance follows, framed in free indirect discourse so that although the narrative is related from a third-person perspective, we seem actually to be hovering within the consciousness of the sisters themselves as they observe this woman parade before them. The roman à clef's distinctive aesthetic of detail then moves seamlessly from spectacle to mounting disgust: "She was impressive, in her lovely pale-yellow and brownish-rose, yet macabre, something repulsive. People were silent when she passed, impressed, roused, wanting to jeer, yet for some reason silenced" (62). This passage powerfully enacts the roman à clef's anarchic ambiguity, layering fiction and fact as we too are invited to jeer at the portrait of this larger-than-life woman even as we wonder about its accuracy.

This same ambiguity, furthermore, emerges within her own consciousness as the narrative takes an unusual and somewhat disorienting plunge into Hermione's subjective experience of the event. She is, on the one hand, aware that "no one could put her down, no one could make mock of her, because she stood among the first, and those that were against her were below her, either in rank, or in wealth, or in high association of thought and progress and understanding" (63). Here, at any rate, the external appearance matches the internal experience of the event; Hermione genuinely does seem to be an almost idealized figure of autonomy completely cut off from the crass snobbery and admiration of the crowd. On the other hand, Lawrence simultaneously suggests that, like the fascinated observers, she too experiences a macabre repulsion at herself that she can neither describe nor understand: "Even walking up the path to the church, confident as she was that in every respect her appearance was complete and perfect, according to the first standards, yet she suffered a torture, under her confidence and pride, feeling herself exposed to wounds and to mockery and to despite. She always felt vulnerable, vulnerable, there was always a secret chink in her armour. She did not know herself what it was. It was a lack of robust self" (63). Hermione's problem appears to be her celebrity, her overinvestment in a public and marketable persona that has effectively mutilated some more authentic sense of self. In buying, as it were, her own public image, she has destroyed the otherwise authentic self her autonomy appears to shelter. She is then brutally exposed to the reader as little more than an empty carapace concealing "a deficiency of being within her" (64).

The text's critique of Hermione as the representative of a fully and dangerously commodified world is further heightened by its equally aggressive (re)construction of Garsington as Breadalby. Like Huxley's palace of Vezza, the house is transparently recognizable as the Morrells' country estate; in the initial typescript a scene is even set beneath "an enormous, beautifully balanced ilex tree."[46] This was a signature feature at Garsington (Huxley's own arboreal title, for example, also alludes to it) and Lawrence only struck it from the typescript at a relatively late date, likely in an attempt to guard against the threatened libel suit. Initially, the estate emerges as an idealized locale. The Brangwen sisters are delighted by an invitation Hermione issues to them and, again, in the free indirect discourse of the novel, both they and the narrator imagine "a magic circle drawn about the place, shutting out the present, enclosing the delightful, precious past, trees and deer and silence, like a dream" (139). This romantic image, however, is under constant pressure, as we gradually become aware that it too is riven by the very anxieties it otherwise appears to exclude. Birkin engages, for example, in an increasingly aggressive critique of the place where the talk has become "powerful and destructive" (146). Thus, when one of the guests, Joshua Malleson, interjects the clichéd observation that "knowledge is, of course, liberty," Birkin waspishly responds, "in compressed tabloids," emphasizing the mass-mediated nature of the platitude. Gudrun then imagines the distinguished sociologist as "a flat bottle, containing tabloids of compressed liberty" (141–42). Transformed from an intellectual giant into a bottle of patent medicine, he and Breadalby as a whole stand exposed—like Hermione at the wedding—as captives to their own allegedly inauthentic public image.

This lengthy chapter brings the book's critique of coterie culture to an appallingly violent climax when we are later plunged into Hermione's consciousness, watching her attain a "consummation of voluptuous ecstasy" as she bashes Birkin over the head with an ornamental paperweight (163). Aside from nearly killing him, the event proves epiphanic for Birkin, who is "shattered . . . like a flask that is smashed to atoms" (164). Freed at last from the same carapace that he earlier claimed surrounded Hermione, he finds a new sense of identity and staggers from the house into the "perfect cool loneliness, so lovely fresh and unexplored" of the countryside (165). Cut loose from Hermione and the anxieties about cultural capital she embodies, he can now begin to pursue the narrative of regeneration that consumes the rest of the book. Although even Birkin seems to confess the rightness of Hermione's actions in striking him and thus essentially renewing his sense of self, as readers we are nevertheless horrified by the image of this woman so thwarted and self-obsessed that she seeks to murder her lover. Throughout *Women in Love*, she is a deadly serious threat to the artist's potential freedom, offering him a false sense of autonomy made all the more treacherous by the self-delusions of those who believe they have escaped the deadening force of bourgeois art, society, and culture. As a celebrity lionhunter, in fact, she concentrates all of these forces in a single empty yet profoundly aggressive being who wants to make the world over in the image of her own hollowness.

Unlike *Crome Yellow, Those Barren Leaves,* and the raft of other Garsington novels published in the 1920s, *Women in Love* does not resort to satire. It maintains instead a resolute seriousness in both its portrait of Morrell and its condemnation of her world. Huxley's deployment of the roman à clef as a "marionette theatre" may have been profoundly hurtful to his patron, but it nevertheless transformed her into an essentially comic figure—one among many, including even the author himself. Thus, the intersection of mass and elite marketplaces in these novels becomes a symptomatic element of their larger satirical aims. Like the modestly historicizing critique of the romance generated by the roman à clef in the eighteenth century, here the genre's structural ambiguity allows Huxley to fold himself, his friends, and his book into a broadly comic analysis of the cultural marketplace. One can laugh at the portrait of Morrell with the same corrosive laughter Huxley invites us to direct at his narrative alter egos as well as at our own hypocritical ability to savor the pleasures of the roman à clef. Lawrence's seriousness, however, which we now also largely associate with his stature as a canonical modernist writer, leads him to reject the interplay between diegetic and extra-diegetic narratives that Huxley deliberately courts. Insisting that we take Birkin's flight from Hermione seriously and that we thus allow for the possibility of a genuine romantic utopia, he seeks to distance the text from its historical antecedents and thus suppresses its extra-diegetic pleasures. Thus, rather than a roman à clef derived from Lawrence's own experiences, *Women in Love* suppresses its "conditional fictionality" in order to seek the imprimatur of an autonomous novel—a work of art that in both form and content offers a (hypocritical) alternative to the artificial worlds of Breadalby and Garsington.

In a slim 1927 Garsington roman à clef entitled *The Aesthetes*, W. J. Turner articulates a similar anxiety about autonomy and consumption. This now obscure text makes little effort to conceal its infectious ambiguities, and its cover features a delicate line drawing by John Mavrogordato of faceless yet well-dressed figures gathered in an elegant drawing room. Its cover, like it elliptical title, promises a taste of scandal, the blank faces openly hinting that these are real portraits that have been decorously masked. An ilex tree is even faintly visible through the window in the background, offering an even more pointed allusion to Morrell's own coterie—at least for those with the knowledge to decipher the image (figure 6.1).[47] The book's

Fig. 6.1. Dust jacket for W. J. Turner's *The Aesthetes*.

narrative unfolds as a dialogue about art and society, recounting an evening debate at "Wrexham," the cipher for Garsington. "Art," the narrator notes, "has taken the place of politics as the favorite topic at week-end parties at country houses," and he promises not to neglect the details of the conversation he is about to relate since "irrelevant details are the sauce of the argument."[48] Such minutiae, of course, are essential to the roman à clef's aesthetics of detail, since, for those in the know, they reveal recognizable portraits of the Garsington and Bloomsbury circles, including Huxley, Lawrence, Clive Bell, Lytton Strachey, Desmond McCarthy, and others.

The party sets out to ask, "What *is* Lady Caraway?" (38). This question immediately declares the book's status as a roman à clef by introducing the fictional double of Morrell as an absent center around which various figures weave their gossipy responses. One character, emphasizing Caraway's notoriety, insists that the party needs to puncture their hostess's public persona: "She is known only to tourists or sight-seers. They look at her and go away—and write books about her" (49). Like Hermione at the wedding in *Women in Love,* the text intimates that the authentic Caraway has never been seen and may have disappeared entirely beneath the "chalky mask" of her make-up and reputation (47). She has become, another character insists, an "unknown reality," a stereotyped "freak," a "psychological sport," and even "a work of art" (47–48, 41–42). In the tradition of the roman à clef, the text is both playful and ambiguous, lamenting the fact that the real Lady Caraway has been lost while simultaneously emphasizing its own complicity in transforming her into a publicly circulated image suitable for both this sort of intimate gossip and for the mass consumption of "tourists" who might read a book like *The Aesthetes.*

Morrell was understandably furious when the book appeared, particularly since Turner initially sought to dedicate it to her. Objecting strenuously, Morrell pointed out that such a dedication "might put the idea [that the book is a roman à clef] into people's heads."[49] Like Huxley, Turner offered up the somewhat feeble defense that he had not actually written a roman à clef, but a "Platonic dialogue" and that he had "taken great pains to make clear that its central figure and its dialogue are necessarily fantastic creations."[50] In what became a familiar pattern in the often anguished correspondence following the publication of such texts, he attempted to stake out the moral and aesthetic high ground by assuring Morrell that she could not be so poor a reader as to see an image of herself in the text: "I think I have taken such pains to make my central idea clear that only a poor intelligence could misunderstand it. However we know that such exist and as it is impossible to make one's work absolutely fool-proof we could help to escape misunderstanding [by dedicating it to her]."[51] This ruse, however, did little to placate Morrell. Her correspondence with Turner ended immediately on the book's publication, and a decade later she wrote angrily to accuse W. B. Yeats of betraying her when he mentioned the book in an introduction to a collection of poetry. A flurried exchange of letters ensued in which Yeats tried desperately to defend himself, but he ultimately failed as this friendship too suddenly cooled.

The Aesthetes is, in fact, the last of the Garsington romans à clef and its focus extends well beyond Morrell, who by 1927 was already vanishing into the myth of wartime Garsington. Like Huxley and Lawrence, Turner also tackles what he considers the essentially derivative, even "conditional," nature of the modern novel. The conversation thus turns to Lady Caraway only after one of the characters laments the failure of the romantic aesthetic that depends on endless innovation as a way of escaping the constraints of a stultifying modernity: "Anyone can provide one sensation by bankrupting himself in a single go and, naturally, the more there is to him the bigger the sensation. But I can't burn my house down every night, and the romantics soon find this out and treat us to sham bonfires, stage flares which deceive nobody of intelligence" (37). This is a stinging critique of the strand of modernism derived from Pound's command to "Make it new," so that innovation for its own sake becomes a charade, a stereotyped performance staged for public consumption rather than a genuine form of art.

As a roman à clef, of course, *The Aesthetes* is founded on this conception of "conditional" art, depending on what it freely acknowledges to be an alternative mode of artistic creativity that no longer insists on a rigid distinction between factual history and romantic fiction: "Things are always what we make them. We may look upon Lady Caraway in various ways and the question is can we make a work of art of her? For this purpose we shall not be creative in the sense the artist is creative, we shall be creative in that secondary sense in which the aesthete, the appreciator, or discoverer of the work of art is creative" (42). In an otherwise forgettable book, this is a remarkable critique of modernism's presumption of autonomy. Turner insists instead on what he calls a "secondary" creativity that derives from the artist's ability to mix fact and fiction in a new kind of narrative alchemy. Rather than "sham bonfires" of ecstatic invention, such a practice instead allows for actual people and events to be reprocessed through an art interested in the autonomy of neither Victorian realism nor Eliotic impersonality.

Rather than treating the roman à clef as a degraded genre laden with gossip and scandal, Turner offers it instead as the potentially rich alternative to a romanticism that had become staid, dull, and conventional. This concept of secondary creativity, furthermore, is not unique to Turner since it pervades *Women in Love* as well, generating a subtle but nevertheless powerful counter-narrative to Birkin's romantic utopianism. Shortly before Hermione strikes her lover in the head, after all, she finds him in his room copying a "Chinese drawing of geese" (144). She is briefly fascinated by this and first insists on the painting's value as a piece of cultural capital, telling Birkin that "The Chinese ambassador gave it me" (144). When he remains unimpressed and absorbed in his work, she resorts instead to the same kind of romantic idealism Turner critiques, asking—in a moment clearly framed to expose her vacuousness—why he is merely copying a piece of art instead of creating "something original" (145). He then passionately defends the same kind of "secondary creativity" Turner would later extol: "One gets more out of China, copying this picture, than reading all the books. . . . I know what centres they live from—what they perceive and feel—the hot, stinging centrality of a goose in the flux of cold water and mud—the curious bitter stinging heat of a goose's blood, entering the blood like an inoculation of corruptive fire—fire of the cold-burning mud—the lotus mystery" (145). While clearly articulated in the familiar tropes of romantic intensity that characterize his later flight into the woods, this passage nevertheless insists simultaneously on the value of the copy for regenerating these lost experiences. Reproduction rather than pure invention grants Birkin this special knowledge and the text insists on this secondary creativity as a powerful corrective to the reified "originality" Hermione desires. The tools and techniques of the roman à clef, which consist precisely of the "copying" of original people into sometimes transformative aesthetic figures, are defended in the text at the very moment that Lawrence himself is deploying them in his own imaginative appropriation of Ottoline Morrell. Just as Turner insists that such an art should be connected more to discovery than to invention, so too readers who recognize the portrait of Lawrence's own patron glimpse an alternative to Birkin's endlessly frustrated attempts to escape bourgeois modernity through a vacuous romantic modernism.

Despite his productive experimentation with the roman à clef as an alternative to modernist impersonality, however, Lawrence diligently resisted any attempt to root *Women in Love* in the events of his own life. Some of this defensiveness clearly arose from the fear that those he attacked would seek recourse in a libel court. In his correspondence with Catherine Carswell, Lawrence clearly expresses this anxiety: "Do you think it would really hurt her [Morrell]—the Hermione?" he asks. "You see, it really isn't her at all—only suggested by her. It is probable she will think Hermione has nothing to do with her."[52] Morrell, who received a copy of the typescript shortly after Lawrence posted this letter, was indeed so devastated she began to take steps to suppress the book through a libel suit. His initial concern about his patron then quickly gave way to aggression and rage, as he wrote to S. S. Koteliansky that "the Ott is really too disgusting with her threats of legal proceedings etc."[53] Like Huxley, Woolf, and Turner, he refused to concede that he constructed a portrait of Morrell and instead wrapped himself in a hypocritical mantle of the very aesthetic autonomy *Women in Love* revealingly critiques, attacking her in starkly gendered terms as a vain and ignorant woman. Ironically, he even accused her of deliberately transforming the text into a roman à clef, since she "would like the thing to appear, for self-advertisement—and her sheep-faced fool of a husband would like to denounce it, for further self-advertisement."[54]

Such vitriol is not at all uncommon in Lawrence's letters. During this period he heaped scorn on Morrell, in particular, whom he often blamed for derailing the text; but at the same time he appears to have made subtle but significant changes to the typescript in order to strengthen his defense in a potential legal action. Not only is the famous Garsington ilex tree changed, but so too is Hermione's physical appearance altered, her distinctive "red brown" hair replaced by "heavy fair hair."[55] This is, furthermore, the same kind of change Lawrence made to two other characters in the book also drawn directly from his life: Halliday and the Pussum. As Lawrence himself admitted, these two figures from London's bohemia were based on real people (Philip Heseltine and Minnie Channing) and both won damages of £60 as well as the suppression of the first English edition after threatening Lawrence's publisher with a lawsuit of their own.[56] Thus, even as Lawrence raged against the Morrells and others who claimed to recognize themselves, he nevertheless implicitly acknowledged the legal risks he had run by making such subtle yet telling changes to the beleaguered manuscript.

As the vehemence of his letters suggests, however, there was more at stake here for Lawrence than just defending himself against a possible action for defamation. Even his presumably confidential notes to friends adamantly deny that he has simply reworked his own relationship with Morrell in the book and thus drawn extensively on his own time at Garsington. The reasons for this emerge from the roman à clef's taint as an inferior or secondary genre too closely linked to the presumably degraded values of the marketplace. Lawrence, after all, found himself in an awkward situation as he sought to find a publisher and thus a commercial market for a book that otherwise vehemently condemns the commercialization of culture. Writers like Turner and Huxley also struggled with this apparent hypocrisy, but the corrosive power of satire enfolds both them and the reader within its critique, suggesting effectively that there may be no alternative to art's commodification. That is, they could teasingly employ the roman à clef precisely because neither of them clung to the romantic conception of the novel as a redoubt of disinterested aesthetic autonomy. In fact, they skillfully deployed the roman à clef to launch potent critiques of the novel as well as attempts to preserve it and other forms of art in an idealized sphere splendidly isolated from the marketplace. Thus rather than indulging in the "sham bonfires" of a romanticism that they acknowledge is merely a segment of a highly specialized market, they instead openly pursued a "secondary creativity" that did not set them in radical—and artificial—opposition to commodity culture. Indeed, this can help explain why subsequent critics never quite managed to include a writer like Huxley in the modernist canon. The apparently derivative nature of his texts simply couldn't be squared with the impulse to "make it new."

Lawrence, however, rejected satire's self-inoculating comforts and instead tried to carve out an autonomous space for art. As a result, his works—though not as structurally innovative as, say, *Ulysses*—nevertheless partake of the same impulse to embrace the romance of invention and could thus be more easily accommodated to modernism's founding myths. This lands him, however, in a troubling paradox since he deploys the "secondary creativity" of the roman à clef in *Women in Love* even as he rails against it. Thus, in a letter to Kot written after Morrell threatened to sue, Lawrence asks, "Why did I give myself away to them—the Otts and Murries etc!"[57] He saw himself, in other words, as a cultural commodity, a reified object that had been brought into the crucible of Garsington and consequently subsumed by the covert flows of social, cultural, and economic capital coursing through it. Though Birkin in *Women in Love* condemns Breadalby as a prison, it is, in fact, a starkly gendered marketplace, and Lawrence felt himself sullied there by the same forces he strove idealistically to critique.

Morrell's own friends and confidants were well aware of the contradictory position in which Lawrence suddenly found himself as he finished *Women in Love*. Katherine Mansfield and Dorothy Brett both urged their friend and patron to use this knowledge in defending herself against Lawrence's portrait. In January 1917 Brett wrote urging Morrell to follow Mansfield's advice: "I think Katherine on the whole right. She knows Lawrence through and through—and her idea is that ridicule kills more quickly than anything else with him. To say 'Well your [sic] a bit behind the times, Gilbert got his out first and everyone's a bit tired of that kind of stuff etc.'"[58] Morrell is urged here, in effect, to treat *Women in Love* like a roman à clef in the lighthearted mode of Gilbert Canan's *Pugs and Peacocks*, thereby dismissing not only the serious content of the novel but also implicitly suggesting that Lawrence himself is merely seeking to trade economically on his relationship with Morrell and Garsington. "Anything else," Mansfield wrote, "will only make him feel like Christ whipping out the money changers."[59] By insisting on Lawrence's "secondary creativity," Brett suggests that Morrell could turn the brutal figure of Hermione against its creator, implying that is was actually he who greedily transformed Garsington's promise of autonomy into an already outmoded commodity.

We have no idea if Morrell really attempted such a rebuttal, though there is little evidence of it in her correspondence. Lawrence, meanwhile, did mount a powerful defense against precisely this kind of allegation. Shortly after Ottoline and her husband approached his agent in February 1917 and warned him that they might take a libel action against the book, its author responded with what would become an increasingly refined aesthetic defense of its form. "Really," Lawrence writes, "the world has gone completely dotty! Hermione is not much more like Ottoline Morrell than Queen Victoria, the house they [the Morrells] claim as theirs is a Georgian home in Derbyshire I know very well—etc. Ottoline flatters herself.—There *is* a hint of her in the character of Hermione: but so is there a hint of a million women if it comes to that."[60] This is clearly the disingenuous argument of an author eager to avoid a libel case, and he defends his work here as pure fiction, insisting that the characters (if not the physical setting) are drawn entirely from his imagination. Only at the end does he allow for the obvious fact that he has indeed drawn on Morrell, but in doing so he links this to a larger aesthetic and philosophical claim about the universalism of a certain kind of woman. Lawrence had, in fact, developed a similar, albeit much more nuanced, argument in a now famous letter to Edward Garnett: "You mustn't look in my novel for the stable old ego of the character. There is another ego, according to whose action the individual is unrecognizable, and passes through, as it were, allotropic states which it needs a deeper sense than any we've been used to exercise, to discover are states of the same single radically-unchanged element."[61] Here he effectively develops a preemptive defense against the charge of secondary creativity by insisting that he has developed a new concept of ego and character rooted in some deeper, universal concept of self. Thus, as Lawrence constructs his various characters, we should all to some extent recognize bits and piece of ourselves in this deep subjective structure. Such an argument, of course, has proven to be one of modernism's most effective defenses, and this passage has long been used essentially to regulate the reception and circulation of Lawrence's text by focusing our attention solely on the diegesis itself—and dismissing the book's plain manipulation of the roman à clef. *Women in Love* may indeed gesture to the world off the page, but it claims to do so in a philosophical rather than satirical mode. Thus, Lawrence could claim that it potentially libels all of its readers, like those million of women he links to Hermione, and is therefore actionable by none of them. His aesthetic, in other words, manipulates the roman à clef in order to transform real women into abstract symbols, evacuating them of historical specificity while at the same time isolating his book from the charges of mere imitation or appropriation.

The authors of almost all of the Garsington romans à clef engaged in similar kinds of disingenuous strategies, publicly asserting the entirely fictional nature of texts whose principal charm and value lies precisely in their manipulation of the genre's anarchic skepticism. Like Turner's rather too blatant request to dedicate *The Aesthetes* to Morrell, the various denials issued by these writers typically served only to emphasize all the more coyly their often satiric portraiture. This, in turn, explains again why these delightful books have now become so obscure: one of their primary pleasures consists in their topical references to personalities and places that have been masked by the passage of time. As we have seen, Huxley's books, in particular, offer a sharp and corrosive critique of literary modernism and its institutions; but it is available only when we read them as romans à clef—as deliberate attempts to challenge the novel's claim to imaginative autonomy. To recover this critique, however, we have to access a densely woven web of extra-diegetic connections. Without these tendrils stretching delicately between fact and fiction, the works seem somewhat flat, uninspired, or merely frivolous. Michael Dirda, in his introduction to the 2001 Dalkey Press edition of *Crome Yellow*, awkwardly acknowledges this, insisting on the quality of the book and mentioning, as if in passing, that its characters may have been derived from real figures. After carefully cataloging their sources, however, he then dismissively asks, "Who cares?" before describing the text's vivid and memorable personalities.[62] His rhetorical question is a clear and anxiously dismissive attempt to isolate *Crome Yellow* from its generic identity as a roman à clef, to cut it off from its extra-diegetic connections in order to revive it as a novel. While the book is no doubt a delightful read, however, Dirda—like many other critics—effectively suppresses its most striking and innovative elements since they seem to be the product of a merely secondary creativity.

By insisting so ardently that readers ignore *Women in Love*'s secondary creativity, Lawrence managed far more successfully than the other Garsington writers to focus his readers' attention almost entirely on the diegesis. This finally proved the most effective response to the strategies suggested by Mansfield and Brett, since the book has been canonized and thus preserved precisely as a novel and not a roman à clef. Rather than a portrait of Morrell, Hermione has indeed become one of a million women, a textual representation of some larger ego who is finally assessed and condemned on the text's own terms. When we insist on deciphering the roman à clef's function in *Women in Love,* however, a more ambiguous and perhaps even more troubling view of the text emerges. In glimpsing the figure of Morrell behind Hermione, we see her less as an abstract symbol of feminine aggression and more as a point of agonized condensation for Lawrence's own troubled relationship to the literary marketplace. Brutally condemned in the book as an acquisitive lionhunter, this woman becomes—as Alice Jardin argues more generally—a symbol of the sort of cultural commodification that Lawrence figures as a threat to his romantic aspirations and aesthetic autonomy. As we have seen in the image of Birkin copying those Chinese geese, his anxieties about the failure of this ideal are subtly figured in the text itself, but they snap into sharp focus only when we realize that Lawrence himself was also copying what he saw. Like Huxley and the others, he too experimented with the roman à clef as a way of resisting and indeed transforming the news/novel divide, but he finally suppressed this most striking element of his work to secure its publication. That is, Lawrence gained the modernist "imprimatur" in a way that Huxley, for example, did not, because he managed to preserve that "interested disinterestedness" Bourdieu argues is so essential to the creation of a market for elite cultural goods. Indeed, *Women in Love* is a novel—and thus a work of what might be called primary creativity—only to the degree that it obscures its innovative experimentation with the roman à clef.

Like Joyce and Lewis, of course, Lawrence may have been initially forced into this position because the laws governing the field of cultural production made it nearly impossible to acknowledge openly the derivative nature of his work. Even Turner, who managed to articulate a defense of secondary creativity, nevertheless relied upon the roman à clef's "conditional fictionality" to afford himself some limited protection. In reading works like *Women in Love, Those Barren Leaves,* or any of the other Garsington-inspired books as pure fiction, however, we participate in one of modernism's most powerful and pervasive myths about its own imaginative supremacy. When the extra-diegetic tendrils of these works are suppressed, they participate in the gender tropism Jardine, Friedman, and Felski describe in which "WOMAN" becomes an abject symbol of commodity culture. Thus Hermione, Amy Caraway, and Mrs. Aldwinkle remain effectively hollow, aggressive, and finally sadistic symbols of an allegedly rapacious modernity threatening a literary creativity and autonomy encoded entirely as male. They become, in short, abject lionhunters: wealthy, powerful, and influential women who symbolically concentrate the encroachment of commodity culture on a presumably autonomous male aesthetic sphere.

By recovering the extra-diegetic dimensions of these texts, however, we gain an alternative vision of modernist cultural production as directly and critically engaged with the cultural marketplace. At one level, in acknowledging the figure of Morrell behind her various textual personas, we see the Garsington novelists deliberately exploiting the roman à clef's scandalous potential so they can market their access to Britain's cultural and aristocratic elites. A close reading of these texts, however, reveals another level of critical self-consciousness connecting the roman à clef to modernism's larger critique of the realist novel and its institutions. That is, rather than the "tissue of personalities" Henry James dismissed, the genre gives writers like Lawrence and Huxley an opportunity to explore the limits of romantic autonomy and develop an aesthetic of "secondary creativity" of the sort Turner describes. The various literary portraits of Morrell certainly harmed the woman who so ardently supported the men who created them, and even Lawrence in 1928 acknowledged that "the so-called portraits of Ottoline can't possibly be Ottoline—no one knows that better than an artist."[63] As the object of their sometimes stinging if lightly veiled and vehemently denied critique, she becomes less a stereotypical lionhunter than a complicated figure for a new mode of literary experimentation that could not be adequately accommodated by the emergent narratives of modernist autonomy. She became for them a symbolic and, eventually, an economic commodity, one they eagerly traded in the literary marketplace; but she also stubbornly signified the failure of their own conquest of autonomy and the potentially derivative nature of their creativity. "We hurt you too much," Brett wrote to Morrell in 1917 after the Garsington novels and paintings began to appear. In recovering the roman à clef's operations, we can simultaneously see the ways in which Morrell herself hurt writers like Huxley and Lawrence into a critical knowledge of modernism's contradictions and limits. More than a mere lionhunter, she instead became the catalyst for crucial narrative innovations that have been suppressed or misrecognized in our own insistence on the novel's aesthetic supremacy.

Gender, Genre, Power: Jean Rhys

For the writers gathered around Ottoline Morrell at Garsington Manor, their patron became a dense site of symbolic entanglement. The satiric and even deranged images they created of her were, in part, attempts to negotiate their own anxieties about the nature of aesthetic creativity within a highly segmented literary marketplace in which the coterie functioned merely as one profit center among others. Their depiction of Morrell, furthermore, has proven so durable precisely because she was not a writer or an artist herself, despite a somewhat desultory attempt to craft a set of memoirs; she has remained largely a symbol deployed by male writers eager to heap on her the perceived sins of their own inevitable commodification. Seen in this light, Morrell becomes a tragic figure, her fortune and her prestige finally insufficient proof against the male artist's ability to appropriate and exploit the symbolic resonance of her gender as a woman and thus transform her from a patron into a lionhunter.

This close link between women and the marketplace, of course, pervades modernist aesthetic production from Joyce's *Ulysses* to Picasso's *Les Demoiselles d'Avignon*. For women writers themselves, however, cultural commodification and the utopian promise of aesthetic autonomy often had a sharply different resonance. The struggle simply to access the public sphere often meant that they had far less anxiety than their male counterparts about the allegedly corrosive effects of the marketplace and precious little nostalgia for an autonomous sphere often resembling the hermetic drawing rooms many of them sought to escape. Even Virginia Woolf, who so eloquently and powerfully articulated the need for women writers to have a room of their own, failed adequately to address the simultaneous need for women to participate in the marketplace in order to gain a public voice and claim to financial independence. The owner and operator of the Hogarth Press, as well as a novelist who made careful note of the profits reaped by both her serious and her lighter fiction, she clearly engaged with the marketplace as a site of empowerment and autonomy.[64] And yet, in *Three Guineas,* written near the end of her career and in the midst of crises both personal and political, she oddly begins to articulate a disgust with the market and a plea for isolation of the sort Birkin defends in *Women in Love*. She urges women "not to commit adultery of the brain" by merely writing "for the sake of money."[65] "Money," "advertisement," and "publicity" she continues, are "adulterers" and drawing unexpectedly on the discourse of chastity she asks women writers "not to allow your private face to be published, or details of your private life; not to avail yourself, in short, of any of the forms of brain prostitution which are so insidiously suggested by the pimps and panderers of the brain-selling trade."[66] This becomes, of course, part of Woolf's larger defense of the "Outsider": an attempt to construct both a real and imaginative space not entirely unlike Morrell's Garsington or her own Bloomsbury where art can be quarantined from the apparently abusive powers of commodity culture.

Such an attempt to link the body and mind of the woman artist through the metaphor of prostitution is troubling, in part, because it ignores what Christine Froula has described as Woolf's successful excavation of "modernism's hidden brothels."[67] Focusing on George Duckworth's sexual abuse of Woolf, Froula eloquently uncovers how the novelist and her sister successfully "vivisected" the "socioeconomic marriage system" and trained "an analytic gaze on the project of freedom that engendered many of modernism's experiments and reforms."[68] These women, who found themselves sexually exploited and unable to access the liberties available to their male friends, pursued a heroic personal and aesthetic quest to recover the autonomy of their bodies while nevertheless insisting on the unjust nature of the system that subjected them to Duckworth's abuse. As Froula furthermore notes, Woolf herself readily deployed the roman à clef in early fictional sketches like "Memoirs of a Novelist" and "Phyllis and Rosamond," both short pieces that cannily exploit the genre's skepticism about fact and fiction and thereby allow their author "to soar over the concealing walls of the private house into public speech."[69] As "public speech," of course, these sketches are strictly delimited because their "speech" is deliberately ambiguous, their charges of sexual abuse and exploitation cloaked behind the roman à clef's double-registers.

Many other women writers in the period found themselves in a position similar to Woolf's: subject to sexual and abuse and manipulation, uncertain about how to access the public sphere with the same freedom and confidence as the men around them, and yet eager to claim a room of their own. Lacking the considerable cultural resources Woolf commanded, their challenge, as Deborah Parsons describes it, was "not so much to enter but to survive in the urban environment" where they too found themselves subject to the "hidden brothels" Froula analyzes.[70] No figure is more emblematic of the way this gendered modernity is configured within modernism's countercultural metropolis than Jean Rhys, whose four novels set in Paris and London during the 1920s and 30s describe an often terrifying struggle to survive on the fringes of a male bohemia where women were mistresses and models to be traded and abandoned. Rhys's work powerfully acknowledges what Froula productively describes as the "gender of free speech" within coteries that otherwise venerated personal liberation and experimentation. Exploiting the conventions of the roman à clef, Rhys offers a critically veiled critique of elite modernist culture that exposes its gendered conception of liberation while simultaneously appropriating the power of the marketplace to access the means of cultural production.

By focusing explicitly on Rhys's strategic manipulation of the roman à clef, we can understand not only the most daring innovations of a book like *Quartet*, but the sociohistorical reasons for its brief notoriety and subsequent descent into obscurity. Typically read as an odd yet haunting account of a woman's masochistic surrender to a bizarre love affair and her consequent destruction, the work has become comfortably canonized as a powerful feminist critique of a still brutally patriarchal Parisian bohemia. The key required to open its hidden subtext— namely that the brutal H. J. Heidler is really Rhys's onetime lover and mentor Ford Madox Ford—was available to a number of its initial readers who reveled in watching the most sordid details of private life become public property. Recovering this key thus alters our most basic assumptions about the work, particularly that it is primarily a record of one woman's intense suffering and brutalization. When reframed as a roman à clef, it becomes something quite different: an empowering act of public vengeance in which the novel's masochistic protagonist becomes a tool for its sadistic author who pillories Ford's bohemian pretensions, bourgeois morality, and infantile sexuality.

In 1966 Jean Rhys emerged from more than three decades of poverty and obscurity to publish *Wide Sargasso Sea,* a novel that won an array of literary awards while prompting many critics to group her among the best living novelists.[71] Shortly thereafter her publishers, Andre Deutsch in London and W. W. Norton in the United States, sought to capitalize on Rhys's fame by republishing the four novels she had written in the 1920s and '30s, as well as an expanded edition of her first collection of short stories. Greeted by an emerging generation of feminist scholars who sought to enlarge the modernist canon beyond the "men of 1914," Rhys immediately became something of a countercultural icon: a bold, original, woman writer from the romanticized bohemian Left Bank of early twentieth-century Paris. The fact that by the 1950s she had been entirely forgotten and was living on the fringes of the welfare state in rented rooms and off-season holiday cottages only helped burnish her image as an unfairly neglected artist. Unlike the sophisticated Virginia Woolf, Rhys did not have access to the kind of cultural and social networks that helped preserve the former's reputation and eventually facilitated her entry into the canon. Indeed, but for the success of *Wide Sargasso Sea,* it is likely that Rhys's books would have remained among what Raymond Williams called "the neglected works left in the wide margin of the century."[72] She now, however, holds an important place in modernism's literary history, a position consolidated by the publication of her letters, the production of a number of biographies, the adaptation of several of her works for film and radio, and—most telling of all—the creation of a considerable critical apparatus for scholars, students, and fans of her work, including a journal entitled the *Jean Rhys Review.* She is a constitutive site for the New Modernist Studies—a writer whose critical assimilation has helped redraw modernism's boundaries.

The reviewers and scholars who evaluated her republished novels in the 1960s and 70s may have been breaking with the canons inspired by the New Criticism, but they did not abandon its critical insistence that authorial intention be strictly separated from the textual artifact. Such a critical procedure, however, distorts seriously both the cultural utility of Rhys's texts as well as some of their most stunning formal innovations. Like Joyce, Lawrence, Lewis and so many others, she too drew explicitly on the roman à clef's infectious and anarchic powers to upset the institutions of the novel. Marya Zelli from *Quartet* and Sasha Jensen from *Good Morning Midnight* can easily be read as only lightly fictionalized images of Rhys's own increasingly desperate and depressing life in Paris. *Quartet,* in particular, was initially published, circulated, and reviewed as a roman à clef detailing the disastrous love affair linking Stella Bowen, Ford Madox Ford, Jean Lenglet, and Rhys. The reviewers who helped reawaken interest in the early novels, however, steadfastly ignored these contexts, carefully eliding them in order to craft Rhys in the image of a "properly" autonomous modernist artist.

Shirley Hazzard in the 1971 *New York Times Book Review,* for example, makes no direct reference to the real events or people behind the events in the novel, alluding to them instead only cryptically: "This is the English-speaking Montparnasse of Ford Madox Ford and Hemingway; and a perfectly dreadful little corner of a foreign field it is."[73] *Quartet,* of course, records not just the Paris of Ford and Hemingway, but the real lives and loves of the two men themselves—the former as the brutal and misogynistic H. J. Heidler and the latter as the impoverished but sympathetic Cairn. Writing in the Sunday *Times* of London, Vernon Scannell similarly elides any direct mention of *Quartet* as a roman à clef, noting elliptically that while "Jean Rhys's style . . . may owe something to Ford Madox Ford, whom she knew in Paris in the Twenties, [it] is wonderfully appropriate, limpid yet astringent, mixing easily the formal and the colloquial."[74] Ford's name again appears here, but as a friend and inspiration rather than the target of the novel's considerable rage. Indeed, the only reviews accompanying the 1969/71 release of *Quartet* that allude to the novel's "conditional fictionality" are those in the *Financial Times,* which notes Rhys's "Colette-like style," and in the *Guardian,* where the unsigned article rates Rhys "higher than Colette."[75] These two references to the popular author of several romans à clef describing the scandalous life of a young French woman, allude only obliquely to the fact that while *Quartet* may indeed engage in high modernist experiments in point of view and narrative technique, it is also a vicious and scandalous roman à clef that indicts both Ford and Bowen as hateful sexual predators.

Even the increasingly rich body of Rhys scholarship generated since the late 1960s has generally avoided a direct engagement with *Quartet* as a roman à clef. In his foundational work, *Jean Rhys: A Critical Study,* Thomas F. Staley argues that the novel "developed out of an intensely private world—a world whose sources of inspiration were neither literary nor intellectual."[76] He references Ford's role in Rhys's life, but when it comes to the text itself, he contends that she works in the modernist mode of impersonality, even if the novel itself fails "to achieve complete aesthetic detachment."[77] The traces of the roman à clef, in other words, are not acknowledged as part of a deliberate and self-conscious aesthetic strategy, but instead cast as a first novel's minor defects. Even less formalist critics than Staley brush aside the overtly biographical nature of the novel, as Veronica Gregg does when she states that while "the affair with Ford gave Rhys material for her fiction," it would nevertheless be "a mistake to reduce narrative experiment to an autobiographical fallacy."[78] Gregg seems oblivious to the fact that this autobiographical mode may be the source of Rhys's most striking and innovative experiments in the social utility of genre. Other critics, of course, have acknowledged a much more direct link between Rhys's life and her works, as Nancy R. Harrison does in *Jean Rhys and the Novel as Women's Text*. Using the awkward device of square brackets to construe a theory of what she calls "[auto]biography," Harrison suggests that Rhys "steps, not down, but away from the centrist position of authority, effectively bracketing out her 'self,' the autobiographical 'I,' to share the writing of her text with her readers."[79] This approach labors doggedly to imbricate life and art, to make the personal political, but it accomplishes this only by ignoring the fact that Rhys was, in fact, writing not a nebulously defined "[auto]biography," but a roman à clef. Paul Delany, in the explicitly titled "Jean Rhys and Ford Madox Ford: What Really Happened?" begins by stating that he intends to settle the facts of the case, but then quickly swerves aside by acknowledging "the extreme and inescapable textuality of the affair."[80] Taking cover behind the canons of professionalism, he claims that "the literary critic . . . is not concerned with the truth of an account, but how well it is told."[81] Once again, literary autonomy, the intentional fallacy, and narrative impersonality are implicitly invoked so that *Quartet* can be preserved as a highbrow modernist masterpiece turned forever inward on itself.

For Rhys herself, however, as well as for the critics and readers who first encountered this book in 1927, *Quartet* was anything but the kind of cold masterpiece scholars would later describe. The text is a roman à clef of the best sort, recounting her affair with Ford Madox Ford, her struggles with Ford's partner at the time, Stella Bowen, and the fallout of these events in her own marriage to Jean Lenglet, who was in prison for fraud. The names are changed, of course, but only lightly: Ford the literary editor who prided himself on discovering new talent, becomes a vicious and lascivious art dealer named Heidler (a vague but distinct echo of Ford's real last name, Hueffer). Bowen becomes Lois Heidler; Jean becomes Stephan; and Rhys becomes Marya. The story related in the book follows the events of its author's life closely, so much so that she later confessed to her biographer that she could no longer distinguish between the two.[82] The "key" to unlocking the identities of these characters was thus left in relatively plain sight—particularly for the many Parisian expatriates who witnessed the affair—and became all the more obvious as first Ford, in *When the Wicked Man*, then Bowen, in *Drawn from Life*, and even Lenglet, in *Sous les verrous* (later translated and redacted by Rhys under the title *Barred*), wrote their own memoirs (Bowen) and romans à clef (Ford and Lenglet) about the affair.[83]

More pressing, however, than the specific details of who slept with whom and who treated whom most brutally, is the way in which Rhys's work was framed and marketed explicitly as a scandalous roman à clef—one designed less to win praise as an elite work of autonomous art than to titillate readers with the sordid details of an affair among Parisian bohemians. For Rhys, this was both an aesthetic and commercial strategy; when her first story, "Vivienne," appeared in Ford's *transatlantic review*, she composed a note saying that it had been drawn from a larger work entitled *Suzy Tells*. Such a title clearly promises something in the vein of Colette—a lightly disguised autobiography that teasingly reveals the decadent scandals of Left-Bank life. When Ford actually published the piece, however, he altered this perhaps too obvious allusion to the roman à clef's infectiousness, retitling it *Triple Sec*; and he also convinced the young author to publish the work not under her own name—Ella Lenglet—but under the pseudonym by which we now know her: Jean Rhys. Ford, in short, helped Rhys to conceal the keys to this roman à clef a bit more effectively and in so doing, to invest herself more fully in the "interested disinterestedness" constituting the field of modernist literary production.[84]

Early readers and reviewers, however, could not be so easily put off the scent of scandal, and though *Triple Sec* was never published, Rhys's works of the 1920s and 30s—*The Left Bank and Other Stories, Quartet, Voyage in the Dark*, and *After Leaving Mr. Mackenzie*—were all greeted as autobiographical romans à clef. The jacket copy for the 1931 *After Leaving Mr. Mackenzie* noted that the author "has lived in several European capitals, has given English lessons, and worked spasmodically as a mannequin, a sculptor's model and a nursery governess."[85] These details describe almost exactly the lives of the various protagonists in Rhys's novels, a fact sourly noted by a reviewer in the 1931 *Boston Transcript* who concluded that "her own biography, judging by what the publishers tell us . . . is far more interesting than her heroine's story."[86] The jacket cover of her first novel, released originally as *Postures* in Britain and then retitled *Quartet* when it was published in the United States, further insists that the book is a roman à clef, coyly informing its readers that the author is writing under a "nom du plume"—presumably to prevent anyone from guessing the real identity of the characters in the book.[87] Like those legal disclaimers designed to guard against libel suits, this hint that the writer's name has been deliberately concealed only further compounds the reader's sense that something scandalous has been hidden in the pages of the novel and must be rooted out with even greater vigor.

Gretchen Mount in the 1929 *Detroit Free Press* called the book "an outstanding example of the sort of thing which has been of late issuing from a group of Americans who live in the Montparnasse quarter of Paris, write for *Transition,* and spend their time loafing around Sylvia Beach's book shop."[88] The reviewer for the *New York Herald Tribune* is even more precise, calling *Quartet* a chronicle of "that curious corner of Paris where the spurious rubs shoulders with the real."[89] Offering here a telling description of the roman à clef's provocative skepticism, this review openly acknowledges the ways in which most bohemian art can be used as a social tool or even a weapon. By rubbing together "the spurious" and the real, Rhys self-consciously puts her book to work: as a moral tale, an act of revenge, an ethnography of Parisian bohemia, and a potentially profitable tell-all autobiography.

Rhys, in other words, knew exactly what she was doing, and proved herself an even more canny self-marketer then Ford, exploiting what one of her characters in the story "La Grosse Fifi" describes as the English desire to seek out immorality and then be horrified by it: "How rum some people are!" she writes. "They ask to be shocked and long to be shocked and hope to be shocked, but if you really shock them . . . how shocked they are!"[90] *Quartet* exploits the profitability of shock by explicitly critiquing Ford's own "brand" of autonomous and impersonal modernism. The romantic image of the Left-Bank bohemian struggling with his or her art in lonely isolation becomes merely a hollow pose, one duplicitously struck to conceal an otherwise very bourgeois pursuit of social and cultural capital. In the text, when Heidler first seduces Marya, she resists his advances, surrendering to them only after he assures her that her own morality is painfully outdated, that she is "too virtuous."[91] Later, Lois further reassures Marya that anything so conventional as monogamy or marriage is merely a Victorian artifact and that she is making too much trouble about the unusual affair: "It's fatal making a fuss," Lois tell Marya, "We're making a great fuss about nothing at all, aren't we? Drama is catching, I find" (81, 82). This distinct—and here obviously stereotyped—adherence to bohemian sensuality is almost immediately given the lie, however, as the erotic entanglements grow increasingly explosive.

The Heidlers, in fact, worry a great deal about what the other residents of Montparnasse think of their relationship, and are at great pains to conceal the fact that the unconventional affair is taking an enormous emotional toll on all of them. The pose is so convincing that it initially even deceives Marya herself. Sharing a railway carriage with the couple, she is "haggard, tortured by jealously, burnt up by longing" (98). Looking at Lois and H. J., however, "it seemed . . . she had hypnotized herself into thinking, as they did, that her mind was part of their minds and that she understood why they both so often said in exactly the same tone of puzzled bewilderment: 'I don't see what you're making such a fuss about.' . . . And then they wanted to be excessively modern, and then they'd think: 'After all, we're in Paris'" (97–98). Ironically, it is Marya—the destitute ex-showgirl with the imprisoned husband—who cannot seem to be bohemian enough, her own moral qualms about the affair consistently dismissed as unfashionably out of date. The affair's gradual dissolution, however, quickly exposes the cynicism of the Heidlers' performance as Marya is moved to a hotel where she is provided with a small allowance and expected to make herself sexually available for H. J.'s afternoon visits. Lois nevertheless frets about the fragility of her own expatriate reputation, asking Marya anxiously, "You are not going to talk to anybody in Paris about this, are you?" (107). In the book's diegesis, Marya plays along, keeping her mouth shut, accepting her ignominious position as Heidler's mistress, and preserving the secret revelation that H. J. himself "looks exactly like a picture of Queen Victoria" (114).

Marya's continued, abject silence throughout the text—even as she is later sent away, then beaten and abandoned by her husband—has led critics to see her as an icon of women's suffering, a case-study in masochism, and even a colonized writer "lacking authentic selfhood in European terms."[92] Such readings, however, require us to treat the book exclusively as a novel, ignoring its attempted extension into the public sphere and consequent social utility for Rhys herself. Marya does indeed suffer at the hands of Heidler, remaining trapped by his order to keep up appearances, but the text itself willfully and powerfully violates this self-serving edict. To the extent that readers recognize Ford in Heidler, *Quartet* becomes instead an act of aggression, a public confession of all the hidden sins that Heidler and Ford both wanted to conceal. Marya, that is, becomes abject only when the text is insulated from any kind of biographical reading and treated instead as an autonomous work of art—precisely the kind of work that both Heidler and Ford admired as the quintessential product of Parisian modernism. As *Quartet* itself reveals, however, such autonomy can all too easily be counterfeited, since it passes through the same messy interface between fact and fiction as the roman à clef. Rhys uses the book's experiment with the social power of genre to expose a very public contest for cultural and social authority in which the line between public and private as well as that between real people and fictional characters becomes increasingly blurred.

As *Quartet* begins to draw to a close, it increasingly foregrounds its own generic structure. Sent to Cannes by Heidler and provided with only a small allowance, Marya writes a letter to him expressing her love and begging for money to escape.

This letter is interpolated into the text in a direct gesture to the roman à clef's eighteenth-century origins. Indeed, it comes to serve as a figure for the novel itself, since immediately after posting it Marya realizes that "he's given her [Lois Heidler] my letter to read, of course. It's like being stripped and laughed at" (161). The revelation that her private writing has become an entertaining and publicly circulated document prompts her to begin plotting a profitable means of escape. Realizing that "nobody owes a fair deal to a prostitute" (161), she plans "to be clever and cunning or she wouldn't get any money at all" (177). In the textual diegesis, her plans to blackmail Heidler collapse, as she first suffers the humiliation of knowing that Lois has seen her letter and then is finally left battered and unconscious by her husband.

The roman à clef's distinctive social life, however, moderates this otherwise bleak ending as we realize that Rhys has, in fact, quite cunningly gotten money out of Ford. Exposed in *Quartet* as a brutal and abusive misogynist whose bohemian ideals are merely a hypocritical pose, Ford now stands before the public eye as Marya feared she would, "stripped and laughed at." The book successfully extracts it own social and economic capital from him—not through the blackmail that Marya planned, but through its publication. The initial reviews of the text greeted it precisely in this vein, and Ford himself felt it necessary to reply in 1932 with his own retelling of the same events in *When the Wicked Man*, which he prefaced with a warning: "I publish this novel in England only with reluctance and under the action of a *force majeure* as to whose incidence I cannot be explicit."[93] The incident he refers to, of course, is the publication of *Quartet*, and he responded in the only way he could without admitting its potential truth: with a roman à clef of his own. In so carefully adopting the form for her own purposes, Rhys preserves the genre's playful confusion of the fictional and the biographical. Ford was unlikely to respond in public, with a libel action for example, because Rhys could all too easily withdraw into the very aesthetic autonomy her mentor so ardently defended by claiming the whole text was merely a fictional invention. In the world of expatriate Paris and beyond, however, the book became a powerful indictment of Ford's misogyny, snobbery, and hypocrisy. *Quartet*, furthermore, struck not only at Ford but at the entire pretense of bohemian modernism, exposing the fraudulent myth of the romantic artist and the autonomous literary text. Staley argues that "Rhys wrote precisely of what it was like to be down and out in both Paris and London[;] her fiction was not a literature of social engagement."[94] This critical commonplace can be true, however, only to the extent that we treat *Quartet* as the kind of elite cultural production it deliberately critiqued rather than as a roman à clef.

Rhys's book found its way into our canons through a willed blindness to its illicit generic codes, as well-meaning critics still steeped in New Critical reading practices transformed it from a scandalous tell-all account of Ford's womanizing and hypocrisy into a record of masochistic self-immolation. An unsigned review of the book in the *Emporia Kansas Gazette* accepts the book on precisely these terms, producing a reading that has now become generally accepted (if not so colorfully described) by recent commentators: "Quartet . . . starts on a high note and plunges downward for 228 pages, hitting the bottom on the last page with a dull thud. . . . You will read it at one sitting and then you will put cigarette ashes in the grand piano, the cat in the goldfish bowl, and your own illusions about the sweetness of life in an unmarked grave. . . . Original? Yes. Vivid? To brutality. Well done? Beautifully."[95] The review then concludes with a more stubborn question: "But why was it written?" The answer, of course, is that Rhys wrote the book to exact exquisite revenge for the very suffering and betrayals it describes. This is a simple enough answer, but its implications are far-reaching. Reading *Quartet* deliberately and unapologetically as a roman à clef radically reframes our understanding of the book by shifting our critical pleasures and attention away from the unredeemed tragedy of the text's diegesis to its success as an innovative and largely successful act of social and economic revenge.

Were *Quartet* unique in this regard it would remain at most a curiosity, but as I have argued throughout *The Art of Scandal*, the extra-diegetic perspectives so essential to the reception and circulation of the roman à clef provide a potent yet largely unexamined point of contact between gender, genre, and power in the early twentieth century. By reading the works of male writers like Huxley and Lawrence through this interpretive lens, we discover not only a familiar anxiety about aesthetic autonomy, but a simultaneous desire to access the economic rewards of the literary marketplace by trading on their connection to an elite coterie. Exploiting the ambiguities of the roman à clef, texts like *Those Barren Leaves* and *Women in Love* attempt to claim financial rewards while simultaneously directing the blame for their "secondary creativity" and their ultimately failed bid for autonomy on the abject figure of the lionhunter. Morrell's various "fictional" ciphers symbolically condense a commodity culture brutally damned and satirized at the diegetic level of the text. The real woman not only disappears into her textual representation, but the open secret of her lightly veiled identity provides the writers themselves with the profits of the very marketplace they otherwise critique.

Rhys too exploits the genre's doubled registers, but she does so strategically in order to reveal the ways women writers struggled to access a public sphere in which free speech was starkly delimited by gender. Within the diegesis of *Quartet*, this means that women remain essentially silenced and disempowered, their bid for sexual and personal liberation within the city cast as a masochistic failure. By reading this text as a roman à clef, however, we see the ways Rhys not only sells out Ford and his circle to a reading public eager for such narratives, but simultaneously insists that modernism itself is a vital segment of the cultural marketplace rather than a point of resistance to it. At the intersection of gender and genre, the roman à clef thus provided a powerful and engaging experimental forum in which male and female writers alike sought creatively to negotiate art's renunciation of its own autonomy—that transformative cultural movement Horkheimer and Adorno contend is so distinctive of the modern culture industry. It is here, in short, in the elite coteries and rough bohemias of the early twentieth century, that the legal and aesthetic constraints governing the boundary between fact and fiction begin to fray, becoming entangled in a mass-mediated cultural marketplace that trades in the open secrets and hidden pleasures of the roman à clef.

Notes

Chapter 1: Introduction

1. Richard Poirier, *A World Elsewhere: The Place of Style in American Literature* (Madison: University of Wisconsin Press, 1966), 7.

2. Brett Bourbon, *Finding a Replacement for the Soul* (Cambridge, MA: Harvard University Press, 2004), 50.

3. Truman Capote, *Playboy* (December 1976), 50.

4. Margaret Drabble, *Ms.* (April 1983), 32.

5. Alex Kuczynski, "Too Good Not to Be True," *The New York Times*, April 25, 2004, 9.1.

6. "Thanks to Ehrlichman and *The Company*, Truman Capote and *Answered Prayers*, and Elizabeth Ray and *The Washington Fringe Benefit*," the reviewer writes, "the roman à clef may become not only the form the bestselling novel takes in 1976 but the symbol of a rather shoddy year that could just possibly go down in history as the Age of Psst!-Have-You-Heard?" (Melvin Maddocks, "Now for the Age of Psst!" *Time*, June 28, 1976).

7. Cited in H. Montgomery Hyde, *The Trials of Oscar Wilde* (New York: Dover, 1973), 196–97.

8. H. G. Wells, *The World of William Clissold* (London: Earnest Benn, 1926), iv.

9. Sewell Stokes, *Pilloried!* (London: Richards Press, 1930) 12.

10. Ibid., 16.

11. Wells was notorious for writing romans à clef, the most scandalous of which was the 1923 book, *Men Like Gods*, which contains a brutal portrait of Winston Churchill as Rupert Caterskill. This helped prompt both his disingenuous preface to the *World of William Clissold*, as well as the following note in the front matter: "If you are the sort of person who will not accept it as a novel, then Mr. Wells asks that you leave it alone. You are not getting sly peeps at something more real than the reality of art, and your attempts to squint through will only make you squint very unbecomingly." Wells's frustration may also have resulted from the fact that he was himself so regularly enfolded into other romans à clef, most famously as Hypo Wilson in Dorothy Richardson's *Pilgrimage*, but also as Broadbent in G. B. Shaw's *John Bull's Other Island* and, later, as Max Town in Anthony West's *Heritage*.

12. D. H. Lawrence, "Review of the World of William Clissold, by H. G. Wells," in N. H. Reeve and John Worthen, eds., *The Cambridge Collection of the Works of D. H. Lawrence: Introductions and Reviews* (Cambridge: Cambridge University Press, 2005), 277.

13. H. M. Paull, *Literary Ethics: A Study in the Growth of Literary Conscience* (London: T. Butterworth, 1928), 250.

14. Ibid. By the late twentieth century, however, at least one guidebook, Jerome H. Sharp's *Making Shapely Fiction* (New York: W. W. Norton, 1991), was urging budding writers to consider the genre's possibilities: "If you have lived among interesting and famous people," he advises, "a *roman à clef* is a way to recreate them as fictional characters. That allows you freedoms of interpretation and invention not available to contemporary biographers." This book nevertheless cautions that using the form might "involve you in complex lawsuits about exploitation of a person's 'commercial value,' libel, and invasion of privacy" (207).

15. Paull, 248.

16. I do not use the term "public sphere" here and throughout *The Art of Scandal* in a strictly Habermasian sense to describe the real space between private life and public authority instantiated in eighteenth-century Britain. Instead, I use it to refer to the essentially utopian idea held by modernist writers themselves that a disinterested space might exist which is defined not, as Nancy Fraser puts it, by "market relations but rather [by] discursive relations, a theater for debating and deliberating rather than for buying and selling." Nancy Fraser, "Rethinking the Public Sphere: A Contribution to the Critique of Actually Existing Democracy," in *Habermas and the Public Sphere* (Cambridge, MA: MIT Press), 110.

17. Ibid., 250.

18. The narrator in *Ravelstein* (New York: Viking, 2000), in a metafictional acknowledgment of Saul Bellow's own roman à clef about Allan Bloom, thinks, "It was wonderful to be so public about the private" (31).

19. In *Reading 1922: A Return to the Scene of the Modern* (New York: Oxford University Press, 2001), Michael North insists on an analytic shift "from the production to the reception of literary modernism" (30). Genre, of course can operate both as a set of deliberately created markers as well as pragmatic codes invoked in the act of reception. It thus serves as a link between creation and consumption, a way of attending to the way literary forms traffic between readers and authors. In *Literature as System: Essays toward the Theory of Literary History* (Princeton, NJ: Princeton University Press, 1971), Claudio Guillén writes that "genre is an invitation to form," but it is ultimately the *reader* as well as the writer who must answer it (121).

20. Guillén, 120.

21. On the novel's mediation of public and private spheres, see Ian Watt, *The Rise of the Novel* (Berkeley: University of California Press, 1957) and D. H. Miller, *The Novel and the Police* (Berkeley: University of California Press, 1988). Seminal studies of the novel and domesticity include Nancy Armstrong, *Desire and Domestic Fiction* (New York: Oxford University Press, 1987) and Jane Tompkins, *Sensational Designs: The Cultural Work of American Fiction, 1790–1860* (New York: Oxford University Press, 1985). For an analysis of the novel and social taste see my own *Am I a Snob? Modernism and the Novel* (Ithaca, NY: Cornell University Press, 2003) and Jonathan Freedman, *Professions of Taste: Henry James, British Aestheticism, and Commodity Culture* (Palo Alto, CA: Stanford University Press, 1990).

22. Northrop Frye, *Anatomy of Criticism: Four Essays* (New York: Atheneum, 1967), 307.
23. Ibid., 309.
24. Ibid., 308.
25. Robert Scholes, "Language, Narrative, and Anti-Narrative," in W. J. T. Mitchell, ed., *On Narrative* (Chicago: University of Chicago Press, 1981), 207.
26. Ibid.
27. Jacques Derrida, "The Law of Genre," *Glyph* 7 (1980): 224.
28. Wai Chee Dimock, "Introduction: Genres as Fields of Knowledge," *PMLA* 122.5 (2007): 1380.
29. Gérard Genette, *Fiction and Diction* (Ithaca, NY: Cornell University Press, 1993), 24.
30. *The Selected Letters of Gustave Flaubert,* ed. and trans. Francis Steegmuller (New York: Farrar, Straus, and Giroux, 1953), 309.
31. Ibid., 319.
32. Ann Ardis, *Modernism and Cultural Conflict, 1880–1922* (Cambridge: Cambridge University Press, 2002), 10.
33. Pierre Bourdieu, *The Field of Cultural Production* (New York: Columbia University Press, 1993), 73.
34. Two such bibliographical studies have been published and I am indebted to the detective work evident in both: Earle Walbridge, *Literary Characters Drawn from Life: Romans à clef, Drames à Clef, Real People in Poetry* (New York: H. W. Wilson, 1936) and William Amos, *The Originals: An A–Z of Fiction's Real-Life Characters* (Boston: Little, Brown, 1985). A select bibliography of romans à clef published in English between 1890 and 1940 can be found after the endnotes.
35. The most famous example of this within modernism is Djuna Barnes's 1928 *Ladies Almanack*. Only 1,050 copies were initially printed privately: fifty were hand-colored and distributed to members of Natalie Barney's circle, while the rest were informally sold on the streets of Paris.
36. Paull, 248.

Chapter 2: True Fictions and False Histories

1. Daniel Defoe, *Robinson Crusoe*, vol. 1 (London: John Stockdale, 1790), xii.
2. Daniel Defoe, *Robinson Crusoe*, vol. 2 (London: John Stockdale, 1790), iii. Defoe's tone here is complex and his extensive defense of the book's veracity may well have an ironic element to it. For many of the book's early readers and critics, however, the invocation of this convention was taken quite seriously and helped stave off charges of romantic excess.
3. Virginia Woolf, *The Voyage Out* (London: Penguin 1992), 224.
4. Cited in Ion Williams, *Novel and Romance 1700–1800, A Documentary Record* (London: Routledge and Kegan Paul, 1970), 75.
5. J. Paul Hunter, *Before Novels: The Cultural Contexts of Eighteenth-Century Fiction* (New York: W. W. Norton, 1990), 44.
6. John Barclay, *Argenis* (Paris, 1621).
7. As Ernest M. Baker notes in *The History of the English Novel*, v. 3 (New York: Barnes and Noble, 1924; rpt. 1950), the book "had immediate and enormous vogue," leading to the publication of its key or "clavis" in 1623–21. In addition to being translated into numerous languages, it was the source for several dramas and became the model for several subsequent romans à clef.

8. Cited in Baker, 19.

9. Osbert Sitwell, *Triple Fugue* (London: Duckworth, 1914), n.p. Chapter 3 provides a lengthier discussion of this preface in the context of modern libel law, since one of Sitwell's targets did indeed recognize herself and threatened a libel suit that promptly led to a hasty withdrawal and redaction of one of his collections.

10. John Richetti, "Popular Narrative in the Early Eighteenth Century: Formats and Formulas" in Richard Kroll, ed., *The English Novel, volume 1: 1700 to Fielding* (London: Longman, 1998), 79.

11. For a detailed account of the politics of Manley's novels and her attempt to use them to enter the public sphere see Ruth Herman, *The Business of a Woman: The Political Writings of Delarivier Manley* (Newark: University of Delaware Press, 2003).

12. Cited in Ros Ballaster, *Seductive Forms: Women's Amatory Fiction from 1684–1740* (Oxford, UK: Clarendon, 1992), 117.

13. William Warner, "Realist Literary History: McKeon's *Origins of the Novel*," *Diacritics* 19.1 (Spring 1989): 69.

14. Cited in Ion Williams, 62.

15. Ibid.

16. Ibid., 67.

17. Hunter, 84.

18. Bourbon, 62.

19. Ballaster, 127, citing April London.

20. Marie-Laure Ryan, *Narrative as Virtual Reality: Immersion and Interactivity in Literature and Electronic Media* (Baltimore: Johns Hopkins University Press, 2001), 103.

21. Deidre Lynch, *The Economy of Character: Novels, Market Culture, and the Business of Inner Meaning* (Chicago: University of Chicago Press, 1998), 77.

22. Lennard J. Davis, *Factual Fictions: The Origins of the English Novel* (New York: Columbia University Press, 1983), 5.

23. Hunter, 66.

24. Ibid., 67.

25. Ibid., 58.

26. Ibid., 303, 316.

27. Nancy Armstrong, *Desire and Domestic Fiction: A Political History of the Novel* (Oxford: Oxford University Press, 1987). Armstrong relies heavily on a detailed and revealing analysis of the ways in which eighteenth-century domestic manuals were essentially incorporated into novels as part of the fictional lives of exemplary characters rather than as direct interpellations.

28. Hunter, 303.

29. Davis, 21, 24.

30. David A. Fleming, "Barclay's *Satyricon*: The First Satirical Roman a Clef," *Modern Philology* 65.2 (November 1967): 98.

31. Cited in English Showalter, *The Evolution of the French Novel, 1641–1782* (Princeton, NJ: Princeton Univ. Press), 162.

32. Cited in Davis, 35.

33. Cited in Baker, vol. 3, 27.

34. Davis, 35.

35. Ibid., 115.
36. Ballaster, 151.
37. Davis, 211.
38. McKeon, 93.
39. Ibid., 59.
40. Ibid.
41. Ibid., 60.
42. Warner, 71.
43. McKeon, 119.
44. William Hazlitt, "The Dandy School," in A. R. Waller and Arnold Glover, eds., *The Collected Works of William Hazlitt, Volume XI* (London: J. M. Dent, 1904), 343.
45. This is one of only several romans à clef penned about Byron. Samuel C. Chew in *Byron in England: His Fame and After-Fame* (New York: Charles Scribner's Sons, 1924) lists six others, including works by Shelley, Peacock, and others.
46. Cited by James L. Ruff, Introduction, *Glenarvon* (Delmar, NY: Scholars' Facsimiles and Reprints, 1972), viii.
47. John Clubbe, "*Glenarvon* Revised—and Revisited," *The Wordsworth Circle* 10 (1979): 208, 207.
48. Barbara Judson, "*Roman à clef* and the Dynamics of Betrayal: The Case of *Glenarvon*," *Genre* 33 (2000): 153. This extremely useful study of the roman à clef makes an important case for recovering Lamb's work from the margins of Byron's biography. Judson's definition of the genre itself, however, differs from my own, particularly since she focuses primarily on the effects of anonymous authorship and treats the roman à clef as a sub-genre of the novel rather than a narrative mode in its own right.
49. Similarly, Thomas Henry Lister's 1826 *Granby: A Novel* (London: H. Colburn, 1826) drew heavily on the celebrity of Beau Brummel in articulating its own figure of a dandy.
50. Nathaniel Hawthorne, *The Blithedale Romance* (Boston: Tickner, Reed, and Fields, 1852), v.
51. Ibid.
52. Debby Applegate, "Review Essay: *Roman à clef,*" *American Literary History* 7 (1995): 156.
53. Cited in Richard Broadhead, "Veiled Ladies: Toward a History of Antebellum Entertainment," *American Literary History* 1 (1989): 286.
54. As Applegate notes, "Melville was haunted by the relation of fiction to his personal life, from his early battles to establish the 'sober veracity' of *Omoo* and *Typee,* to his later efforts to throw off his reputation as Mr. Omoo and Typee Melville, to public questioning of his sanity in the critical reception of *Pierre* and *The Confidence Man*"(155).
55. Emily Brontë, *Wuthering Heights* (Oxford: Oxford University Press, 1981), 24.
56. Garrett Stewart, *Dear Reader: The Conscripted Audience in Nineteenth-Century British Fiction* (Baltimore: Johns Hopkins University Press, 1996), 12. He goes on to describe this curious dynamic and the odd syntactic structures it creates: "The impulse of classic fiction is to address your attention even when no second-person grammar gets in the way of story, as well as to narrate your place in its discourse even when no one (else)—no character—is made to read"(20).
57. Ford Madox Ford, The *English Novel: From the Earliest Days to the Death of Joseph Conrad* (Philadelphia: J. B. Lippincott, 1929), 54.

58. Bourbon, 53.

59. Charles Dickens, "Leigh Hunt: A Remonstrance," *All the Year Round* (December 24, 1859). In a private letter, Dickens took a much different tone, calling Skimpole "the most exact portrait ever printed in words." Cited in Stephen F. Fogle, "Skimpole Once More," *Nineteenth-Century Fiction* 7.1 (1952): 3.

60. Lynch, 28.

61. Ibid., 8.

62. Terry Eagleton, *The English Novel: An Introduction* (London: Blackwell, 2005), 1.

63. Eagleton, 2, 1.

64. M. M. Bakhtin, *The Dialogic Imagination,* trans. and ed. Michael Holquist and Caryl Emerson (Austin: University of Texas Press, 1981), 3.

65. Ibid., 39.

66. For a fascinating account of the ways in which the novel's synthetic powers grew from its deft manipulation of the anthology, see Leah Price, *The Anthology and the Rise of the Novel: From Richardson to George Eliot* (Cambridge: Cambridge University Press, 2003). Following the anthology through the various subgenres of the nineteenth century, she claims that nearly all "borrowed the discontinuous structure of the anthology—and made a bid, at least, for its social functions. Some took on its ambition to compile a national literary memory, others its project of disciplining narrative greed, others its campaign against solipsistic reading." The roman à clef, in fact, may have been so deeply suppressed during this period precisely because its sources are narrower and it thus cannot perform this assimilative function as efficiently as the novel.

67. George Levine, *The Realistic Imagination: English Fiction from Frankenstein to Lady Chatterly* (Chicago: University of Chicago Press, 1981), 8.

68. Bourbon, 53.

69. Marie-Laure Ryan, 92.

70. Caroline Levine, *The Serious Pleasures of Suspense: Victorian Realism and Narrative Doubt* (Charlottesville: University of Virginia Press, 2003), 17.

71. Alan Rauch, *Useful Knowledge: The Victorians, Morality, and the March of Intellect* (Durham, NC: Duke University Press, 2001), insists on the novel's power to generate a system of knowledge capable of almost entirely suppressing the stubborn distinction between word and world: "Novels establish elaborate guidelines of knowledge to direct the reader through the system; the narrative thread that emerges from comparisons with the 'real' or from gaps in the knowledge-structure relies on the confusion that exists (if only briefly) between fact and fiction" (17).

72. Eagleton, 4.

Chapter 3: Open Secrets and Hidden Truths

1. Francine Prose, "The Splatterer's Wife," *New York Times Book Review,* September 3, 2000.

2. Judith Ryan, *The Vanishing Subject: Early Psychology and Literary Modernism* (Chicago: University of Chicago Press, 1991), 1.

3. These include the period's two best-selling novels: George Du Maurier's *Trilby* (New York: Harper and Brothers, 1894) and Marie Corelli's *Sorrows of Satan* (London: J. B. Lippincott, 1895). The former, first serialized in *Harper's Magazine* in 1894, contains a

devastating portrait of James McNeil Whistler that had to be removed under threat of a libel suit. This fictional double nevertheless haunted Whistler for the rest of his life and is even mentioned at the opening of his obituary in the *Times* of London (July 18, 1903).

4. Brian Masters, *The Life of E. F. Benson* (London: Chatto and Windus, 1991), 104.

5. Josef Breuer and Sigmund Freud, *Studies on Hysteria* (New York: Basic Books, 1957), xxix.

6. Edmund Wilson, *Axel's Castle: A Study in the Imaginative Literature of 1870–1930* (New York: Charles Scribner's Sons, 1931), 184.

7. Martin Jay, "Modernism and the Specter of Psychologism," *Modernism/modernity* 3.2 (1996): 93.

8. Ibid., 104.

9. Arthur Baumann, "The Functions and Future of the Press," *Fortnightly Review* 107 (April 1920): 624. For a more detailed discussion of fascination in the popular press with "personality" journalism about figures both public and private, see Patrick Collier, *Modernism on Fleet Street* (Hampshire, UK: Ashgate, 2006), 32–37.

10. In T. S. Eliot's famous essay on Joyce's *Ulysses*, "*Ulysses*, Order and Myth," in *The Selected Prose of T. S. Eliot*, ed. Frank Kermode (New York: Harcourt, 1975), Eliot writes that what he calls the "narrative method," and with it the novel, "ended with Flaubert and James" only to be replaced by a deeper "order and form" made available through "the mythical method" (76).

11. Sigmund Freud, *Dora: An Analysis of a Case Study of Hysteria* (New York: Collier Books, 1963), 7. Further references will be cited parenthetically in the text.

12. Steven Marcus, "Freud and Dora: Story, History, and Case History," in Bernheimer and Kahane, eds., *In Dora's Case: Freud-Hysteria-Feminism* (New York: Columbia University Press, 1985), 79.

13. Sigmund Freud, in *The Origins of Psychoanalysis: Letters to Wilhelm Fleiss* (New York: Basic Books, 1954), 326, writes that *Dora* was, in fact, "a continuation of the dream book," prompting Charles Bernheimer to suggest that this "authorize[s] us to read the case as a symptomatic continuation of his ongoing self-analysis, as a fragment of the analysis of *his* case of hysteria"—see Charles Bernheimer, "Introduction," in Bernheimer and Kahane, eds., *In Dora's Case*, 17.

14. Freud's later works rarely draw on actual case histories. When he does seek to append clinical evidence for his claims, furthermore, he resorts to a much more abstract kind of writing that does not substitute fictional pseudonyms for real names. This passage from a 1915 essay, "The Unconscious," in *General Psychological Theory: Papers on Metapsychology* (New York: Macmillan, 1963), is typical: "Dr. Viktor Tausk of Vienna has placed at my disposal some observations that he has made in the initial stages of schizophrenia, which are particularly valuable in that the patient herself was eager to explain her utterances further." Having distanced himself from the actual scene of treatment, Freud then employs a somewhat more conventional anonymous third-person to describe one of these patients: "One of Tausk's patients, a girl who was brought to the clinic after a quarrel with her lover, complained that her eyes were not right, they were twisted (143–44).

15. Sigmund Freud, "Some Remarks on a Case of Obsessive-Compulsive Neurosis," in *The "Wolfman" and Other Cases* (New York: Penguin, 2003), 125.

16. Allegedly, the "Ratman" would answer the phone using this name rather than his own.

17. Freud, "Some Remarks on a Case of Obsessive-Compulsive Neurosis," 126.

18. Hippocratic Oath.

19. James Braid, *Neurypnology; or, the Rationale of Nervous Sleep Considered in Relation with Animal Magnetism* (London: John Churchill, 1843), 204. For a useful compendium of primary sources relating to the history of psychiatry, see the website maintained by Ed Brown at http://bms.brown.edu/HistoryofPsychiatry/hop.html (accessed October 14, 2008).

20. Wittmann went on to work as a laboratory assistant for Marie Curie in whose service she lost three limbs to radiation poisoning. Her life has been creatively reinvented in Per Olov Enquist, *The Story of Blanche and Marie*, trans. Tina Nunnally (London: Secker, 2006).

21. I am grateful to Professor Elana Newman at the University of Tulsa and Professor Harold Kudler at Duke University for their help in guiding me through the evolution of the psychological case study.

22. Available online at http://bms.brown.edu/HistoryofPsychiatry/rp1886.html (accessed October 13, 2008).

23. Richard von Kraft-Ebbing, *Psychopathia Sexualis* (F. J. Rebman, 1894), iv, v. Further references will be cited parenthetically in the text.

24. In *Epistemology of the Closet* (Berkeley: University of California Press, 1990), Eve Sedgwick argues that "a whole cluster of the most crucial sites for the contestation of meaning in twentieth-century Western culture are consequentially and quite indelibly marked with the historical specificity of homosocial/homosexual definition, notably but not exclusively male, from around the turn of the century." Lodged at the intersection between the public and the private, the roman à clef is uniquely positioned to explore this epistemology. As this chapter argues, it effectively queers both the novel and the psychiatric case study in order to render homosexuality as the constitutive secret upon which is staked what Sedgwick calls "the subject—the thematics—of knowledge and ignorance themselves, of innocence and initiation, of secrecy and disclosure" (72, 74).

25. Michel Foucault, *The History of Sexuality*, vol.1 (New York: Vintage, 1990), 17.

26. Havelock Ellis, *Studies in the Psychology of Sex*, vol. 1 (New York: Random House, 1941), xxxv. Further references will be cited parenthetically in the text.

27. In a letter of October 14, 1900, to Wilhelm Fleiss, written shortly after Dora arrived in his exam room, Freud too invokes this same lock and key metaphor that implicitly evokes the roman à clef: "it has been a lively time and I have a new patient, a girl of eighteen; the case has opened smoothly to my collection of picklocks" (325). Freud, *The Origins of Pscyhoanalysis: Letters to Wilhelm Fleiss, Drafts, Notes* (New York: Basic Books, 1977).

28. The excised material was privately published under Symonds's name in London in 1896 as *A Problem in Modern Ethics, Being an Inquiry into the Phenomenon of Sexual Inversion Addressed Especially to Medical Psychologists and Jurists* (London: n.p., 1896).

29. Freud, "Some Remarks on a Case of Obsessive-Compulsive Neurosis," 125.

30. Neil Herz, "Dora's Secrets, Freud's Techniques," in Bernheimer and Kahane, 234.

31. Jen Shelton, *Joyce and the Narrative Structure of Incest* (Gainesville: University of Florida Press, 2006), 30, 27. Like Shelton, a number of critics argue that Freud's attempt to mix fact and fiction in this narrative depends on the text's ability to suppress the facts of her abuse. "Dora had been traumatized, and Freud retraumatized her," writes Patrick J. Mahoney, in *Freud's Dora: A Psychoanalytic, Historical, and Textual Study* (New Haven: Yale

University Press, 1996), 149. For a thorough assessment of similar analyses, see Bernheimer and Kahane, eds.

32. Freud, "Some Remarks on a Case of Obsessive-Compulsive Neurosis," 125.

33. He writes: "There is never any danger of corrupting an inexperienced girl. For where there is no knowledge of sexual processes even in the unconscious, no hysterical symptom will arise; and where hysteria is found there can no longer be any question of 'innocence of mind' in the sense in which parents and educators use the phrase" (42).

34. Colleen Lamos, *Deviant Modernism: Sexual and Textual Errancy in T. S. Eliot, James Joyce, and Marcel Proust* (Cambridge: Cambridge University Press, 1998), 137.

35. Tim Armstrong, *Modernism, Technology, and the Body: A Cultural Study* (Cambridge: Cambridge University Press, 1998), 94.

36. Sedgwick, *Epistemology of the Closet*, 71.

37. Wilde, "The Decay of Lying," in Richard Ellmann, ed., *The Artist as Critic: The Critical Writings of Oscar Wilde* (Chicago: University of Chicago Press, 1968), 305. Further references will be cited parenthetically in the text.

38. Michael Patrick Gillespie, *Oscar Wilde and the Poetics of Ambiguity* (Gainesville: University of Florida Press, 1996), 14.

39. Such works technically fall into the complex generic category of the *drame à clef*, which, because of drama's more immediate relationship to indexical reality, has its own unique history running only roughly parallel to the roman à clef. As a result, I deal with it here only in passing.

40. Oscar Wilde, *The Picture of Dorian Gray* (Oxford: Oxford University Press, 1981), 11. Further references will appear parenthetically in the text.

41. In *Letters of Oscar Wilde*, Rupert Hart-Davis, ed. (London: Hart-Davis, 1962), Wilde famously writes to Ralph Payne, "Basil Hallward is what I think I am, Lord Henry what the world thinks me"—(352).

42. "The Decay of Lying" captures here the importance of treating the roman à clef as a pragmatic rather than typologically delimited form. Critics traditionally read it not as a roman à clef, but as a Platonic dialogue, its classical abstraction shifting attention from characters to their ideas. But Vivian can also function quite easily as a disguise for Wilde himself and in doing so shifts the reader's attention to the interplay between person and persona. As we'll see in chapter 5, W. J. Turner tried to shield himself from the charge of having written a potentially libelous roman à clef by arguing that he too had crafted nothing more than an abstract dialogue, despite the fact that most readers easily recognized in it a callous portrait of Ottoline Morrell.

43. *The Picture of Dorian Gray* first appeared in the July 1890 issue of *Lippincott's Monthly* magazine, before being revised and expanded into a novella published by Ward, Lock and Company in April 1891. The "Preface" was published first in the *Fortnightly Review* before being added to the 1891 book. The differences between the two versions are significant. Nevertheless, both versions depend heavily on the roman à clef and I quote throughout from reviews of both editions.

44. Wilde, *Letters*, 435.

45. Garelick, 128.

46. W. Graham Robertson, *Time Was: The Reminiscences of W. Graham Robertson* (London, 1931), 135–36. For a detailed and deeply informed account of the green carnation event,

see Neil McKenna, *The Secret Life of Oscar Wilde: An Intimate Portrait* (New York: Basic Books, 2005), 169–71.

47. Cited in McKenna, 170.

48. Frank Harris, *Oscar Wilde* (publisher? Michigan, 1959), 106, 107.

49. Robert Hichens, *The Green Carnation* (New York: D. Appleton, 1895), 151. Further references will be cited parenthetically in the text.

50. Wilde and Douglas themselves both suspected Ada Leverson. As McKenna notes, Max Beerbohm wrote to her as well, saying, "I am not surprised that [they] think anything so witty as the 'Green Carnation' must have been written by you" (304).

51. Wilde, *Letters*, 617.

52. Well aware of the damage his book had done, Hichens wrote in an introduction to the 1948 edition of *The Green Carnation* (London: Robin Clark, 1992),that he had been inspired almost entirely by *Dodo*: "I am sure I should never have written it if I had not met 'Dodo' Benson on the Nile, and been pricked into a desire to emulate his success" (xvi). Hichens even relates a story that seems to indicate Douglas had endorsed the book and claims that he unsuccessfully sought to have the book withdrawn immediately following Wilde's arrest.

53. See, for example, Michael S. Foldy, *The Trials of Oscar Wilde* (New Haven: Yale University Press, 1997); Regina Gagnier, *Idylls of the Marketplace: Oscar Wilde and the Victorian Public* (Stanford: Stanford University Press, 1986); and H. Montgomery Hyde, *The Trials of Oscar Wilde* (New York: Dover, 1962).

54. Merlin Holland, *Irish Peacock and Scarlet Marquise: The Real Trial of Oscar Wilde* (London: Fourth Estate, 2003), 72. Further references will be cited parenthetically in the text.

55. Harris, *Oscar Wilde*, 338.

56. Oscar Wilde, *De Profundis and Other Writings* (London: Penguin, 1973), 105.

Chapter 4: Libel

Detailed bibliographic information for this chapter's epigraph is as follows: William Congreve, *The Way of the World* (London: Jacob Tonson, 1700), n.p. Osbert Sitwell used this passage as an epigraph for his 1924 edition of *Triple Fugue*. It does not, however, appear in subsequent editions of the book.

1. Cited in Philip Ziegler, *Osbert Sitwell* (New York: Knopf, 1999), 123. *Triple Fugue* contains satiric portraits of, among others, Ottoline Morrell as Lady Septuagesima Goodley, Edmund Gosse as Professor Criss-cross, and Edward Marsh as Mattie Dean.

2. Osbert Sitwell, *Triple Fugue* (London: Duckworth, 1927), 182.

3. Clipping from *The Spectator* (July 19, 1924), from the Osbert Sitwell Collection, Harry Ransom Humanities Research Center (hereafter HRHRC), vertical file 16.

4. Clipping from *The Outlook* (June 21, 1925), HRHRC, vertical file 16.

5. Clipping from *The Times Literary Supplement* (June 19, 1924), HRHRC, vertical file 16.

6. *Parmiter v. Coupland* (1840).

7. From Dorothy Sayers, *Murder Must Advertise* (New York: Harper Collins, 1993), n.p. This disclaimer appears in most contemporary editions of this still popular novel, which was based upon the author's experiences working at Pim's, the London advertising agency. When the book was originally published, however, it contained an "Author's Note" that

read: "If, in the course of this fantasy, I have unintentionally used a name or a slogan suggestive of any existing person, firm or commodity, it is by sheer accident, and is not intended to cast the slightest reflection upon any actual commodity, firm, or person."

8. Consider, for example, those many episodes of the long-running American television show *Law and Order*, which are claimed to be "ripped from the headlines" even while they open with the disclaimer that no real people or actual events are being portrayed. This disclaimer only appears at the beginning of the show (rather than being crammed into the closing credits) when lightly fictionalized versions of real events are indeed being portrayed.

9. Aaron Jaffe, *Modernism and the Culture of Celebrity* (Cambridge: Cambridge University Press, 2005), 20.

10. Ibid., 20.

11. Sitwell, *Triple Fugue,* n.p.

12. Osbert Sitwell, *Dumb Animal* (London: Duckworth, 1930), 243.

13. Ibid., 264.

14. Cited in Ziegler, 126.

15. In the early stage of negotiation, Sitwell's attorney advised in a letter that "It seems pretty clear Mrs. W. is not in league with Mr. W or any of his masters and there does seem to be a reasonable chance that if it is quietly [disposed of] the others won't hear of it; while if we attempted to fight Mrs. W. the publicity would have been so tremendous that we should have had his whole pack on our tracks" (Osbert Sitwell Collection, HRHRC, correspondence folder 39.7). The implication here is clearly that Sitwell should avoid publicizing the libel charge lest other people connected with the school also consider legal action.

16. Cited in John Pearson, *Façades: Edith, Osbert, and Sachervell Sitwell* (New York: Macmillan, 1978), 338. The case against Hilton Fyfe was successful because his comments concerned only the Sitwells' reputation and had nothing to do with the book he was reviewing. Thus, they were not protected by the legal exceptions carved out for criticism and fair comment.

17. This infamous poem roundly condemned the king's friends for abandoning him when his affair with Wallis Simpson (then married) became public and was circulated only privately before being obtained by *Cavalcade*. The magazine planned to publish a bowdlerized version anonymously (leaving out any reference to the king), essentially daring the author to come forward. Sitwell thus found himself in a troubling predicament. If he launched a copyright suit to claim his authorial rights (and thereby suppress the poem), he would simultaneously expose himself to a series of libel suits. Eventually, he prevailed though an out-of-court settlement on the copyright case. For a full history of this complicated affair, see Osbert Sitwell, *Rat Week: An Essay on the Abdication* (London: Michael Joseph, 1986).

18. Major studies on modernism's agonistic relationship to obscenity law include Katherine Mullin, *James Joyce, Sexuality, and Social Purity* (Cambridge: Cambridge University Press, 2003); Allison Pease, *Modernism, Mass Culture, and the Aesthetics of Obscenity* (Cambridge: Cambridge University Press, 2000); and Paul Vanderham, *James Joyce and Censorship: The Trials of Ulysses* (New York: New York University Press, 1997). Paul Saint Amour helps correct this liberation narrative in *The Copywrights: Intellectual Property and the Literary Imagination* (Cornell: Cornell University Press, 2003), an analysis of copyright law, while Claire A. Culleton, *Joyce and the G-Men: J. Edgar Hoover's Manipulation of Modernism*

(London: Palgrave Macmillan, 2004) offers a rich archival examination of political censorship in the United States based on FBI files.

19. John Ruskin, *Fors Clavigera*, in *The Works of John Ruskin*, ed. E. T. Cook and Alexander Wedderburn, 39 vols. (London: Allen, 1903–12), 29:160. This passage then appears as the prologue to Whistler's own entertaining account of the affair, *The Gentle Art of Making Enemies* (New York: Putnam, 1890).

20. Cited in Whistler, *Gentle Art*, 11. For a full description of this infamous incident, see Linda Merrill, *A Pot of Paint: Aesthetics on Trial in* Whistler v. Ruskin (Washington, DC: Smithsonian Institution Press, 1992).

21. Pierre Bourdieu, *The Rules of Art: Genesis and Structure of the Literary Field*, trans. Susan Emmanuel (Stanford: Stanford University Press, 1997), 47.

22. Typescript note, untitled, from the Richard Ellmann Collection, McFarlin Library Special Collections, University of Tulsa, series I, folder 89.

23. The quote in the preceding heading is from *Rex v. Woodfall* (1774).

24. Francis Holt, *The Law of Libel: In Which Is Contained A General History Of This Law In The Ancient Codes, And Of Its Introduction, And Successive Alterations, In The Law Of England* (London: W. Reed, 1812), 49.

25. For a more detailed history of defamation's historic roots, see Peter Carter-Ruck, *Libel and Slander* (London: Archon, 1972), 35–38.

26. W. Blake Odgers, *A Digest of the Law of Libel and Slander with the Evidence, Procedure, and Practice, both in Civil and Criminal Cases, with Precedents of Pleadings* (Boston: Little Brown, 1881), 459. Until British defamation law was reformed in 1952, this remained the standard reference work and was dramatically employed by the newspaper editor and M. P. Noel Pemberton Billing in the infamous "Black Book Case" (*Rex. v. Billing*) in 1918. The jingoistic and homophobic Billing wrote in his muckraking newspaper, *The Vigilante*, that German agents possessed a book containing the names of 47,000 British men and women who could be blackmailed because of their homosexuality. The case generated sensational headlines and drew in the actress Maud Allen as well as H. H. Asquith and his wife Margot (the infamous "Dodo"). Billing acted by all accounts with extraordinary talent in his own defense, regularly turning to Odger's book in order to wage his case. His ever more outrageous claims, however, ultimately proved no match for his command of the law. For more on this case, see Joseph Dean, *Hatred, Ridicule or Contempt: A Book of Libel Cases* (New York: Macmillan, 1954), 19–38.

27. Holt, *Law of Libel*, 33.

28. In the United States, defamation law has been locked in a long-standing conflict with the First Amendment's guarantee of free speech, though it was not until very recently that the Supreme Court partially vitiated libel protections by insisting instead on an individual's right to privacy rather than to a good name. In two key cases—*New York Times v. Sullivan* (1964) and *Masson v. New Yorker Magazine* (1991)—the Court decided that the right to free speech must be given the widest possible latitude, particularly in matters of public interest. Thus, the majority decision from the 1991 case held that "when . . . the plaintiff is a public figure, he cannot recover unless he proves by clear and convincing evidence that the defendant published the defamatory statement with actual malice, i.e. with knowledge that it was false or with reckless disregard of whether it was false or not" (*Masson v. New Yorker Magazine* [1991] 501 U.S. 496, 510). This wide leeway is granted only to writing

about a public figure, meaning that this high standard of malice does not apply to private individuals who retain considerable rights to bring an action for libel provided they can demonstrate that their rights as private rather than public figures have been violated.

This particular resolution of the legal tension between the ancient right to a good name and the democratic right to free expression, however, is relatively unique to the United States. The 1937 Constitution of Ireland (*Bunreacht na haÈireann*), for example, states in article 40, section 3 that "The State shall, in particular, by its laws protect as best it may from unjust attack and, in the case of injustice done, vindicate the life, person, good name, and property rights of every citizen," thus explicitly granting its citizens protection from defamation. In this, Ireland is much closer to the long tradition of common law precedents that have treated libel as a potentially damaging threat to the operation of a just society.

29. The Society for the Suppression of Vice in Great Britain helped secure passage of the Obscene Publications Act in 1857. This new law offered one of the first legal definitions of obscenity and effectively severed such publications from the category of libel. Blasphemy remains a part of libel law and is still infrequently invoked. In 1977, for example, a criminal charge was filed following a public reading of James Kirkup's "A Love that Dare Not Speak Its Name," a poem suggesting Jesus was gay. This portion of libel law has never been repealed, but has largely been replaced by the Racial and Religious Hatred Act of 2006. The last person imprisoned for blasphemous libel was John William Gott, who served nine months in 1922 for publishing two pamphlets, "Rib Ticklers, or Questions for Parsons" and "God and Gott."

30. For a useful summary of changes in British and Irish libel laws over the centuries, see the report by the Law Reform Commission in Ireland entitled *Consultation Paper on the Crime of Libel*, http://www.lawreform.ie/publications/data/volume10/lrc_65.html (consulted October 13, 2008). This document was prepared as part of an effort to reform the Irish Free State's constitution and, in part, to help resolve some of the tensions between libel and free speech.

31. Cited in Joseph Dean, *Hatred, Ridicule or Contempt: A Book of Libel Cases*, 10.

32. Edward Coke, *The Selected Writings and Speeches of Sir Edward Coke, Volume 1*, ed. Steve Sheppard (Indianapolis: Liberty Fund, 2003), 125. Excerpts are available at the *Online Library of Liberty*, http://oll.libertyfund.org/index.php?option=com_staticxt&staticfile=show.php%3Ftitle=911&chapter=106331&layout=html (consulted October 13, 2008).

33. This question from a debate in the House of Lords is cited in the *Consultation Paper on the Crime of Libel*, 18 n.51.

34. In 1927, for example, Captain Peter Wright published a book entitled *Portraits and Criticisms*, which alleged that the deceased Prime Minister, W. E. Gladstone, had consorted regularly with prostitutes. As a matter of law, the dead cannot be libeled, but the outraged family wanted to rebut these claims, so they published an incendiary letter calling Wright "a liar, a coward, and a foul fellow." As they had hoped, he responded with a libel suit that then afforded them the opportunity to rebut his claims about the former prime minister in a widely publicized case. Wright himself ultimately failed in his own suit and was ordered to pay all costs.

35. Pearson, *Façades*, 430.

36. Dan B. Dobbs, *The Law of Torts* (St. Paul, Minn.: West Group, 2000), 1120.

37. Cited in Dean, 11.

38. Lennard J. Davis, *Factual Fictions: The Origins of the English Novel* (New York: Columbia University Press, 1983), 95.

39. Eric Barendt, "Defamation and Fiction," in Michael Freeman, ed., *Law and Literature: Current Legal Issues, vol. 2* (Oxford: Oxford University Press, 1999), 481.

40. The quote in the preceding heading is from Lord Coleridge in *Gibson v. Evans* (1889), cited in H. Montgomery Hyde, *Their Good Names: A Collection of Libel and Slander Cases* (London: Hamish Hamilton, 1970), 13.

41. This phrase comes from an Irish case, *Bolton v. O'Brien* (1885) 16 L.R. Ir. 97, 108, but the same principle holds in British law as established in *White v. Tyrell* 5 I.C.L.R., 477. For a fuller discussion of this issue and the larger comparative context, see Una Ni Raifeartaigh, "Fault Issues and Libel Law: A Comparison between Irish, English and United States Law," *International Comparative Law Quarterly* 40 (1991), 763–83.

42. William Wimsatt, "The Intentional Fallacy," *The Verbal Icon: Studies in the Meaning of Poetry* (Lexington: University of Kentucky Press, 1954), 3–20.

43. Odgers, 127.

44. In Ireland similar changes were made by the Defamation Act of 1961. Great Britain again updated its libel and defamation laws with passage of a new Defamation Act in 1996, helping bring some elements into alignment with the European Union.

45. Cited in Odgers, 128.

46. Peter F. Carter-Ruck, *Libel and Slander* (London: Archon Books, 1973), 67.

47. Odgers, 26, 113.

48. Ibid., 91.

49. This Education Act required municipalities to set up schools supported, in part, by local tax dollars. A decade later, attendance became mandatory for children up to the age of 10, and in 1891 the local boards were required to provide these schools without charge to the students. The result was an explosion of literacy, which, coupled with the political reforms of the 1867 and 1884 Reform Acts, led to a rapid democratization of the public sphere.

50. New developments in paper and printing technology in the late 1870s and early 1880s led to the widespread introduction of halftone images. This made illustrations relatively cheap and easy to produce, and there was a subsequent boom not only in illustrated magazines, but in the advertisements which helped fund their expansion to a mass audience. For a concise yet detailed history of these innovations and their effects, see the first chapter of David Reed, *The Popular Magazine in Britain and the United States: 1880–1960* (Toronto: University of Toronto Press, 1997), 27–49.

51. The law narrowly defined a registered newspaper as "any paper containing public news, intelligence, or occurrences, or any remarks or observations therein printed for sale, and published in England or Ireland periodically, or in parts or numbers at intervals not exceeding twenty-six days between the publication of any two such papers, parts, or numbers." It also included advertising weeklies, or "any paper printed in order to be dispersed, and made public weekly or oftener, or at intervals not exceeding twenty-six days, containing only or principally advertisements." The full version is online at the *UK Statute Law Database,* http://www.statutelaw.gov.uk/content.aspx?LegType=All+Primary&PageNumber=91&NavFrom=2&parentActiveTextDocId=1055484&ActiveTextDocId=1055484&filesize=27346 (accessed October 13, 2008).

52. From the trial transcript, as cited in Dean, 165.

53. The fear of the serious consequences of libel trials like this one deserves more serious attention from film historians seeking to explain the periodic vogue for historical costume dramas. Particularly in the wake of the Yousoupoff case, it simply became too risky to make films about recent and contemporary historical events.

54. Cited in Dean, 131.

55. The newspaper's apology was somewhat less than sincere, suggesting just how absurd its editors found the action for libel: "It hardly seems necessary for us to state that the imaginary Artemus Jones referred to in our article was not Mr. Thomas Artemus Jones, barrister, but, as he has complained to us, we gladly publish this paragraph in order to remove any possible misunderstanding and to satisfy Mr. Thomas Artemus Jones we had no intention whatsoever of referring to him (cited in Dean, 131).

56. Lord Goddard, cited in Dean, 134.

57. Barendt, 486.

58. The 1952 Defamation Act essentially codified these judicial opinions, formally creating the category of "unintentional libel" as part of the statute and thereby lifting the most ominous aspect of the "terror to authorship" created by the Artemus Jones case.

59. Barendt, 494.

60. Cited in Dean, 147.

61. Orwell's *Such, Such Were the Joys*, for example, was not published until 1968 for fear of potential libel suits. As Bernard Crick notes in *George Orwell: A Life* (London: Secker and Warburg, 1980), Orwell's publisher, Victor Gollancz, published *Down and Out in Paris and London* only after some changes were made to the original text and despite the warning from his reader (Gerald Gould) that the book was "full of possibilities of libel, running to thousands of pounds" (140).

62. Humphrey Carpenter, *Brideshead Generation* (London: Weidenfeld and Nicolson, 1989), 185.

Chapter 5: The Novel at the Bar

1. Aramis, "The Scandal of *Ulysses*," *Sporting Times*, 34 (April 1, 1922): 4.

2. James Joyce, *Ulysses* (California: Collectors Publication Edition, n.d.). This is a pirated edition, printed sometime in the late 1960s, which advertises an array of pornographic novels and magazines, often with delightfully lurid illustrations.

3. Katherine Mullin, *James Joyce, Sexuality and Social Purity* (Cambridge: Cambridge University Press, 2003), 3.

4. James Joyce, *Selected Letters of James Joyce* (New York: Viking, 1975), 285.

5. *U.S. v. Ulysses*, 5 F. Supp. 182 (District Court, Southern District of New York, December 6, 1933, sec. VI; reprinted as "Foreword," *Ulysses* (New York: Random House, 1961), xiii.

6. Cited in Jeffrey Meyers, *The Enemy: A Biography of Wyndham Lewis* (London: Routledge and Keegan Paul, 1980), 18.

7. Cited in C. J. Fox, ed., *Enemy Salvoes: Selected Literary Criticism* (London: Vision, 1975), 23–24.

8. Meyers, 29.

9. Wyndham Lewis, "Preliminary Aside to the Reader; regarding Gossip, and its pitfalls," *Modernism/Modernity* 4 (1997): 183.

10. Hugh Kenner, "Joyce and Modernism," in *James Joyce*, ed. Harold Bloom (Philadelphia: Chelsea House, 2003), 101.

11. Cited in Frank Budgen, *James Joyce and the Making of Ulysses* (New York: Harrison Smith and Robert Hass, 1934), 69.

12. James Joyce, *Finnegans Wake* (New York: Penguin, 1939), 179, 182.

13. Cited in Richard Ellmann, *James Joyce* (Oxford: Oxford University Press, 1982), 310. The various manuscript copies of the story contain several different versions of this passage, which was continually rewritten in an effort to secure publication. For a full record see Michael Groden et al., eds., *The James Joyce Archive* (New York: Garland, 1977–79), 4:181–269. The final version of the text of Joyce's *Dubliners* (New York: Viking, 1967) simply refers to the queen as Edward VII's "old mother" (132).

14. Joyce, *Dubliners*, 132.

15. Ellmann, 314. As we saw in the previous chapter, a civil suit could not be brought since it is not possible to libel the dead. In this case, however, it seems likely that the concern is with *libellis famosus*—the more serious criminal charge of libeling the head of state.

16. Ellmann, 315.

17. James Joyce, *Letters of James Joyce* (New York: Viking, 1966), 2: 291.

18. Holt, *The Law of Libel*, 84.

19. Ellmann, 328.

20. Ellmann, 329–30.

21. Roberts demands that Joyce take out two sureties against the possibilities of a libel suit, each providing a thousand pounds of insurance for the publisher. The outraged Joyce wrote to Nora, "No one admires me as much as that" (*Selected Letters*, 202).

22. *Collected Letters of James Joyce*, 1:64.

23. In the published text of *Dubliners* as well as in the manuscript and typescript drafts preserved in the *James Joyce Archive*, the name of the railway company in "A Painful Case" is never directly used. Since Joyce mentions this specific objection in a letter, however, it is reasonable to assume that some version of the story did name the company specifically. Just as he excised the description of Queen Victoria as a "bloody old bitch," literally pasting a new version into his notebook, so Joyce may also have deleted this specific reference to the railroad company in an effort to shore up his defense against a libel charge. See *Collected Letters of James Joyce*, 2:312.

24. Ellmann, 331.

25. Ibid.

26. The decorous dash whose absence Kenner notes, is actually everywhere evident in the text since Joyce originally sought to use it (as he would in *A Portrait* and *Ulysses*) in place of quotation marks to identify direct discourse.

27. Stanislaus Joyce, *The Dublin Diary of Stanislaus Joyce* (London: Faber and Faber, 1962), 105.

28. Herbert Gorman, *James Joyce: His First Forty Years* (New York: B. W. Huebsch, 1944), 119, 134.

29. *Ulysses* was suppressed in Great Britain not at trial but through the actions of the Home Office. For a detailed description of these proceedings, see Carmelo Medina Casado, "Sifting Through Censorship: The British Home Office *Ulysses* Files (1922–1936)," *James Joyce Quarterly* 37 (2000): 479–508.

30. Cited in *Irish Times*, October 9, 1954.

31. James Joyce, *Ulysses*, ed. Hans Walter Gaber et al. (New York: Random House, 1986), 1.150–54. All subsequent references to this edition of the text will appear parenthetically, citing episode and line numbers.

32. *New York Times* (September 23, 1957), 27.

33. Claire Culleton, *Names and Naming in Joyce* (Madison: University of Wisconsin Press, 1994), 107. St. John Gogarty admitted in his review of *Finnegans Wake*, "Roots in Resentment: James Joyce's Revenge," *The Observer* (May 7, 1939), that Joyce had succeeded brilliantly in his libelous campaign: his "style has its beginnings in resentment," the review contends, and he effectively "had his revenge" on the Dublin literary establishment.

34. Ellmann, 530.

35. Ibid., 507.

36. Clive Hart, "James Joyce and Sentimentality," *James Joyce Quarterly* 41 (2003): 35–36.

37. Typescript page titled "Ulysses" from the Richard Ellmann Collection, McFarlin Library Special Collections, University of Tulsa, series I, folder 89.

38. William Empson, *Using Biography* (Cambridge, MA: Harvard University Press, 1984), 225. For Hayman's influential theory of the "Arranger," which is designed to mediate between authorial intention and the intentional fallacy, see David Hayman, *Ulysses: The Mechanics of Meaning* (Madison: University of Wisconsin Press, 1982).

39. Sebastian D. G. Knowles, *The Dublin Helix: The Life of Language in* Ulysses (Gainesville: University of Florida Press, 2001), 7.

40. As is so often the case in *Ulysses,* the card itself presents a difficult textual crux. Even its potentially libelous content is unclear, since when Bloom initially reads it he sees only the two letters, yet when Josie Breen recites its contents she says "u.p: up" (8.258). She may simply be running the letters together, or the card itself may contain the colon and word "up" as well as the letters. The card later resurfaces in "Circe" (8.485) when Alf Bergan recites it, but since this is an essentially hallucinatory event, it does not resolve this curious aporia, which leaves us not only unsure of the card's meaning, but of its contents as well.

41. Robert Byrnes, "'U.P.: up' Proofed, *James Joyce Quarterly* 21 (1984): 175–76.

42. Like many fictional characters, Bloom's origin can be vaguely traced to a number of potential sources all reworked imaginatively by Joyce in a synthetic act of creation that is actually quite unusual in all the works that appear after *Dubliners*. Among these sources were the Triestine novelist Ettore Schmitz (who published his own autobiographical works under the penname Italo Svevo) and the Dubliner Alfred Hunter, who helped rescue Joyce after a night of drinking and who may have been the initial inspiration for *Ulysses*. For more on Schmitz see John McCourt, *The Years of Bloom: James Joyce in Trieste, 1904–1920* (Dublin: Lilliput, 2001); for Hunter see Ellmann, 162.

43. Joyce used the pseudonym "Stephen Daedelus" to sign his the first version of "The Sisters" in 1904, thus only further compounding the interplay of real and fictional names that complicate this episode.

44. Ellmann, 364, argues that "according to friends" Joyce took this theory of Shakespeare's plays more seriously than Stephen does, further emphasizing the perhaps obvious fact "that *Ulysses* divulges more than an impersonal and detached picture of Dublin life."

45. Mark Shechner, *Joyce in Nighttown: A Psychoanalytic Inquiry into Ulysses* (Berkeley: University of California Press, 1974), 27, contends that "Shakespeare, then, is only the pretext of 'Scylla'; James Joyce is the text."

46. Ulick O'Connor, *Oliver St. John Gogarty: A Poet and His Times* (London: J. Cape, 1963), 84.

47. A complete description of this case is provided by Conrad L. Rushing, "The English Player's Incident: What Really Happened?," *James Joyce Quarterly* 37.3–4 (2000): 371–88.

48. Cited in Meyers, 219.

49. Wyndham Lewis, *Satire and Fiction* (London: The Arthur Press, 1930), 43.

50. Meyers, 108.

51. This book has a particularly complicated history, having been written in 1915 and initially published in *The Egoist* (immediately following Joyce's *A Portrait of the Artist as a Young Man* as the magazine's "Serial Story") before appearing as a book in 1918. A decade later, Lewis then substantially revised the initial text, eliminating some of its stylistic experiments to render it more recognizable as a novel. Therefore, no standard edition of this work does (or indeed could) exist.

52. Gregory Castle in *Reading the Modernist Bildungsroman* (Gainesville: University Press of Florida, 2006) argues that texts like *Portrait* actually fail as *Bildungsromane* since their characters do not "achieve inner culture or harmonious socialization." They nevertheless do exploit "the formative and transformative power of failure in powerful new ways" to create alternative concepts of subjectivity and its articulation within a decentered modernity.

53. Paul Peppis, "Anti-Individualism and the Fiction of National Character in Wyndham Lewis's *Tarr*," *Twentieth-Century Literature* 40.2 (1994): 238, 241.

54. Wyndham Lewis, *The Letters of Wyndham Lewis,* ed. W. K. Rose (London: Methuen, 1963), 49.

55. Ibid., 49–50.

56. Cited in Quentin Bell and Stephen Chaplin, "Ideal Home Rumpus," *Apollo* (June 1966).

57. Cited in Paul O'Keeffe, *Some Sort of Genius: A Life of Wyndham Lewis* (New York: Random House, 2001), 136.

58. "Manifesto," *Blast* 1 (1914), 15. A digital edition of this journal is freely available online through the Modernist Journals Project at www.modjourn.org (consulted October 14, 2008).

59. Ibid., 33.

60. Wyndham Lewis, *Apes of God* (New York: Harper Collins, 1984), 120,121. Further references will be cited parenthetically in the text.

61. Ezra Pound, "After Election," in Forrest Read, ed., *Pound/Joyce: The Letters of Ezra Pound to James Joyce, with Pound's Essays on Joyce* (New York: New Directions, 1970), 241.

62. Cited in Lewis, *Satire and Fiction,* 35.

63. Ibid., 34.

64. Lewis, *Letters,* 149.

65. Cited in Meyers, 170.

66. Lewis, *Satire and Fiction,* 46.

67. Hugh Kenner, *Wyndham Lewis* (London: Methuen, 1954), 97.

68. Wyndham Lewis, "The Meaning of the Wild Body," in Bernard Lafourcade, ed., *The Complete Wild Body* (Santa Barbara: Black Sparrow Press, 1982), 158.

69. Vincent Sherry, "Anatomy of Folly: Wyndham Lewis, the Body Politic, and Comedy," *Modernism/Modernity* 4.2 (April 1997): 124.

70. Mark Perrino, "Marketing Insults: Wyndham Lewis and the Arthur Press," *Twentieth-Century Literature* 40.1 (1995): 59.

71. Ibid., 73.

72. Lewis, *Letters*, 149.

73. For a discussion of modernism's complex relationship to the collector's market, see Lawrence Rainey, *The Institutions of Modernism: Literary Elites and Public Culture* (New Haven: Yale University Press, 1998).

74. Lewis, *Satire and Fiction*, 33. In so openly revealing the book's key, in fact, Richardson herself ran the risk of being named in a libel suit as well.

75. Ibid., 7.

76. Ibid., 8.

77. Perrino identifies a "legalistic denial of libel that envelopes Satire and Fiction," when the text, in fact, dares its targets to enter into a court and thereby identify themselves.

78. Lewis, *Satire and Fiction*, 7.

79. Meyers, 158.

80. One year after the publication of the Arthur Press edition, Grayson and Nash produced the first trade edition of the text, their concerns about a potential libel suit now allayed by the lack of legal action. Though this new edition could itself have been the subject of a suit, the existence of the earlier edition would suggest that little harm had been done and that any damage award would be minimal.

81. Tyrus Miller, *Late Modernism: Politics, Fiction, and Art between the Wars* (Berkeley: University of California Press, 1999), 62.

82. Ibid., 63, 42–43.

83. Wyndham Lewis, *Blasting and Bombardiering* (London: Eyre and Spottiswoode, 1937), 9–10.

84. Lewis, "Preliminary Aside to the Reader," 185.

85. Lewis, *Blasting and Bombardiering*, 13.

86. Wyndham Lewis, *Doom of Youth* (New York: Haskell House Publishers, 1973), xix. Further references cited parenthetically in the text.

87. O'Keeffe, 315.

88. In Ezra Pound's copy of this book, held by the Harry Ransom Humanities Research Center, this passage is clearly marked in pencil. Although it's not clear when this was done, it does suggest that the case had some notoriety.

89. Cited in Meyers, 215.

90. Cited in O'Keeffe, 317.

91. Charles Prentice, an editor at Chatto, was furious when he learned that Lewis had been signing contracts with other publishers while his own firm was in the midst of mounting an expensive libel defense. Chatto eventually sued Lewis for breach of contract and won the return of a £100 advance paid out following the publication of *Snooty Baronet*. For a description of this incident, see Meyers, 216–17.

92. Wyndham Lewis, *Filibusters in Barbary: Record of a Visit to the Sous* (London: Grayson and Grayson, 1932), 151, 156.

93. Cited in O'Keeffe, 337.

94. O'Keeffe, 339.

95. The Bennett character, Samuel Shodbutt, is actually referred to on one page of the manuscript by the initials "SB" rather than "SS." See Walter Allen, "Introduction," *The Roaring Queen* (London: Secker and Warburg, 1973), 7.

96. Cited in O'Keeffe, 292.

97. Ibid., 363.
98. Lewis, *Letters*, 240–41.
99. Ibid.

Chapter 6: The Coterie as Commodity

1. Hugh Ross Williamson, "Honest at a Discount," *The Bookman* (June 1931), 144.
2. Ibid.
3. In Somerset Maugham's preface to *Cakes and Ale* (New York: Penguin, 1948), he disingenuously writes: "I am told that two or three writers thought themselves aimed at in the character of Alroy Kear. They were under a misapprehension. This character was a composite portrait: I took the appearance from one writer, the obsession with good society from another, the heartiness from a third, the pride in athletic prowess from a fourth, and a great deal from myself" (7). Maugham confesses here that he has copied from life, but nevertheless tries to preserve a claim to autonomy by asserting that in mixing real portraits he has produced something fundamentally new.
4. William Soskin, *The New York Evening Post* (March 31, 1931).
5. Williamson, 144.
6. Andreas Huyssen, *After the Great Divide: Modernism, Mass Culture, Postmodernism* (Bloomington: Indiana University Press, 1986), offers the most compelling description of this division. It is, he argues, a constitutive part of the modernist imagination, albeit one shot through with contradiction and what Robert Scholes calls "paradoxy" in *Paradoxy of Modernism* (New Haven: Yale University Press, 2006).
7. Theodor Adorno and Max Horkheimer, *The Dialectic of Enlightenment*, trans. John Cumming (New York: Continuum, 1982), 157.
8. This well-known image graphically represents the connections between various writers analyzed in her anthology by drawing a line between each name that was cross-referenced elsewhere in the book. The resulting "tangled intricacy" of connections makes visible the ways in which we too often simplify modernism and its sites of production. See Bonnie Kime Scott, *The Gender of Modernism: A Critical Anthology* (Bloomington: Indiana University Press, 1990), 10.
9. Virginia Woolf, "The Patron and the Crocus," *The Common Reader* (San Diego: Harcourt, Brace, and World, 1953), 212–13.
10. Aaron Jaffe, *Modernism and the Culture of Celebrity* (Cambridge: Cambridge University Press, 2005), 168.
11. Rita Felski, *The Gender of Modernity* (Cambridge, MA: Harvard University Press, 1995), explores the ways in which women were reconfigured as consumers at the end of the nineteenth century, becoming in the process a metaphoric "vehicle for expressing ambivalent responses to the social and economic transformations of commodity capitalism" (88).
12. Susan Stanford Friedman, *Penelope's Web: Gender, Modernity, H. D.'s Fiction* (Cambridge: Cambridge University Press, 1990), 2–3.
13. Virginia Woolf, *The Diary of Virginia Woolf*, Anne Olivier Bell and Andrew Macneillie, eds. (New York: Harcourt Brace, 1978–84), 2:243.
14. Ibid.
15. Richard Shone, *The Art of Bloomsbury: Roger Fry, Vanessa Bell, and Duncan Grant* (Princeton University Press, 1999) implicitly compares these works to the roman à clef's

ambiguities, noting that Grant yoked together "unexpected elements and allusions . . . to vivify objective transcription." As a result he walked a tenuous "tightrope stretched between fact and fantasy" (14). Shone includes a reproduction of this portrait, now held in a private collection.

16. With typical honesty, Woolf confides her hypocrisy to her diary in 1923: "What puts me on edge is that I'm writing like this here, & spoke so differently to Ott. I'm over peevish in private, partly in order to assert myself. I am a great deal interested suddenly in my book. I want to bring in the despicableness of people like Ott: I want to give the slipperiness of the soul" (*Diary*, 2:244).

17. Michael Holroyd, *Augustus John: A Biography* (London: Heinemann, 1974), 278.

18. Cited in Sandra Darroch, *Ottoline: The Life of Lady Ottoline Morrell* (New York: Coward, McCann and Geoghegan, 1975), 235.

19. *Everyman*, December 3, 1920, HRHRC, Box 35.3.

20. *The Star*, December 3, 1920, HRHRC, Box 35.3.

21. Aware of this, Morrell refused to purchase the portrait by John as well. In February 1921 he wrote to her gently inquiring about her interest in the piece: "I still have your portrait. People don't often buy other people's portraits. It's rather a cruel presentment as you know and yet I like it." This is followed by two lines crossed out in red crayon: "I think I had priced it at L500 at the show but you can have it for much less. Would L200 be too much?"(Morrell Papers, HRHRC, box 11, folder 2). She nevertheless bought another portrait and hung it prominently to help deflect the sense of scandal, prompting John himself to remark that "whatever she may have lacked, it wasn't courage" (Holroyd, 278).

22. The *OED* defines a "lionhunter" as "one who is given to lionizing celebrities." The term dates to the middle of the nineteenth century and is perhaps most famously deployed by Charles Dickens, who named a celebrity-obsessed character in *The Pickwick Papers* "Mrs. Leo Hunter."

23. These include Jayne Marek, *Women Editing Modernism: "Little" Magazines and Literary History* (Lexington: University Press of Kentucky, 1995); Georgina Taylor, *H. D. and the Public Sphere of Modernist Women Writers 1913-1946: Talking Women* (Oxford: Oxford University Press, 2001); Shari Benstock, *Women of the Left Bank: Paris, 1900-1940* (Austin: University of Texas Press, 1986); and George Bornstein, *Material Modernism: The Politics of the Page* (Cambridge: Cambridge University Press, 2001).

24. Lois Cucullu, *Expert Modernists, Matricide, and Modernist Culture* (New York: Palgrave, 2004), 6.

25. Ibid., 33.

26. Bourdieu argues that "the literary and artistic world is so ordered that those who enter it have an interest in disinterestedness" (*Field*, 40). In laying claim to a radical aesthetic autonomy and pursuing art for its own supposed ends and internal rewards, the artist tries deliberately to lose the game of economic success by displaying his or her indifference to it. Profits, prizes, and authority (or rather economic, cultural, and social capital) must be not simply ignored or refused, but vehemently condemned.

27. Virginia Woolf, *Letters of Virginia Woolf, Volume Three,* Nigel Nicholson and Joanne Trautman, eds. (New York: Harcourt, Brace, Jovanovich, 1977), 195. Ironically enough, Woolf was as this very moment composing *Orlando,* her most deliberate roman à clef, which experiments brilliantly with the destabilized boundary between fact and fiction.

28. Aldous Huxley, *Aldous Huxley: Selected Letters,* James Sexton, ed., December 3, 1921 (Chicago: Ivan R. Dee, 2007), 107–8.

29. Ibid.

30. The book, like most of Huxley's work, nevertheless remains in print and still has a significant audience beyond the academy. It has recently been reissued as a Dover paperback (2004) and appeared under the Dalkey Archive imprint in 2001 with an introduction by Michael Dirda.

31. Huxley, *Selected Letters,* December 3, 1921, 107–8.

32. Aldous Huxley, *Those Barren Leaves* (Chicago: Dalkey Archive, 1997), 22. Further references will be cited parenthetically in the text.

33. Cardan describes parasites this way: "They're quiet, they're gentle, they're rather pathetic. They appeal to the protective maternal instincts. They generally have some charming talent—never appreciated by the gross world, but recognised by the patron, vastly to his credit of course (that flattery's most delicate). They never offend like the buffoon; they don't obtrude themselves, but gaze with doglike eyes; they can render themselves, when their presence would be tiresome, practically non-existent. The protection of them satisfies the love of dominion and the altruistic parental instinct that prompts us to befriend the weak" (29).

34. Huxley uses a similar conceit in *Crome Yellow* (Chicago: Dalkey Archive, 2001), where a Huxley-like character discovers that a young woman has been meticulously recording the people and events around her at a great country estate. The discovery effectively shatters his own aesthetic pretensions and, perhaps not accidentally, refers to Defoe's own manipulation of the roman à clef in *Robinson Crusoe*: "It seemed, somehow, impossible that other people should be in their way as elaborate and complete as he in his. . . . The red notebook was one of those discoveries, a footprint in the sand. It put beyond a doubt the fact that the outer world really existed" (121).

35. Leah Price, "Introduction: Reading Matter," *PMLA* 121.1 (January 2006), 12.

36. The most concise history of the text with a useful stemma can be found in David Farmer, Lindeth Vasey, and John Worthen's introduction to their edition of *Women in Love* (Cambridge: Cambridge University Press, 1987), xx–lxi. For an earlier, but more detailed history, see Charles L. Ross, *The Composition of the Rainbow and Women in Love: A History* (Charlottesville: University of Virginia Press, 1979).

37. Cited in Farmer et al., xliii.

38. D. H. Lawrence, *The Letters of D. H. Lawrence,* George J. Zytaruk and James T. Boulton, eds., January 3, 1915 (Cambridge: Cambridge University Press, 1979–93), 2:298. In the draft of *Women in Love,* Hermione is also described as "strange like a priestess"—a line struck from the final text.

39. Lawrence, *Letters,* February 11(?), 1915, 2:281.

40. Lawrence, *Letters,* June 20, 1915, 2:359.

41. The prospectus is in an ALS by Dora Carrington dated October 27, 1916, HRHRC, Morrell Collection, Folder 4.1.

42. Dorothy Brett, ALS, December 14, 1916, HRHRC, Morrell Collection, Folder 4.1, HRHRC, Morrell Collection, Folder 3.3.

43. Siegfried Sassoon, *Siegfried's Journey: 1916–1920* (London: Faber and Faber, 1945), 22.

44. Dorothy Brett, ALS, February 10, 1917, HRHRC, Morrell Collection, Folder 4.1, HRHRC, Morrell Collection, Folder 3.5.

45. D. H. Lawrence, *Women in Love* (London: Penguin, 1982), 62. Further references to this edition will be cited parenthetically in the text.

46. The ilex tree appears in the autograph copy held in the Lawrence collection at the HRHRC, Folder 25.2, notebook, 24. In the published edition, it becomes a much less distinctive "cedar tree."

47. Three years later a similar conceit was used as cover art for a book of gossip columns, *And the Greeks,* written by Charles Graves (the brother of Robert Graves) for *The Daily Mail*. It features a collection of people seated around a card table whose faces have all apparently been erased—their identities presumably obscured so that Graves can dish all the more deliciously about their lives and habits.

48. W. J. Turner, *The Aesthetes* (London: Wishart and Co., 1927), 3. Further references will be cited in the text.

49. Cited in Darroch, 251.

50. W. J. Turner, ALS, April 23, 1927, Morrell Collection, HRHRC, Folder 35.3.

51. Ibid.

52. Lawrence, *Letters,* 3:44.

53. Lawrence, *Letters,* 3:109.

54. Lawrence, *Letters,* 3:220. This passage appears in a letter to Cynthia Asquith (the famous "Dodo") seeking her patronage to support a private edition of the book. Lawrence continues to remain concerned about libel because, as we have seen, although such private editions might provide protection against obscenity charges they provided no such refuge from the civil tort of defamation.

55. Lawrence, typescript draft of *Women in Love,* HRHRC, Folder 25.2, notebook, 11.

56. For a detailed description of this incident, as well as the subsequent textual changes to the hair and eye color of Halliday and the Pussum, see Farmer, xlix.

57. Lawrence, *Letters,* 3:112.

58. Dorothy Brett, ALS, January 15, 1917, Morrell Collection, HRHRC, Folder 3.5.

59. In an undated letter to Morrell, Katherine Mansfield wrote, "I am *sure* there is only one way to answer him. . . . It is to laugh at him—to make fun of him—to make him realise he has made a fool of himself" (ALS, n.d., Morrell Collection, HRHRC, Folder 14.4).

60. Lawrence, *Letters,* 3:95.

61. Lawrence, *Letters,* 2:182–83.

62. Michael Dirda, Introductionto Aldous Huxley, *Crome Yellow* (Chicago: Dalkey Archive, 2001), v.

63. Cited in Darroch, 268.

64. Following the publication of *Orlando,* for example, Woolf's diaries carefully record the substantial fees she could command for articles and reviews while savoring the fact that she had "become two inches & a half higher in the public view" (*Diaries,* 3:201). For a lengthy discussion of Woolf's ambivalence about her success and her manipulation of the roman à clef in *Orlando,* see chapter 4 of my *"Am I a Snob?": Modernism and the Novel* (Ithaca, NY: Cornell University Press, 2001).

65. Virginia Woolf, *Three Guineas* (London: Horgarth, 1986), 93, 94.

66. Ibid., 94.

67. Christine Froula, "On French and British Freedoms: Early Bloomsbury and the Brothels of Modernism," *Modernism/modernity* 12.4 (2005): 572.

68. Ibid., 572, 577.

69. Ibid., 567.

70. Deborah Parsons, *Streetwalking the Metropolis: Women, the City, and Modernity* (Oxford: Oxford University Press, 2000), 124.

71. *Wide Sargasso Sea* won the prestigious W. H. Smith Award in 1966, was subsequently dramatized and broadcast, was translated into a number of languages, and has since become a crucial text in postcolonial studies. See Carol Angier, *Jean Rhys: Life and Work* (London: Andre Deutsch, 1990), 525–67.

72. Raymond Williams, *The Politics of Modernism* (London: Verso, 1989), 35.

73. Shirley Hazzard, *New York Times Book Review*, clipping in Jean Rhys Collection, University of Tulsa, box 3, folder 13.

74. Vernon Scannell, *The Times*, Jean Rhys Collection, University of Tulsa, box 3, folder 13.

75. *Financial Times*, Jean Rhys Collection, University of Tulsa, box 3, folder 13.

76. Thomas F. Staley, *Jean Rhys: A Critical Study* (London: Macmillan, 1979), 36.

77. Ibid., 35.

78. Veronica Gregg, *Jean Rhys's Historical Imagination: Reading and Writing the Creole* (Chapel Hill: University of North Carolina Press, 1995), 107.

79. Nancy R. Harrison, *Jean Rhys and the Novel as Women's Text* (Chapel Hill: University of North Carolina Press, 1988), xvi.

80. Paul Delaney, "Jean Rhys and Ford Madox Ford: What Really Happened?" *Mosaic* 16.4 (Fall 19983): 16.

81. Ibid., 16.

82. Carol Angier, *Jean Rhys: Life and Work* (London: Andre Deutsch, 1990), 159.

83. Ford Madox Ford, *When the Wicked Man* (London: Jonathan Cape, 1932); Stella Bowen, *Drawn from Life* (London: Virago, 1984); Edouard de Nève (Jean Lenglet), *Sous les verrous* (Paris: Librarie Stock, 1933); Jean Lenglet, *Barred* (London: Desmond Harmsworth, 1932). The title of Rhys's novel may have proved more prescient than she thought, for the quartet grew to include not only the four original parties to the affair, but the four texts that its disastrous consequences spawned. Among these, only Bowen's is not a roman à clef; it is instead a memoir that publicly named Rhys and Ford, portraying both of them in a very poor light. Ford's 1932 *When the Wicked Man* went quickly out of print and has long been condemned by critics as a feeble effort—largely, I suspect, because it is too obviously a salvo lobbed back at Rhys. Lenglet's *Sous les verrous* was later translated into English and redacted (in a somewhat self-serving way) by Rhys, appearing as *Barred* in 1932 under the pseudonym Edward de Nève.

84. As the editor of *transatlantic review*, Ford was a major broker of cultural capital who played an essential role in helping to market literary modernism as an anticommercial commodity. Altering Rhys's name revealed both his canny understanding of this market as well as his ability to commute the presumably degraded roman à clef into a properly sanctified work of art. For a detailed study of Ford's complicated relationship to the marketplace and his attempt to carve out a profitable site of relative aesthetic autonomy within it, see Mark Morrison, *The Public Face of Modernism: Little Magazines, Audiences, and Reception, 1905–1920* (Madison: Wisconsin University Press, 2000).

85. Jean Rhys Collection, University of Tulsa, box 1, folder 5.

86. *Boston Transcript*, Jean Rhys Collection, University of Tulsa, box 1, folder 5.

87. Jean Rhys Collection, University of Tulsa, box 3, folder 13.

88. Gretchen Mount, *Detroit Free Press*, Jean Rhys Collection, University of Tulsa, box 3, folder 13.

89. *New York Herald Tribune*, Jean Rhys Collection, University of Tulsa, box 3, folder 13.

90. Jean Rhys, *The Left Bank and Other Stories* (London: Jonathan Cape, 1927), 169.

91. Jean Rhys, *Quartet* (New York: W. W. Norton, 1997), 78. Further references will be cited parenthetically in the text.

92. Gregg, 11.

93. Ford, *When the Wicked Man*, 9.

94. Staley, 84.

95. *Emporia Kansas Gazette*, Rhys Collection, University of Tulsa, box 3, folder 13.

Select Bibliography of Modernist Romans à Clef

This is not meant to be a comprehensive bibliography, in part because the infectious and unstable nature of the roman à clef makes it almost impossible to generate a definitive list. Instead, I have chosen a broad sampling of seventy texts to indicate just how pervasive the genre was in the early decades of the twentieth century at all levels of cultural production. Thus detective novels, sentimental fiction, and other types of genre writing are mixed here with more familiar works from the traditional canon of high modernism. This list includes only books written in English, leaving aside the equally broad number of romans à clef written in other languages, including works by Proust, Mann, and de Beauvoir.

Aldington, Richard. *Stepping Heavenward: A Record*. London: Chatto and Windus, 1931.
Arlen, Michael. *The Green Hat: A Romance for a Few People*. London: W. Collins Sons, 1924.
Barnes, Djuna. *Ladies Almanack: Showing Their Signs and Their Tides, Their Moons and Their Changes, the Seasons as It Is with Them, Their Eclipses and Equinoxes, as Well as a Full Record of Diurnal and Nocturnal Distempers*. 1st ed. Paris: printed for the author, 1928.
———. *Ryder*. New York: H. Liveright, 1928.
Beckett, Samuel. *Dream of Fair to Middling Women*. Dublin: Black Cat Press, 1992.
Benson, E. F. *Dodo: A Detail of the Day*. London: Methuen, 1893.
Butler, Samuel Streatfeild R. A. *The Way of All Flesh*. London: Grant Richards, 1903.
Cannan, Gilbert. *Mendel, A Story of Youth*. London: T. Fisher Unwin, 1916.
———. *Pugs and Peacocks*. London: Hutchinson, 1921.
Cather, Willa. *The Song of the Lark*. Boston: New York, 1915.
Douglas, Norman. *South Wind*. London: Martin Secker, 1917.
Du Maurier, George. *Trilby, a Novel*. New York: Harper and Bros., 1894.
Ford, Ford Madox. *When the Wicked Man*. New York: H. Liveright, 1931.
Greene, Graham. *It's a Battlefield*. London: William Heinemann, 1934.

193

H. D. *Asphodel*. Durham, NC: Duke University Press, 1992.
———. *Hermione*. New York: New Directions, 1981.
Hall, Radclyff. *The Well of Loneliness*. London: Jonathan Cape, 1928.
Hemingway, Ernest. "Mr. and Mrs. Elliot." In *In Our Time*. New York: Charles Scribner's Sons, 1924. 83–89.
———. *The Sun Also Rises*. New York: Charles Scribner's Sons, 1926.
Hichens, Robert Smythe. *The Green Carnation [a Novel]*. London: Heinemann, 1894.
Huxley, Aldous. *Crome Yellow*, 1921.
———. *Point Counter Point*. London: Chatto and Windus, T. and A. Constable, 1928.
———. *Those Barren Leaves*. London: Chatto and Windus, 1925.
Isherwood, Christopher. *Goodbye to Berlin*. London: Hogarth Press, 1939.
Joyce, James. *A Portrait of the Artist as a Young Man*. London: Egoist, 1916.
———. *Ulysses*. Paris: Shakespeare and Co., 1922.
Lawrence, D. H. *Women in Love*. London: Martin Secker, 1921.
Leslie, Shane. *The Cantab*. London: Chatto and Windus, 1926.
Lewis, Wyndham. *The Apes of God*. London: Arthur Press, 1930.
———. *The Roaring Queen*. London: J. Cape, 1936.
———. *The Roaring Queen*. London: Secker and Warburg, 1973.
———. *Snooty Baronet*. London and Toronto: Cassell, 1932.
———. *Tarr*. London: Egoist, 1918.
Loy, Mina. *Insel*. Santa Rosa, CA: Black Sparrow Press, 1991.
Mackenzie, Compton. *Extraordinary Women: Theme and Variations*. London: Martin Secker, 1928.
———. *Vestal Fire*. London: Cassell, 1927.
Maugham, W. Somerset. *Cakes and Ale: The Skeleton in the Cupboard*. London: Heinemann, 1930.
———. *The Moon and Sixpence*. London: Heinemann, 1919.
Moore, George. *The Lake*. London: Heinemann, 1905.
Mordaunt, Elinor. *Gin and Bitters*. New York: Farrar and Rinehart, 1931.
O'Sullivan, Vincent. "Anna Vaddock's Fame." *Rhythm* 2 (1911): 1–7.
Powell, Dawn. *The Locusts Have No King*. New York: Charles Scribner's Sons, 1948.
———. *Turn Magic Wheel*. New York: Farrar and Rinehart, 1936.
Revermort, J. A. *Cuthbert Learmont: A Novel*. London, 1910.
Rhys, Jean. *After Leaving Mr. Mackenzie*. London: J. Cape, 1931.
———. *Postures*. London: Chatto and Windus, 1928.
———. *Voyage in the Dark*. London: Constable, 1934.
Richardson, Dorothy Miller. *The Tunnel*. London: Duckworth, 1919.
Shaw, Bernard. *John Bull's Other Island*. London: A. Constable, 1909.
Sinclair, May. *Mary Oliver: A Life*. London: Macmillan, 1919.
Sitwell, Osbert. *Dumb Animal*. London: Duckworth, 1930.
———. *Triple Fugue*. London: Duckworth, 1914.
Smith, Stevie. *Novel on Yellow Paper; or, Work It Out for Yourself*. London: J. Cape, 1936.
Stein, Gertrude. *Q.E.D.* (1903). In *Fernhurst, Q.E.D., and Other Early Writings*. New York: Liveright, 1971. 51–134.
Trefusis, Violet. *Broderie Anglaise*. Paris: Plon, 1935.

Turner, W. J. *The Aesthetes*. London: Wishart, 1927.
von Arnim, Elizabeth. *Elizabeth and Her German Garden*. London: Macmillan, 1898.
———. *Vera*. London: Macmillan, 1921.
Waugh, Evelyn. *Vile Bodies*. London: Chapman and Hall, 1930.
Wells, H. G. *Men Like Gods*. London: New York, Cassell, 1923.
———. *The World of William Clissold; a Novel at a New Angle*. London: Ernest Benn, 1926.
West, Rebecca. *The Judge: A Novel*. London: Hutchinson, 1922.
Wilde, Oscar. *The Picture of Dorian Gray*. London: New York, Ward, Lock, 1891.
Williamson, Henry. *The Gold Falcon: Or the Haggard of Love*. London: Faber and Faber, 1933.
Wilson, Edmund. *I Thought of Daisy*. New York: Charles Scribner's Sons, 1929.
Wolfe, Thomas. *Look Homeward, Angel: A Story of the Buried Life*. New York: Charles Scribner's Sons, 1929.
———. *Of Time and the River: A Legend of Man's Hunger in His Youth*. New York: Charles Scribner's Sons, 1935.
Woolf, Leonard. *The Wise Virgins: A Story of Words, Opinions and a Few Emotions*. London: E. Arnold, 1914.
Woolf, Virginia. *Mrs. Dalloway*. London: Hogarth Press, 1925.
———. *Orlando: A Biography*. London: Hogarth Press, 1928.
———. *To the Lighthouse*. London: Hogarth Press, 1927.

Index

Adorno, Theodor, 125–126, 166
aesthetic autonomy, 3–5, 9–10, 15–17, 20, 27, 31–41, 44, 47, 58–62, 64–66, 70–74, 78, 80–81, 84–85, 90–91, 97, 104–106, 113–117, 125–129, 131–133, 136–140, 142–145, 148–166
aesthetics of detail, 15, 27, 38, 69, 80–81, 95–97, 100, 102–103, 109–111, 122, 135–136, 143–147, 150, 161–162
Ardis, Ann, 16
Arlen, Michael, 11, 119
Armstrong, Nancy, 28
Arthur Press, 116
Asquith, H. H., 45, 178 n.26
Asquith, Margot, 6, 45, 178 n.26, 189 n.54. *See also* Benson, E. F.
Austen, Jane, 38, 39
autobiography, 12, 32, 37, 42, 43–44, 138, 159–162

Bakhtin, Mikhail, 39–41
Barclay, John, 23–24, 29
Barendt, Eric, 78, 83, 84
Barnes, Djuna, 169 n.35
Bauer, Ida, 48–49, 54–58. *See also* Freud, Sigmund
Bauman, Arthur, 48

Beach, Sylvia, 89, 99, 130–131, 162
Bennett, Arnold, 185 n.95
Benson, E. F., 11, 45–46, 63
Best, Richard, 73
Bildungsroman, 12, 106–108, 184 n.52
biography, 3–6, 69–70
Blast, 107–108
Bloomsbury, 91, 107–108, 110–111, 114, 122, 127, 147, 156
Bloxham, John Edgar, 65
bohemia, 107–108, 112–117, 127, 128, 150, 157–159, 161–166
Bolton v. O'Brien, 79, 87
Bourbon, Brett, 3, 27, 40
Bourdieu, Pierre, 16, 73, 85, 132, 187 n.26
Bowen, Stella, 159, 160–161, 162–164
Braid, James, 50–51
Brett, Dorothy, 142, 151, 153, 155
Breuer, Joseph, 46
British Broadcasting Corporation, 97–98
Brontë, Emily, 36–37
Bussy, Rabutin, Roger de, 29
Bussy, Simon, 130–131
Byron, George Gordon, 35

Campbell, Roy, 116–117, 122
Cannan, Gilbert, 132, 142, 151

Canning v. William Collins and Co. Ltd., 85–87
Capote, Truman, 4
Carr, Henry, 105
Carrington, Dora, 110, 142
Carson, Edward, 66–67
Carswell, Catherine, 149
Carter-Ruck, Peter, 80
case studies, 17–18, 44, 46–56, 173 n.14.
    See also Freud, Sigmund
celebrity, 7–8, 35–36, 42, 43–44, 49–50, 57–58, 60–62, 72–73, 81–86, 113–116, 124–128, 130–132, 134–135, 137–138, 142–144, 146–149, 153–155
Channing, Minnie, 150
Charcot, Jean-Martin, 51
Chatto and Windus, 115–116, 119–120, 122, 185 n.91
Clubbe, John 35
Cole, Horace de Vere, 114
The Company, 4
conditional fictionality, 15, 18, 21, 23–24, 31, 44–46, 57–58, 61–63, 66–68, 78, 80, 83, 86, 98, 113–115, 132, 145, 148, 159
Congreve, William, 69
Cooper v. Wakley, 77–78
Corelli, Marie, 102
coterie culture, 127–128, 136–140, 142–144, 146–149, 156–158
creativity, 148–155
Cucullu, Lois, 131
Culleton, Claire, 98
Cunard, Nancy, 122
Cusak, Michael, 99

Davis, Lennard, 28–31, 78
defamation, 73, 74–78, 105. *See also* libel law *and* slander
Defamation Act (1952), 73, 79, 81–82, 85, 88
DeFoe, Daniel, 21–23, 26, 37
De Libellis Famosus, 76
Derrida, Jacques, 14
The Devil Wears Prada, 4
Dickens, Charles, 37–38, 39
Dimock, Wai Chee, 14–15

Dirda, Michael, 153
Disraeli, Benjamin, 34
Dodd, Reuben J., 97, 104, 123
Douglas, Alfred, 60, 64, 65
Drabble, Margaret, 4
drame à clef, 175 n.39
Duckworth, George, 156–157
Du Maurier, George, 172–173 n.3

E. Hulton and Co. v. Jones, 18, 73, 83–86, 87, 110, 111
Eagleton, Terry, 38–39
Education Act (1872), 81, 180 n.49
Edward VIII, 72
Eglinton, John, 102–104
Eliot, T. S., 48, 109–110, 115, 173 n.10
Ellis, Havelock, 52–54
Ellmann, Richard, 94, 99, 101
Empson, William, 100
ethics and the novel, 6–7, 20, 26

fame. *See* celebrity
Felski, Rita, 128
feminism, 128–129, 155–159, 160, 163–166
Fern, Fanny, 36, 42
Flaubert, Gustave, 16
Fleming, David, 29
Ford, Ford Madox, 19, 37, 91, 128, 157–158, 159–165, 190 n.84
Foucault, Michel, 52
Fox's Libel Act (1792), 78, 86
Freud, Sigmund, 17–18, 46–47, 48–50, 54–58, 64–67, 173 n.14
    Dora: An Analysis of a Case of Hysteria, 17–18, 48–49, 54–58, 64–67
Friedman, Susan Stanford, 128
Froula, Christine, 156–157
Frow, John, 13
Fry, Roger, 107
Frye, Northrop, 12–13

Garelick, Rhonda, 62
Garnett, Edward, 152

Garsington Manor, 127, 128, 129–130, 133–139, 141–149, 151, 153–155, 156. *See also* Huxley, Aldous *and* Lawrence, D. H.
Gaskell, Elizabeth, 21
Genette, Gérard, 15
genre theory, 10–17, 26–27, 159–166
Gertler, Mark, 129
Gillespie, Michael Patrick, 58
Gilson, Charles, 26
Gladstone, W. E., 179 n.34
Gogarty, Oliver St. John, 13, 98–99, 102, 104
Gollancz, Victor, 122
Gorman, Herbert, 97
Gosse, Edmund, 69
gossip, 4, 5, 7, 49–50, 55–56, 91, 111–113, 141–143
Grant, Duncan, 129, 130–131, 136
Grayson and Grayson, 121–122
Grayson, Rupert, 106–107
Gregg, Veronica, 160
Guillén, Claudio, 10, 168 n.19

Habermas, Jürgen, 168 n.16
Hardy, Thomas, 125
Harrison, Nancy, 160
Hart, Clive, 99
Hawthorne, Nathaniel, 35–36
Hayman David, 100
Hazlitt, William, 34
Hazzard, Shirley, 159
Heinemann, William, 65
Hemingway, Ernest, 159
Herz, Neil, 55
Heseltine, Philip, 150
Hichens, Robert, 11, 63–66, 176 n.52
Hippocratic Oath, 50
historical novel, 21
Hogarth Press, 156
Holt, Francis, 74–75, 94
homosexuality, 51–54, 56–57, 63–68, 110, 114, 120
Hunt, Leigh, 37–38
Hunter, J. Paul, 23, 26, 28–29

Huxley, Aldous, 11, 69, 129, 133–140, 142–145, 150–151, 153–155, 165
  Crome Yellow, 132–134, 135, 139, 153, 188 n.34
  Point Counter Point, 12, 132
  Those Barren Leaves, 16, 132, 134–140, 154, 165

impersonality, 26, 91–92, 112–114, 125, 148–149, 159–160
intention of the author, 5, 78–86, 115–116, 122–123, 133–134, 158–159
intentional fallacy, 4, 79, 100, 160

Jaffe, Aaron, 70, 127
James, Henry, 9, 155
Janet, Pierre, 51–52
Jardine, Alice, 128
Jay, Martin, 47
John, Augustus, 90–91, 129–131, 136, 187 n.21
Jones, Artemus, 73, 82–83. *See also E. Hulton and Co. v. Jones*
Joyce, James, 4, 5, 13, 82, 89–90, 92–107, 113, 117–118, 123, 156
  Dubliners, 93–96, 122, 182 n.23
  Finnegans Wake, 93, 96–97, 117
  and lawsuits, 93, 97–98, 104, 105
  and libel law, 82, 92–104
  A Portrait of the Artists as a Young Man, 96–98, 106
  and the roman à clef, 98–104
  Ulysses, 13, 18, 72, 73, 89–90, 92–93, 97–106, 117, 123, 156, 183 n.40, 183 n.42

Kenner, Hugh, 92–93, 110
Knowles, Sebastian, 100
Koteliansky, S. S., 150, 151
Krafft-Ebing, Richard von, 51–52

Labouchére, Henry, 76–77, 81
Lamb, Caroline, 35, 36

Lawrence, D. H., 6, 19, 106, 129, 141–155, 165
  Lady Chatterley's Lover, 22, 123
  and libel law, 141, 144, 149–152
  The Rainbow, 141
  Women in Love, 11, 86, 127–128, 132, 141–145, 148–155, 156, 165
Lawrence, Frieda, 141
Le Fanu and another v. Malcolmson, 80
legal disclaimers, 70, 82–84
Lenglet, Jean, 159, 160–161
Leventhal, A. J., 99, 100
Levine, Caroline, 40
Levine, George, 39–40
Lewis, Wyndham, 18, 73, 82, 90–92, 105–123
  Apes of God, 18, 73, 91–92, 108–117, 119–121, 185 n.80
  Blasting and Bombardiering, 91, 110, 118–119
  Doom of Youth, 105, 119–120, 122
  Filibusters in Barbary, 105, 120–121
  and lawsuits, 107, 108–110, 119–123
  and libel law, 73, 82, 90–92, 105, 107, 109–110, 115–123
  Roaring Queen, 105, 122–123
  and the roman à clef, 90–92, 105–106, 108–123
  Satire and Fiction, 116–117, 122
  Tarr, 106
Libel Act (1843), 76, 87
Libel Act (1952). See Defamation Act (1952)
libel law, 9, 18–19, 65–67, 69–88, 109–110, 115–117, 125, 134, 141–142, 144, 149–152, 164, 177 n.15, 177 n.17, 178–179 n.28, 179 n.34. *See also individual cases*
  as censorship, 72–74, 109–110, 115–117, 118–123, 125, 142, 149–150, 164
  civil type, 75–78, 81, 95–98, 119–123, 119–122, 125, 141, 144, 172–173 n.3
  criminal type, 75–77, 79–81, 93–94
  defined, 70, 74–78
  development of, 74–77
  and film, 81–83
  and freedom of speech, 72, 74–76, 97, 178–179, n.28
  and modernism, 68, 69–74, 78–79, 89–123, 149–150

  rules of evidence and procedure, 75–81, 91, 100–102, 109–110, 179 n.34
Lidwell, George, 94
lionhunter, 131–132, 135–139, 144–145, 154–155, 187 n.22
Lister, Thomas Henry, 171 n.49
Lynch, Deirdre, 27, 38
Lytton, Edward Bulwer, 34

Mackenzie, Compton, 7, 11, 141
Manley, Mary Delarivier, 24–25, 30–31
Mansfield, Katherine, 129, 151, 153
masochism, 128, 163, 166
Masson v. New Yorker Magazine, 178–179 n.28
Maugham, Somerset, 124–125, 186 n.3
Mavrogordato, John, 146
McFie, Thomas, 120–121
McKeon, Michael, 32–34, 39, 40
Melville, Herman, 171 n.54
Menton, John Henry, 101
Miller, Tyrus, 118
modernism, 4, 10–11, 17–20, 24–25, 46–48, 68, 73–74, 78–79, 86, 90–92, 117–118, 123, 125–129, 130–131, 138, 140, 148–166, and *passim*
Mordaunt, Elinor, 125
Morrell, Ottoline, 11, 19, 69, 127–156, 165, 187 n.21
Morrell, Philip, 129, 132–133, 142, 152
Mount, Gretchen, 162
Mullin, Katherine, 90
Myers, Jeffrey, 106

The Nanny Diaries, 4
New Journalism, 81
news/novel divide, 28–31, 46, 61–63, 72–74, 78, 81, 83–84, 97, 112–114, 118, 122, 124–126, 134, 154
Newspaper and Libel Registration Act, 81, 87, 94, 180 n.51
New York Times v. Sullivan, 178–179 n.28
North, Michael, 10
Northern Whig, 94

novel
  history of, 9–10, 17, 18, 23, 26–29, 31–34, 35–40
  legal regulation of, 77–78, 82–86, 103–104, 123
  and libel law, 70–71
  silver-fork sub-genre, 34
  theory of, 12–13, 25–26, 31–33, 38–41, 148, 158–159

obscenity, 53–54, 72, 74, 75, 88–90, 93, 123, 141–142, 179 n.29
Odgers, W. Blake, 74, 79, 80
Omega Workshops, 107
Orwell, George, 86, 181 n.61

Parmiter v. Coupland, 70, 87
Parsons, Deborah, 157
patronage, 127–131, 139–140. See also lionhunter
Paull, H. M., 20
Peacock, Thomas Love, 35
Peppis, Paul, 106
Perrino, Mark, 112, 114
Picasso, Pablo, 156
Porier, Richard, 3
Porter Committee, 87–88
Pound, Ezra, 108–109
Price, Leah, 172 n.66
professionalism, 7, 15–16, 131–132, 160
Prose, Francine, 43
Proust, Michel, 47, 112–113
psychoanalysis, 17–18, 45–56, 108. See also Freud, Sigmund
public sphere, 7

Queensbury, marquis of, 64–65, 66–67

Rasputin the Mad Monk, 82
realism, 7, 20, 32–34, 39–42, 47, 57–58, 66–67, 73, 84, 91–92, 97, 100, 117, 123, 125

Reform Act (1832), 75
Regina v. Hart, 78
Regina v. John Douglas. See Wilde, Oscar
Regina v. Labouchère, 76–77
Rhys, Jean, 19, 127–128, 157–166
  After Leaving Mr. Mackenzie, 161
  Good Morning Midnight, 159
  "La Grosse Fifi," 162
  Quartet, 19, 128, 159–166
  Triple Sec, 161
  "Vivienne," 161
  Wide Sargasso Sea, 158
Richards, Grant, 93–94
Roberts, George, 93–96
roman à clef, 7–11, 15, 17, 25–36, 45–47, 49–50, 52–62, 82–86, 90–92, 102–106, 108–123, 124–129, 140–166, 172 n.66
  and creativity, 144–155, 165–166
  defined, 7–9, 15
  early history of, 9–10, 17, 25–35
  legal regulation of, 79–80, 82–86 (see also libel law)
  and modernism, 10–11, 46–47, 58–62, 86, 90–92, 103–105, 108–123, 124–129, 138, 140–166
  precursors to, 25, 29–31
  and psychology, 45–47, 49–50, 52–58
  and public scandal, 11, 15, 36, 44, 90, 109, 110, 118–121, 124–125, 127, 142–143, 154–155, 157–158, 160–163
romance, 26, 30, 32
Roth, Samuel, 89
Ruach, Alan, 172 n.71
Ruskin, John, 72
Russell, Bertrand, 129
Russell, George, 102–103
Ryan, Judith, 44
Ryan, Marie-Laure, 27, 40

salon. See coterie culture
Sassoon, Siegfried, 129, 142
satire, 12–13, 106, 108–117, 120–123, 138–140, 145, 152
Sayers, Dorothy, 70, 176–177 n.7
Scannell, Vernon, 159

Schmitz, Ettore, 183 n.42
Scholes, Robert, 13–14, 186 n.6
Scott, Bonnie Kime, 126
Scott, Walter, 21
Scudéry, Madeleine, 30–31
Secker, Martin, 141
secrecy, 52, 55–57, 61–62, 64–66, 76, 96–97, 143–144, 136–158, 163–166
Sedgwick, Eve Kosofsky, 52–53, 57, 63, 174 n.24
sexology, 44, 46, 51–54. *See also* case studies
sexual inversion. *See* homosexuality
Shakespeare, William, 102–104
Shaw, George Bernard, 99
Shelley, Mary, 36
Shelton, Jen, 55
Shiff, Sidney, 112–113, 115–116
Simpson, Wallis, 72
Sinn Féin, 94
Sitwell, Edith, 77, 117, 129
Sitwell, Osbert, 11, 24, 69–72, 77, 109–110, 114–116, 129, 132, 177 n.15, 177 n.17
skepticism, 37, 40–41, 44, 57
slander, 75, 81–82
Soskin, William, 125
Staley, Thomas, 159–160
Stewart, Garrett, 37
Stokes, Sewell, 5–6
Strachey, Lytton, 110, 129
Symonds, John Addington, 53–54

Tennant, Margot. *See* Asquith, Margot
Toynton, Evelyn, 43
transatlantic review, 161
Trench, Samuel, 99
Turner, Walter, 132, 146–149, 150–151

Ustinov, Peter, 77

von Arnim, Elizabeth, 11

Walpole, Hugh, 125
The Washington Fringe Benefit, 4–5
Watt, Ian, 27–29
Waugh, Alec, 119–120
Waugh, Evelyn, 10, 86
Wells, H. G., 5, 167 n.11
Whistler, James McNeill, 72, 77, 91, 172–173 n.3
White v. Tyrell, 87
Wilde, Oscar, 17–18, 44, 57–68, 105
  criminal trials of, 5, 17, 53, 65
  "Decay of Lying," 59–60, 175 n.42
  libel suit against Queensbury, 18, 24–25, 60, 65–68, 72, 75, 76
  The Picture of Dorian Gray, 5, 10–11, 24–25, 33, 45, 47, 58–62
William, Raymond, 158
Williamson, Hugh Ross, 124–126
Wilson, Edmund, 47, 112
Wimsatt, William, 4, 79
Wittman, Blanche, 51, 174 n.20
Woolf, Virginia, 22–23, 122, 126–127, 129–130, 132–133, 156–157, 187 n.16, 189 n.64
Woolsey, John, 90
Wyndham, Richard, 116

Yeats, W. B., 148
Youssoupoff v. Metro-Goldwyn-Mayer Pictures Ltd., 82, 87

www.ingramcontent.com/pod-product-compliance
Ingram Content Group UK Ltd.
Pitfield, Milton Keynes, MK11 3LW, UK
UKHW021903240426
12048UKWH00038B/1399